Florida Politics in the Gilded Age
1877 ⧸ 1893

Florida Politics in the Gilded Age
1877 ≠ 1893

Edward C. Williamson

A University of Florida Book
The University Presses of Florida
Gainesville / 1976

Library of Congress Cataloging in Publication Data
Williamson, Edward C. 1916-
  Florida politics in the gilded age, 1877-1893.
  "A University of Florida book."
  Bibliography: p.
  Includes index.
  1. Florida—Politics and government—1865-1950.
I. Title
F316.2.W54   320.9'759'06   75-30634
ISBN 0-8130-0365-2

PRINTED BY THE ROSE PRINTING COMPANY, INCORPORATED
TALLAHASSEE, FLORIDA

Preface

The Republican Reconstruction government remained in power in Florida for eight stormy years. Handicapped by its dependence upon the black vote, the state's poor economic condition, and the hostility of the majority of white citizens, it finally went down in defeat in the disputed election of 1876.

The leadership of the incoming Democrats lay with an oligarchy composed of their county leaders, since the victorious gubernatorial candidate, George F. Drew, was virtually a political unknown before the campaign. The manner in which Drew and the other Bourbon governors met the problems facing them moulded the complex political patterns of present day Florida. That they and the county leaders left few official and personal records was in keeping with their utilitarian philosophy. All who work in Florida history owe a major debt of gratitude to the late Julien C. Yonge of the University of Florida, not only for his collection of newspapers and manuscripts, but for the knowledge that he was always willing to share.

In telling the story of Bourbon politics I am obliged to Dr. James Miller Leake of the University of Florida. Dr. Leake first encouraged me to examine the career of Senator Wilkinson Call. This book is a continuation of a dissertation written under the kindly and encouraging supervision of Dr. Roy F. Nichols of the University of Pennsylvania. Dr. W. E. Baringer of the University of Florida generously evaluated the original manuscript. The grant-in-aid and research professor programs of Auburn University made possible the preparation of the final draft.

Students in New South history classes at Auburn University will easily recognize the interpretations for which I am completely responsible.

Dr. Samuel Proctor, editor, graciously gave permission to quote from several articles which I contributed to the *Florida Historical Quarterly*.

In gathering source material I received considerable assistance from Watt Marchman of the Hayes Memorial Library, Fremont, Ohio, Mrs. Frank W. Pope, Jr., of Daytona Beach, Carlton Smith of Madison, W. Lansing Gleason of Eau Gallie, Mrs. Elizabeth Swann Carroll of Fernandina, and Mrs. William S. Jennings of Jacksonville, all in Florida.

I am indebted to Jane C. Cobb, Auburn Learning Resources Center, for carefully drawn maps of Florida.

I am thankful to Mrs. John C. Ball and Bobbie Olliff, my typists, for their conscientious efforts.

Last and most of all, for her patience, understanding and confidence, I am forever indebted to my wife, Ruthie.

To Ruthie, Susie, and Eddie

Contents

List of Maps

1

Reconstruction Doldrums

Until long after the Civil War, to most Northerners and Europeans Florida was a forbidden land. Associated in the common imagination with the dark Everglades and the bloody Seminole wars, the state's name evoked thoughts of swamps, marshes, canebrakes, and alligators.[1] Adventurous tourists fancied that in visiting Florida they were absenting themselves from civilization.[2] Most immigrants from Europe, coming to the United States through the port of New York, either stayed in the ghettos of the East or homesteaded in the West. Few came south, and few of these individualistic ones selected the sparsely settled peninsula despite its mild climate, fertile land in the public domain, and vast pine, cypress, and hardwood forests.[3]

In common with her sister states in rebellion, Florida recovered slowly from the defeat and destruction caused by the Civil War. Although the state was neither in the path of large armies nor the scene of major battles, damage to property had been considerable, because of the Union efforts to prevent blockade running, destructive raids upon the railway system, and general neglect and decay.[4] Political disintegration was accentuated when in 1865 Confederate Governor John Milton, exhausted and discouraged, committed suicide. As a result, Florida surrendered leaderless, disorganized, and demoralized.[5]

Fortunately, before complete chaos set in, President Andrew Johnson appointed Federal Judge William Marvin provisional

Notes begin on p. 195.

governor.[6] Northern-born and a long-time Unionist resident of Key
West, Marvin immediately acted to relieve uncertainty and to
arouse the defeated from their apathy. To prepare for Florida's
reentrance into the Union, a statewide election was held for delegates to a constitutional convention,[7] which met in Tallahassee
on October 24, 1865. Composed almost entirely of ex-Confederates, the convention was dominated by the old plantation, small
town, port city oligarchy. Philosophically conservative, they
would later be call Bourbons by their political opponents.
Reactionary insofar as the blacks were concerned, their views
were based on paternalistic attitudes rather than racial hatred.
Many of them would become proponents of the New South concept of Henry Grady and John B. Gordon. Northern investors such
as Henry Flagler would find them enthusiastic allies. Confronted
with the necessity and practicality of bringing Florida back into the
Union under Presidential Reconstruction, these ex-Confederates
annulled the Ordinance of Secession, then repealed the state law
which legalized slavery. They rejected Governor Marvin's recommendation that civil rights be extended to the freedmen and
Florida's Civil War debt of $2,100,000 be repudiated. Not until
the convention was notified that repudiation was an inflexible
demand of President Johnson was it voted. The delegates also
reluctantly supported a watered-down civil rights bill.[8] It was
obvious that the role of the Negro had changed but not the attitude
of the white Floridian toward him.

Interest in state government continued at a low ebb. When the
state held its first postwar election to replace Governor Marvin's
provisional administration, Negroes were still denied the franchise,
and only four thousand whites went to the polls to give the Unionists a hollow victory. Since the voting strength in Florida prior
to the Civil War had been fourteen thousand, it was obvious that
the new governor, David S. Walker of Tallahassee, did not have
a clear mandate from the people. A former slaveholder, Walker
was a cousin and successor of long-time antebellum Whig and
Unionist leader General Richard Keith Call.[9] If left to his own
devices, Walker would follow a moderately conservative policy
and not disturb the ex-Confederate control of the state.

The new legislature was more aggressive than the similarly composed convention. The old defeatist attitude was disappearing as
things returned to normal. As a stop-gap, a stringent Black Code

was passed to prevent disintegration of the prevailing two-class system. The legislature selected former Governor Marvin and Wilkinson Call of Tallahassee to represent Florida as United States senators.[10] Though a strong Unionist until Florida seceded, Call, a cousin of Walker and nephew of General Call, had served in the state as a Confederate Army officer during the war.[11] His election climaxed a remarkable comeback for the Call-Virginia-planter faction of the Florida Whigs, considering that the old general, thinking the cause of Whiggery hopeless, had died in 1862 discouraged and frustrated.[12] The ex-Whigs, however, owed their good fortune more to the discrediting of the Democrats in the downfall of the Confederacy than to their own particular activities. The election of Marvin indicated a spirit of compromise on the part of Florida's Presidential Reconstruction legislature. The Key West Unionist was completely untainted by any connection with the Confederacy. Prewar Unionists who had sided with either the North or the South were now united and in control in Florida.

Any possibility that Florida would be reconstructed by the Unionist coalition was ended by a Radical Republican victory in the national election in 1866, which gave the Radicals complete control of Congress. They then passed a series of Reconstruction acts despite Johnson's vetoes. Florida thus did not reenter the Union under the guidance of ex-Whigs and other Unionists. Instead it became part of the Third Military District under the command of Major General John Pope, who voided the Florida Constitution of 1865 and issued a call for a new constitutional convention. In the November 1867 election of delegates to the convention, the freedmen were given the franchise.[13] Unionists Wilkinson Call and William Marvin were denied seats in the Senate, and Governor Walker became a figurehead. Henceforth, most of the Unionists would work with ex-Confederates in the Conservative Democratic party. The Radicals had inadvertently mended the political split among Florida's whites.

While these political changes were taking place, the Freedmen's Bureau under the guidance of Major Thomas W. Osborn was distributing free rations and agricultural supplies to thousands of destitute whites and blacks in Florida. In addition it opened public schools for Negro education. The bureau accomplished much good in the short run, yet in the long run it accelerated the widening of the rift between the planter and his ex-slave.[14] Thus the attempt of the federal government to reweave the pattern of Florida's culture through economic and political changes was not acceptable to the majority of Florida's white population. A way of life calling for white supremacy and a sharp division between the races would not easily be cast aside.

Paralleling the Freedmen's Bureau activities on a religious plane were the efforts of Northern Protestant missionaries, both white and Negro. In antebellum Florida, Negro religious life had been controlled by the traditional white churches. The Northern missionaries effected an end to that control. Before the Civil War, Negro Southern Methodists in Florida numbered 8,110. In Reconstruction this group dwindled to less than five hundred. The Episcopalians also felt the effects of Northern proselyting. While most of the Northern missionaries were undoubtedly religious, several became involved in politics after their sects had made substantial gains in membership.[15] Considering the high illiteracy rate of Florida's freedmen, it is understandable how the educated missionary became a political leader.

These Negro leaders competed for the black vote with newly arrived white Northerners, mostly ex-Union soldiers and former officials of the Freedmen's Bureau. Willing to disregard the color line insofar as the Negro vote was concerned, such men as Dennis Eagan of Madison, the Stearns brothers of Quincy, and Leonard G. Dennis of Gainesville were able not only to develop strong political machines but also to prosper, either as planters or as merchants. Leonard G. Dennis built the only brick building in Gainesville and also owned its largest hotel, the Arlington House. Irish-born Dennis Eagan, in the manner of the old antebellum aristocrats, ran Madison County from his plantation.[16] These carpetbaggers had basically the same code of ethics, ambitions, and scruples as the young politician in the North who controlled the immigrant vote. But whereas the latter was in his element in a materialistic, expanding urban area in which even a Boss Tweed had uptown support, the carpetbagger was a white leader of black men in a static rural society economically dominated by whites firmly committed to white supremacy. Although the main motivation of the carpetbaggers was political and economic, social motivation was extremely important to the white Southerner. Carpetbaggers and their families, therefore, experienced little of the traditional Southern hospitality in Florida's Black Belt.

Northerners, particularly farmers, who came south after the war were inclined to underestimate the Southern yeomanry. To the Yankee it seemed that the natives lacked the energy and ambition needed to develop the land properly. Thus it was expected that the intelligent and industrious Northern farmer would increase the yield perhaps as much as tenfold. The blame for such a low state of being on the part of Southerners was laid on the doorstep of slavery.[17]

Northern businessmen were no strangers to antebellum Florida, and in the Reconstruction era some were attracted to the Republican party. Their stronghold was Jacksonville. Suffering from the "Damn Yankee" label by which defeated natives showed their resentment, this group held high hopes in 1867 of effecting a merger with ex-Whigs and business-minded Democrats to form a party to be known as the Reconstruction or Unionist party, since both Northern and Southern businessmen recognized that the name "Republican" was distasteful in Florida.[18] Harrison Reed, originally a postal agent from Wisconsin and a Johnson Democrat, was political spokesman for the Jacksonville businessmen. Reed even dreamed of enticing former firebrand Senator David L. Yulee into the fold if the party name could be changed from Republican.[19]

Yulee had been the dominant antebellum Democratic political leader. In the early 1850s as spokesman for the small planters and yeoman farmers, he had been a "fire eater" in the slavery controversy with the North. Then in the middle 1850s his interest shifted to railroad building. With the aid of a liberal federal land grant and Wall Street financial support, he constructed the Florida Railroad across a virtual wilderness from Fernandina on the Atlantic Ocean to Cedar Key on the Gulf of Mexico. The Civil War was a trying period of crisis for both Yulee and his railroad, particularly when raiding parties tore it up. However, at the end of the war, despite a brief imprisonment for supporting the Confederacy, he was able to reestablish his relationship with his Northern financial backers and continue his railroad promotion.[20] His politics, henceforth, would be geared to his business interests. He would do business with but not join the Republicans.

Yulee had selected Fernandina as his railroad's eastern terminal because its natural harbor on Amelia Island was the finest on Florida's Atlantic coastline. And as long as the peninsula did not have a direct connection by rail with the rest of the United States, most freight and the growing tourist trade would come by water to either Fernandina or Jacksonville, twenty-four miles to the south. Having made substantial real estate investments on Amelia Island and possessing a railroad monopoly into Fernandina, Yulee hoped that his terminal town would become the metropolis of North Florida, relegating Jacksonville to the subordinate role of port for the St. Johns River boats.[21] Located at the mouth of the St. Johns River and the terminal for the railroad that ran as far west as Tallahassee, Jacksonville was, however, in excellent shape to resist any encroachments on its business that Fernandina might make. From its busy waterfront, river boats left daily for Palatka, Enterprise, and Sanford. The Florida Central Railroad provided competition to Yulee's road in Northeast Florida.

Northern prosperity was reflected in a new impetus to the tourist trade, which by the early 1870s had established its headquarters in Jacksonville's St. James and Grand National hotels. In contrast to antebellum days when antiquarian and invalid came to St. Augustine for quiet and mild winters the trade now catered to the whims and sports (particularly hunting) of the nouveaux riches. Picturesque St. Augustine, the oldest city in the United States and for centuries (1565–1823) the capital of East Florida, was now stagnant. Its empty harbor, blocked by treacherous shoals, served as a grim reminder to Jacksonville of what might happen if it became landlocked.[22]

The sleepiness of St. Augustine was similar to the lethargy of many whites who failed to register for the militarily supervised election in 1867. Fully 30 per cent of Florida's white males failed to qualify, allowing blacks, registering for the first time, to become the majority, 15,500 to 11,151. On the three days in November set aside for voting, white citizens who had registered stayed away from the polls in an unsuccessful attempt to defeat the call for a convention. A complete Republican victory resulted: with 14,503 votes cast, 13,283 were those of Negroes. Of the delegates to the convention, eighteen were Negroes, fifteen carpetbaggers, eleven scalawags, and two Southern Democrats. Not one delegate had previously held an important office in Florida and nearly all were newcomers to the state's politics.[23]

At the Tallahassee convention, the Republicans split into two factions, moderates and radicals. In the early sessions a radical trio of two carpetbaggers and one Negro, all recent arrivals in Florida, seized control of the convention machinery. The moderates, led by Major Thomas W. Osborn, formerly with the Freedmen's Bureau, withdrew to nearby Monticello, regrouped, and formed a rump convention. After writing a constitution to their liking and acting as the nominating convention for the state's Republican party, the Osborn group returned to Tallahassee and in a midnight coup d'état seized the convention chamber. After obtaining the open assistance of the military government, the moderates ejected the radical leadership from the convention. The Monticello constitution which was adopted provided for a strong centralized government with the appointive power residing in the chief executive. This appointive power included almost all county officials as well as cabinet members, and it gave the party which controlled the governorship practically all offices in the state.[24]

Moderate Republicans maintained their control of the state with the election in 1868 of Harrison Reed as governor. Reed continued in his efforts to conciliate the Southern Unionist element by naming one of them to his cabinet. But despite good original intentions, the new governor was soon in difficulty. He quarreled with Osborn, who was elected to the Senate by the Republican-dominated legislature. The quarrel split the moderates. Handicapped further by a hostile legislature and the hatred of the Southern Democrats, Reed endured four attempts at impeachment during five stormy years.[25]

In this period, although the state was practically bankrupt, a coalition of carpetbaggers and Southern businessmen attempted to exploit the internal improvement lands and expropriate the railroads. Railroad promotion centered in the activities of two North Carolina adventurers, George Swepson and Milton S. Littlefield. This shrewd pair arrived in Florida in 1868 carrying with them the construction fund of the western division of the Western North Carolina Railroad, which they proceeded to invest. Obtaining control of three of Florida's bankrupt railroads, they formed the Jacksonville, Pensacola, and Mobile Railroad and persuaded compliant Florida legislatures to vote them $4 million in state bonds. The bonds were placed in the hands of a New York firm which succeeded in selling $3 million of them in Holland at seventy cents on the dollar. An injunction prevented the sale of the remaining $1 million. Of the amount raised by selling the bonds, exactly

$153,938 was used in constructing nineteen and one-half miles of railroad. In 1876 an irate Republican state supreme court declared the bonds unconstitutional and void but allowed their holders to have a statutory lien on the railroads. At the same time authorities in North Carolina took legal action to recover funds misappropriated by Swepson and Littlefield.[26]

The efforts of carpetbaggers and sundry others to grab the public domain for little or nothing ran counter to the vested interests of Northern speculators such as Francis Vose of New York, who had invested in Florida railroads before the war. Vose held a claim against the Florida Internal Improvement Fund. This claim was based on the fund's being used to guarantee the interest on the defaulting bonds of Yulee's railroad. To prevent the Republican government of Florida from supporting new railroad construction at the expense of Internal Improvement Fund lands, Vose went into federal court in 1871 and succeeded in obtaining an injunction to freeze the fund. The injunction forbade Governor Reed and the other fund trustees from selling fund lands until the Vose claim was settled. As a result of this decree, the Internal Improvement Fund was placed in the hands of a receiver.[27] With the state unable to subsidize internal improvements, railroad building was at almost a standstill throughout the remainder of Republican rule in Florida.

The same year as the Vose injunction, the Democratic party, rejuvenated by the leadership of William D. Bloxham, started to make a comeback. In a special election caused by the removal of the Republican lieutenant governor, the mild-mannered Leon County planter ran a close race. The campaign featured Bloxham phrasing platitudes concerning the rights of the Negro while Democratic clubs and vigilantes prevented many freedmen from voting. Because of the state constitution, however, the Republicans controlled the election machinery, and Bloxham was counted out after an apparent win.[28]

By this time, Republican supremacy was endangered by constant intraparty strife. By the end of his term, Reed's prestige as a statewide Republican leader was badly damaged and his influence minimal. The Republican party turned to Ossian Hart, a Jacksonville scalawag and state supreme court judge. Judge Hart was the one native Southerner high in state Republican circles. His father had founded Jacksonville and with Judge Hart as its candidate the Republican party made its strongest appeal to the native white vote. Like former Governor Marvin, Hart had remained a Unionist loyal to the North throughout the war.

The Democratic party selected both its top candidates from Florida's Black Belt planter class. Despite his limited state militia-home guard role during the war, William Bloxham was advanced as the gubernatorial candidate. His running mate was battle-scarred Confederate brigadier Robert Bullock of Ocala. Although the Democrats carried twenty-seven of Florida's thirty-nine counties, the Republicans won by a narrow margin. The twenty-seven Democratic counties were mainly in the thinly populated, predominantly white, rural areas of the panhandle and the peninsula. The Republican counties were in the more populous Black Belt and on the coast.[29]

In the Legislature the lineup followed the results of the gubernatorial election. With their counties represented by Republicans, the Black Belt planters depended on their rural allies from Democratic counties for their needs. The planters concentrated their political activities on regaining the Black Belt counties and controlling state and district conventions.

Republican control in Black Belt counties was broken first in Jackson, where organized violence and murder by vigilante-type organizations not only eliminated both Negro and carpetbag leadership but also victimized some individuals not engaged in any political activity. Law and order became a forgotten issue as the blacks retaliated. But they were not able to maintain their cause against the onslaught of militant Klan-like elements.[30]

The last statewide Republican victory of the Reconstruction era occurred in 1873 when the legislature elected Dr. Simon B. Conover, a Tallahassee carpetbagger, to the United States Senate. Democratic votes provided Conover's margin over both Democratic and Republican opponents: had the twenty-one Democrats who voted for Conover supported Democrat James D. Westcott, Jr., he would have won easily.[31]

In 1875 the legislature elected the first Democrat to the Senate since the Republicans had come to power. Mainly self-educated, Charles W. Jones was an Irish-born ex-carpenter from Pensacola.[32] His mediocre career in the Senate would later end in a mental breakdown.[33] But with his election, though by only one vote, Republican control of the legislature was broken. While internal

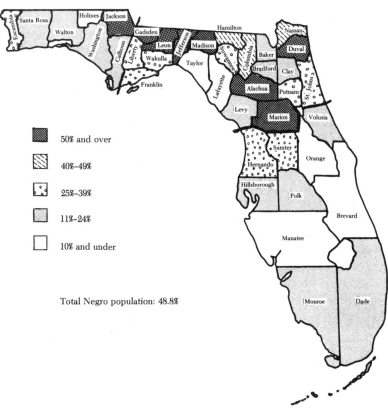

Santa Rosa
Escambia
Holmes
Jackson
Walton
Washington
Gadsden
Hamilton
Nassau
Leon
Madison
Duval
Calhoun
Jefferson
Liberty
Wakulla
Baker
Franklin
Taylor
Suwannee
Columbia
Bradford
Clay
Lafayette
St. Johns
Alachua
Putnam
Levy
Marion
Volusia
Sumter
Orange
Hernando
Hillsborough
Polk
Brevard
Manatee
Monroe
Dade

50% and over

40%-49%

25%-39%

11%-24%

10% and under

Total Negro population: 48.8%

1. Ratio of Negro Distribution by County, 1870. (Statistics from U.S. Census Office, Ninth Census, 1870.)

corruption and the hatred of white Southerners played important roles in its downfall, the Republican party throughout Reconstruction lacked strength because it lacked leadership. With the exception of scalawag Ossian Hart and blacks Jonathan Gibbs and Josiah T. Walls, it depended on Northern carpetbaggers with only a superficial knowledge of the state and the needs of the freedmen. Political rewards for Negroes other than minor offices were rare despite the fact that almost the entire party voting strength was Negro. Jonathan Gibbs of Tallahassee was the only Negro to become a cabinet member, and Josiah T. Walls of Gainesville was the only black representative from Florida in Washington.[34]

The death of Gibbs left Josiah T. Walls the only strong Negro leader in the state. A self-made man of limited education, Walls came to Florida from Virginia shortly after the war and engaged in cabbage growing in Alachua County. Prospering while most of his white neighbors were poverty stricken, Walls reached the economic status of a planter. Entering politics he soon became joint leader of the Alachua County Republican machine, sharing this position with Leonard G. Dennis. In contrast to Walls, Dennis was a corrupt, self-seeking demagogue, forever willing to sacrifice the Negro on the altar of opportunism. In 1870 and 1874 Walls appeared to have been elected to Congress, only to be unseated by his Democratic opponents. In 1872 he received a clear majority of the votes cast. Holding the respect of many Democrats, Walls served his race and party with distinction.[35]

In 1876, with prospects at their brightest since the start of Reconstruction, Florida Democratic leaders decided to put up as strong a ticket as possible. They turned to the Unionist–former Whig branch of their party for all four major candidates. An ex–New Hampshire Yankee, George F. Drew of Ellaville on the Suwannee River, was the unanimous choice to head the ticket as William D. Bloxham (in his most gracious manner) stepped aside. The son of poor farm people, and possessing only a grammar school education, Drew had come south in 1847 to open a machine shop in Columbus, Georgia. A clever mechanic and good business- man, he prospered and at the time of the outbreak of the Civil War was a successful sawmill operator in Columbus. He supplied the Confederate government with lumber and also began a salt- making business near St. Andrews Bay in West Florida. Federal raiding parties destroyed his salt-making equipment in 1862. He then sold his Columbus mill and moved to Adams Station in Lee County, Georgia, to begin another sawmill. He continued to furnish lumber for the Confederate government, and there is strong evidence that he assisted Union sympathizers in running the Confederate lines to escape military service. In late 1863 he was arrested, charged with disloyalty to the Confederacy, and tried before a Confederate Commissioner at Macon. He was then apparently convicted and imprisoned at Savannah until 1864. He seems next to have traded his sawmill for two hundred bales of cotton stored in a Savannah warehouse. His cotton was seized by the Union army and sold. He then entered a claim for the cotton, and after due consideration the United States Court of Claims awarded Drew, "always loyal to the United States," $35,066 as the legitimate owner of the cotton. At the war's end Drew moved to Ellaville, where the firm of Drew and Bucki cut Florida's virgin forests. Prosperity gave him the sobriquet "Millionaire" Drew, although he was by no means as wealthy as that.

With financial success achieved, Drew entered politics as a Democrat and was appointed a Madison County commissioner by Republican Governor Harrison Reed. A fair-minded man with liberal views and no bias against the Negro, Drew was popular with both races in the eastern part of the county. Probably thinking that with this popularity he could buck the Republican county machine successfully, he accepted the Democratic nomination for state senator in 1872. In this contest for political office, his first, he was soundly defeated when Negro voters solidly supported one of their own race. But in 1876, now stout, gray-haired, and fiftyish, the genial "Millionaire Drew" would be well able to finance his own campaign, no small matter in a poor frontier state.[36] He would make a strong appeal to the white voters—and would attract black voters disillusioned by the failure of the Republican administrations to help their status. By nominating Drew the Florida Democrats followed a Southern precedent set in 1874 in Alabama when wealthy George Smith Houston was the Democratic candidate.[37]

Strongly backed by state patronage, carpetbagger Marcellus Stearns, who had succeeded to the governorship following Hart's death in 1874, secured the Republican nomination. Opposition immediately appeared from a small so-called reform element of the Republican party which attempted to run Senator Simon B.

Conover as an independent candidate. But after denouncing Stearns as the corrupt ring candidate and unsuccessfully attempting to get money from the Democrats, Senator Conover mysteriously withdrew in favor of the Gadsden County carpetbagger. In East Florida the Jacksonville businessmen faction seized control from the Negroes at the Republican District Convention. Josiah Walls was pushed aside as the Republican candidate for Congress and replaced by the austere Horatio Bisbee, Jr., a railroad lawyer who numbered David L. Yulee among his clients. Now all major Republican candidates were white despite the overwhelmingly black rank and file.[38]

In the campaign both parties put forth major efforts. Disregarding the Democratic claim to be the reform party and George F. Drew's fair appeal to the people of the state, local bands of white regulators and terrorists were again active. Democratic landlords and employers exerted strong economic pressure and passed out thousands of marked Democratic ballots. New to politics on a statewide level and unable to control his party, Drew was not in sympathy with any undemocratic practices. On the other hand, the Republican state administration (with control of the election machinery) had no intention of making a fair count if the election went for the Democrats. Fraud, chain voting, tissue paper ballots, and intimidation were commonplace on both sides.[39] Captain E. M. L'Engle, a longtime resident of Jacksonville and a prominent businessman with Democratic leanings, wrote his wife on the eve of the election that Tilden's victory was assured but Florida was doubtful. Democrats would cast several thousand more legal votes than the Republicans, but the Republicans controlled the ballot box and duplicate voting by their ignorant rank and file could decide the issue.[40]

First returns indicated that the vote in Florida would be very close. To an anxious nation a partisan state canvassing board announced a Republican victory. Unwilling to accept this verdict and at the same time ignoring proposals for physical action to oust the carpetbaggers from the capital, George F. Drew immediately sought recourse within the law, requesting a writ of mandamus from Chief Justice Edwin M. Randall of the state supreme court. Judge Randall, a Jacksonville carpetbagger but no political ally of Governor Stearns, acted in an impartial manner; he granted the writ and ordered the state canvassing board reconvened. In

the new count Drew won, and ex-Whig Colonel Robert H. M.
Davidson of Quincy was declared the victor in the Congressional
race in West Florida.[41] Horatio Bisbee, Jr., while allowed to take
the Second District seat in Congress, was unseated by his Democratic opponent, Confederate brigadier Jesse Johnson Finley of
Lake City, after serving most of his term.[42]

With the defeat of the Republicans in 1876, Reconstruction in
Florida came to a close. In retrospect it is easy to ascertain that
politics were radically changed by the entrance of the Republican
party into the state and the admission of the Negro to political
participation. Just a decade away from the cotton field, black
political leaders in the legislature showed progress as they presided
over committees, voted on issues, and expressed their opinions
in speeches. A politically conscious Negro community added a
new element to be taken into account in dividing the loaves and
fishes. Before the Civil War, the political lineup had been the Black
Belt planters against the yeoman farmers, the former generally
Whigs, the latter Democrats. When the planters went into the
Democratic party, they did not give up hope of controlling the
Negro's vote as they had previously controlled his life.[43] And in
spite of the strong anti-Negro bias of the yeoman farmers, the
planters were successful in getting the Democratic party to make
a vigorous bid for the black vote in 1876.[44] However, planters
were not the dominant group, and it was questionable just what
reward, if any, the Negroes-for-Drew would receive.

Under Republican administrations, Florida officeholders included a cross section of economic and racial groups. Great strides
were made in black and white education and adherents of the
newly established schools were gained from both parties. The
efforts to establish the Florida Agricultural College at Eau Gallie
were certainly laudable. The state prison at Chattahoochee made
progress toward becoming an institution of correction as well as
punishment. The practice of the Republicans in appointing Democratic cabinet members and county officials had made possible
Democratic participation in the state government far beyond what
is usual for a defeated party.[45]

But while Reconstruction in Florida led to some progress, it also
aggravated the deep emotional hurt which the South had incurred
when it lost the war. The white Southerner would not grant the

Negro social and economic equality and would allow him political equality only under strong federal pressure. In applying this pressure and organizing the Negroes, the Republicans introduced Northern-model political machines into Florida, particularly in Duval and Madison counties. Since they were no different from their Northern counterparts, it was not surprising that the handful of carpetbaggers dominating the state showed more interest in political patronage and economic profits for themselves than in social, economic, and political gains for the Negro. As a member of the majority, the Negro received no more benefit than his immigrant counterpart in the cities of the North. The Negro was ruthlessly used by carpetbaggers and Republican businessmen who desired to replace the old planters as the ruling class of Florida and to control millions of acres of public domain and the railroads. These Northerners soon lost interest in the betterment of the "bottom rail." Often they found their racial views coinciding with those of the white Southerner. Leading Republicans were more often hard-fisted Yankees such as Horatio Bisbee, Jr., than dreamy abolitionists.

In handling the railroads and the public lands, the Republicans followed the antebellum precedents of Whigs and Democrats. The prewar Democratic record is better: while the Democratic railroad builders constructed hundreds of miles of railroad at little personal profit, the faith-bond-backed schemes of the Whigs and the Swepson-Littlefield episode of the Republicans all ended in failure. The circumstances regarding the repudiation of $3.9 million worth of faith bonds by the Territory of Florida at the close of the Whig period in 1842 are startlingly similar to circumstances surrounding the repudiation of the $4 million worth of state bonds in 1876. In both cases European investors were the losers, and in both cases the government of Florida was used as a willing tool by frontier promoters operating primarily for their own personal profit.[46]

With the repudiation of the $4 million in state bonds upheld by the courts, the state debt in 1876 stood at $1,391,600, only a small increase over what it was in 1868 when the Republicans gained control.[47] Florida was much the same poor, agrarian frontier in 1877 as in 1821 when the second Spanish occupation ended. The fight of the Democrats for supremacy was not so much the fight of lily-white reformers against a corrupt political machine as it was the struggle of a desperate people, who had lost a war, to regain their sovereignty from those who had been the enemy and the slave. They would find when they regained political control of the state that the same basic problems remained: those of an agrarian frontier seeking population, capital, transportation facilities, better education, and law and order.

2

The Redemption and the Old Problems

Situated in Florida's Black Belt on a hill covered with old live oaks, Tallahassee's gardens overlooked an expanse of field and forest spreading southward to the old Spanish fort at St. Marks on the Gulf of Mexico. Described by one Northern traveler as "the floral city of the flowery South," the former Apalachee Indian village had been the capital since 1824. Fifty years later, with a population of 2,500, it was a town of leisure and houses rather than industry and factories. Its business district consisted of four blocks of old brick stores on one side of Main Street. Since the capitol itself was only a simple brick structure, it might have seemed to a casual onlooker that a town so rural held its favored position with only a light grasp.[1] But Florida's larger cities, Jacksonville, Pensacola, and Key West, were all located on the state's periphery. Geography and a determined, politically conscious populace in Tallahassee made a change of capital unlikely.

Lawmakers set the gubernatorial inauguration date for January 2, 1877. The artificial niceties of protocol, always sacred to lawyers and politicians, were observed when Republican carpetbagger Chief Justice Edwin M. Randall swore Redeemer George F. Drew into office. Frustrated and disappointed, outgoing Governor Marcellus Stearns chose inauguration day as an appropriate time to drive a team of horses into the country.[2] Though the one-armed Union war veteran had withdrawn from the capital, he still hoped that the state supreme court would declare him the winner.[3]

Studiously ignoring the obvious hostility of the nominal leader

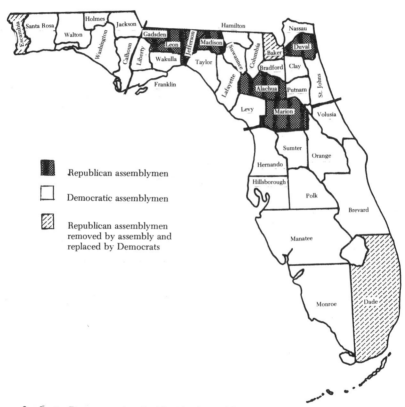

2. Party Representation in Florida Assembly by County, 1877. (Statistics from *Florida Assembly Journal*, 1877.)

of Florida's Republicans, the incoming executive made his inaugural speech a plea for reconciliation. His course, he promised his racially mixed audience, would follow the middle of the road for the next four years, and he assured the state's Negro population that their rights as guaranteed by the Constitution would be fully sustained. His statement that "we are a law abiding people, resolved to perpetuate free institutions," rebuffed extremists on both sides and was a promise to the Negroes that a reign of terror would not occur in Florida. Although some Democrats had anticipated trouble from Republican extremists, the inauguration passed quietly.[4]

The new governor's move toward better racial relationships was viewed with skepticism by even moderate Republicans. The *Daily Florida Union*, which normally spoke for the ex-Northern business group in Jacksonville, gave credence the next day to a wild rumor that Drew was in favor of the reenactment of the Black Code of the post–Civil War era. The *Union*'s editor warned his readers that under this projected circumvention of the Fourteenth Amendment any vagrant, white or black, could be placed on the auction block and sold as a time slave to the highest bidder.[5]

For Drew, getting off to a strong start depended not so much on his conciliating the Republicans as on his leadership of the Democrat-dominated legislature and his handling of state patronage. Coming from the quiet of Ellaville, where the entire community loved him, he would experience for the next four years an entirely different atmosphere in Tallahassee, where William D. Bloxham was the favorite son. Recognizing Bloxham's high standing in the Democratic party and grateful for his support during the campaign, Drew gave him first priority in the cabinet, naming him secretary of state. This appointment was no small favor since Bloxham had neglected planting for politics and was in poor financial straits.[6]

Despite its small size, the politically conscious capital traditionally obtained a good share of Florida's major political posts. It was not surprising that a second resident, George P. Raney, was named attorney general. Though a young man, Raney was a veteran politician. At twenty-two years of age he had represented Franklin County as one of the few Democrats in the legislature of 1868. Moving his law practice to Tallahassee in 1869, he retained his interest in politics, serving as a member of the Democratic State Executive Committee.

Columbus Drew, no relation to the governor, had been a prominent Whig editor and Unionist in Jacksonville in the 1850s. Appointed as the new comptroller, he now emerged from almost twenty years of obscurity. The post of adjutant general rewarded Captain John Jackson Dickison, earlier a Civil War hero and of late a defeated candidate for the assembly from Gadsden County. Guerilla leader of the few Confederate soldiers remaining in the field in Florida in the closing stages of the war and known to the Yankees as "Dixie," Dickison gained his fame by defeating small parties of Union soldiers foraging in the interior of the state.

Hugh A. Corley, junior member of the large Fernandina real estate firm of Williams, Swann, and Corley, was an excellent choice for commissioner of lands and immigration. For the remaining two positions in his cabinet, the governor chose South Florida men, ex-Northerner William P. Haisley of Hillsborough County for superintendent of public instruction, and Walter Gwynn, wartime state comptroller and now an assemblyman from Orange County, for treasurer.[7]

Drew's cabinet was well balanced, perhaps lacking only a West Florida representative. Bitter feelings engendered by Reconstruction had ended the Republican precedent of naming a prominent opposition party member to the cabinet, but the absence of any representative of the Ku Klux Klan–like young Democratic clubs confirmed the fact that the governor would seriously attempt to carry out his promise of conciliatior. Piloted by an ex-Northerner and officered by a preponderantly Southern cabinet, Florida would follow a political middle-of-the-road course under Drew.

No earlier Democratic governor, with the exception of John Milton, had been a top political leader, and all had passed into political oblivion after serving one term.[8] Because the self-made Drew had not been a member of the inner circle who periodically gathered at the party's unofficial headquarters in the office of the *Weekly Floridian*, he was looked on by some as a candidate of expediency. During Reconstruction, the *Floridian*'s editor, Charles E. Dyke, Sr., played the part of a Nestor as he advised, planned, and consulted with the leaders of Democratic county organizations and legislators. Not a native son—he was born in Canada—Dyke came as a young printer to Apalachicola, then a thriving cotton port, in 1839. After a brief stay he moved to Tallahassee to begin a long association with the *Floridian*.[9] For over thirty years, his newspaper had been the infallible authority of the Democratic party from which there was to be no deviation under penalty of being branded a heretic. Editor Dyke saw eye to eye with the Bourbon-planter class on the Southern way of life. The poor boy who arrived from the North in the antebellum era hated the poor boys who arrived from the North after the war, and in his editorial columns he made it clear that these carpetbaggers could either conform to the *mores* or leave, preferably the latter.[10] Anxious to secure the senior Dyke as an ally, Governor Drew named Charles E. Dyke, Jr., as his private secretary.[11] In selecting young Dyke and Bloxham, the independently minded lumberman showed that he was making every effort to work with the old guard alliance of the printer and the planter.

The new cabinet appointments received unexpected praise from Jacksonville's Republican businessmen. Pleased because the extremist elements of the Democratic party had been excluded, the *Daily Florida Union*'s editor saw hopeful indications that Drew would conduct his administration on a moderate basis.[12] But to have split the Democratic party by cutting loose from the party extremists would have been a risky undertaking for Drew, lacking as he did any strong, loyal, personal following throughout the state. As it was, the governor had the support of a legislature safely Democratic in both houses: the senate fourteen to nine, the assembly thirty-two to eighteen.[13] Favorable decisions in disputed elections would further swell the Democratic ranks. The Democratic legislators, however, were primarily responsible to their county political organizations, which were the lifeblood of the Democratic party. Traditionally, the Florida Democratic party operated as a confederation; if Governor Drew attempted to build up a personal machine, he would certainly arouse the resentment of local oligarchs. These men enjoyed their roles as king-makers in the state conventions too much to relish subordinate positions.

Among those particularly sensitive concerning their position in both Florida and the Democratic party were the Scottish Presbyterian farmer-politicians from the thickly forested West Florida panhandle. Stretching along a narrow 135-mile corridor from the Perdido River to the Apalachicola River with few areas of good farming land—a forgotten relic of the Spanish Empire—the panhandle possessed neither railroad nor river to connect it to the rest of the state. In West Florida, the frustration of having at Pensacola the finest harbor on the Gulf of Mexico largely undeveloped and unused produced a strong undercurrent of sentiment in favor of annexation to Alabama. Except for Escambia County, whose Republican legislators would be contested, West Florida sent a solid Democratic bloc of yeoman farmers, small town merchants, and lawyers to the legislature. The West Floridians had played an important part in the redemption of the state, and they showed their strength when G. G. McWhorter, a Milton lawyer, was elected speaker of the assembly.[14] To them the most important issue before the legislature was the construction of a railroad to end their isolation.

The Black Belt, possessing the state's two major railroads and consisting of the planter counties of Middle Florida, stretched across the best farming land of North Florida from a few miles west of the Apalachicola River to Silver Springs. Home of the bulk of the Republican party in Florida, it had in the legislature one Democratic senator and three Democratic assemblymen, all from Jackson County. In antebellum days the Black Belt was the dominant part of Florida, guided by its cotton-growing, politically conscious planters; now it was impotently represented by the minority party. The remainder of Florida, except for Duval, Baker and Dade counties, sent a solid bloc of Democrats to Tallahassee.[15]

Political maneuvering in the senate started on inauguration day when demoted black congressman Josiah T. Walls offered a resolution that all standing committees be elected by a two-thirds vote. The alacrity with which this motion was tabled demonstrated to the Republicans just how far the Democrats would follow the conciliation theme of Drew's speech. In both houses all committee appointments consisted of three Democrats and two Republicans.[16] The Republicans did receive some assurance that they would not be treated in a roughshod manner when, on January 9, a Walls-sponsored resolution denouncing the political murder of Republican State Senator E. G. Johnson of Lake City was passed by the senate, which also adjourned for the remainder of the day in respect to Senator Johnson.[17]

The following day, Governor Drew sent his first message to the legislature, declaring "that government will be the most highly esteemed that gives the greatest protection to individual and industrial enterprises at the least expense to the taxpayer . . . spend nothing unless absolutely necessary." Faced with a deficit of almost $90,000, he advised the sharp cutting of expenditures and held

out little hope for an immediate tax cut. Noting that the penitentiary cost an average of $25,000 a year, he recommended that
it be made self-sustaining or that, alternatively, prisoners be leased
out under conditions most advantageous to the state. Previously,
Republican legislatures had shown no interest in Warden Martin's
efforts to make the prison self-supporting. With only $43,311.70
on hand in the state treasury and $130,961.50 in old bills outstand-
ing from the late Republican administration, the prison would
certainly be under fire in the legislature. The governor dealt next
with the election reform. Under his proposal a reregistration was
necessary to divide the counties into election districts, each voter
being required to vote in his district. This change would have
prevented transient Negroes and those working away from home
from voting.

While Drew's views on economy and changes in election laws
closely followed the Democratic party line, he showed independent thinking in his assessment of the free school system: "It is
cheaper to build schoolhouses and maintain schools than to build
poorhouses and jails and support paupers and criminals." Courageously leaving no doubt where he stood on black education, he
told the legislature that it was the state's responsibility to educate
the Negro so that he might vote intelligently and make a good
citizen. As minor improvements to the free school system, he recommended a modification of funds to encourage rural education
and the unification of textbooks. But his enthusiasm for state-
sponsored schools was limited to the elementary level, and he
advised that the Florida Agricultural College at Eau Gallie be
abandoned. If this action were approved, Florida would continue
to be without a single college. The state-supported seminaries at
Tallahassee and Gainesville were little better than mediocre high
schools.

In the matter of Republican corruption, Drew brought up only
one case of possible fraud, the matter of $39,087 missing in state
warrants issued during Governor Harrison Reed's administration.
This incident involved Democrat Robert H. Gamble, who as
comptroller was responsible for the warrants.

In concluding his message, Drew reverted to the theme of conciliation, calling upon the legislators to "bury the passions of the
past" since all within the state were "one people, with one hope
and one destiny."[18]

The state press gave a mixed reaction to Drew's program. In the columns of the *Weekly Floridian* Charles Dyke commented favorably on all aspects of the message except for the governor's stand on Negro education, which the editor disdainfully characterized as "broad liberality."[19] The staunchly Republican *Daily Florida Union,* smarting because Drew had released his message to the Jacksonville Democratic newspapers in advance, evaluated it as liberal and sensible but superficial. Deprecating Drew's failure to recommend the lowering of taxes, the *Union* editorial observed that past legislatures had listened more to home interests than to governors. In concluding its comments, it warned the blacks that Drew's policy of conciliation might turn out to be a delusion.[20]

Although the legislature and governor were working harmoniously on most matters, five days after the governor's message the Democratic majority answered that it was not ready "to bury the passions of the past." In the disputed Escambia County election where the carpetbagger-Negro machine of Pensacola had a clear majority of a hundred votes, the only possible way the Democrats could upset the verdict was by throwing out the ballots of those residing in the Pensacola Naval Reservation. The right of these citizens to vote had never been questioned in the past, so the assembly committee on privileges and elections recommended that the two Republican assemblymen retain their seats. The report of this committee was the first break in the solidarity of the Democratic front in the legislature. A newly converted Democrat with a Northern Republican background, P. P. Bishop, a Putnam County citrus man, was responsible for the majority report.[21] On the floor of the assembly, the contest degenerated into a straight party issue, and Bishop, whipped back into line, meekly voted with the Democratic majority to unseat the Republicans.[22] The Jacksonville *Daily Florida Union* interpreted the outcome as an indication that the Democrats were working to obtain a two-thirds majority.[23] In the other contested elections, Democrats were invariably seated, with the exception of state prison warden Malachi Martin, who was allowed to continue to represent Gadsden County in the assembly.[24]

As an anticlimax to the return of Democratic control to Florida, on January 18 the Federal troops were withdrawn from Tallahassee.[25] The era in which the state was a conquered territory came officially to a close. The Florida Republican party was now, with the exception of federal patronage, completely on its own. *Nation* magazine indicated that wealthy and invalided Northern men were beginning to influence the tone of Florida politics.[26] However, the few Northern migrants who came into the state were inclined to affiliate with the Democrats.[27] In addition, Republican members of the 1877 legislature were accomplishing little other than verbal harassment of the Democrats. One opportunity for typical heckling by the black senators occurred on January 23 when the Democrats brought forth a measure to vote the state for Tilden. A. B. Osgood, Negro senator from Madison, slyly suggested that the bill be amended to read that the votes for 1872 be recanvassed. Senator T. W. Long of Marion County facetiously offered the title, "a bill to be entitled an act showing the ability and wisdom of the Florida legislature." Senator Robert Meacham, mulatto son of a planter, moved to amend by inserting the words, "an act to count four men in office without being elected." The bill passed without these amendments on a strict party vote.[28] Two previous certificates had already been submitted for the 1876 election. The majority report of the board of state canvassers cast the electoral vote for Hayes; the minority report favored Tilden. Voting on a strictly party line, the Electoral Commission accepted the Hayes certificate.[29] On March 1 Congress ratified this decision.[30]

The most important remaining instrument of Republican origin was the Constitution of 1868. To prevent blacks from electing every official in a Black Belt county, the governor had been given broad appointive powers so that the whites could be represented. Voters elected constables but no other local officials. Leaders from predominantly white counties had long opposed giving the governor such a strong power over patronage. Needing only the formality of confirmation by a friendly senate, Drew possessed the authority to dismiss almost every Republican on the state payroll and to appoint an entire new slate of state and county officials.[31] Faced with the alternatives of either building up a personal political machine or passing the patronage to the politically starved autonomous Democratic county organizations, he chose the latter.[32] The many office seekers who beat a hopeful path to the governor's door found to their disappointment that they must have the local stamp of approval and that a comparatively short journey to the county seat would have been more profitable than the long trek to Tallahassee. As their ranks thinned out in the capitol corridors, they returned home with much less enthusiasm for the new order.[33] In usual cases of patronage, Democratic legislators were consulted regarding new county officers. Even old Unionists had to be approved by the local Democratic leaders. Where no recommendations were made for removal, the incumbents were allowed to remain in office.[34]

Obviously this solution was not applicable to Black Belt counties represented in the legislature by Negroes, scalawags, and carpetbaggers. Instead of consulting Republican legislators on patronage, Drew made it a rule to rely on the Democratic county executive committees to suggest appointees. An exception to this policy was made in Alachua County, however, when opposition to the county committee choices developed within the party. To restore peace, Drew withdrew the names of the nominees from senatorial consideration and instructed Thomas F. King, committee chairman, to have each county club meet separately and either ballot for the county officials or elect three delegates each to a county convention which would select the officials.[35]

Adhering strictly to the Democratic party framework, working with the Bourbons, and putting new life into the local Democratic groups, Drew crushed any last hopes for the restoration of the old Whig-Unionist party. Though the governor had been a Whig-Unionist, the rank and file of his party now were Democrats and former secessionists, and the patronage went to them. Heading a long list of removed officeholders was James A. Finlayson, scalawag sheriff of lawless Jackson County, where hatred between parties and races seemed stronger than anywhere else.[36]

That the governor had no intention of effecting a rapprochement with the Republicans was evident when his secretary bluntly told a disgruntled Republican that Drew would certainly not reward those who were "loudmouthed in the denunciation of the people who supported him."[37] The appeal for conciliation was made directly to the rank and file of the Republicans, not channeled through their political leaders. But apart from losing their state and county offices, the Republicans had little to complain about. There were no organized or spontaneous state-wide reprisals against the defeated Negroes, scalawags, and carpetbaggers by the victorious Democrats. Credit for the peaceful transition, according to the Jacksonville *Daily Florida Union*, went to Drew.[38]

With his lieutenants in Alachua County rapidly losing their offices, Josiah T. Walls brought forward in the senate on January 26 a proposal for home rule. Walls planned to amend the state constitution to permit the election of county officials and the governor's cabinet. If his amendment passed, the Black Belt and port city counties would once more have Republican officeholders. Unable to choose his own cabinet, the governor would be more subservient than ever to the county political machines. If the Democratic leaders were to oppose Walls, they would place themselves in the paradoxical position of defending a wholly Republican document which the Republicans were trying to change. It was ironical that under a constitution made entirely by Republicans, they were practically excluded from holding any office except in the legislature. The Democratic majority quickly killed Walls's proposal.[39] Dyke, Sr., commented on the *Floridian* editorial page that there was no popular demand for a change in the constitution.[40]

But dissatisfaction with the constitution did exist in Democratic ranks. In the assembly on February 5, J. H. McKinne of Jackson County voiced his opinion that the constitution should be amended to eliminate the office of superintendent of public instruction. The other cabinet offices under the McKinne plan were to be elective. Jackson County possessed a large majority of Negro children in its school-age population, and its white yeoman farmers showed little enthusiasm in furthering their education, since an educated Negro citizenry might regain political control. While McKinne's bill was the first direct attack on the state's free school system, William Watkin Hicks, the last Republican superintendent of public instruction, had warned in 1876 of the existence of powerful opposition. However, such opposition failed to materialize, and the proposal was quickly defeated by a temporary alliance of Democrats and Republicans for the free schools.[41]

Even with its yeoman farmer–small town merchant, provincial makeup, the legislature displayed the traditional Florida interest in Latin America. J. V. Harris of Key West, currying the favor of his hometown's large number of Cubans, offered a strong resolution in the assembly calling for the recognition of "Cuba Libre." Later, South Florida cattleman Francis Asbury Hendry advocated in the senate the establishment of a customhouse at the Gulf port of Punta Rassa, from where Jacob Summerlin and he were shipping cattle to the Spanish army in Cuba. With the emphasis on liberty in the lower house and trade in the upper house, the two resolutions passed.[42]

Threatened Democratic investigations of Republican election frauds dwindled down to an inquiry conducted by a special assembly committee into the activities of Leonard G. Dennis and W. K. Cessna, two legislators from Alachua County. If the vote of Alachua, where the Republicans were victorious, had been thrown out by the original canvassing board, Samuel J. Tilden would have carried Florida and been elected President. In a peculiar decision the special committee absolved Dennis but found Cessna guilty; however, when the issue came to a floor vote on February 17, Cessna was acquitted by a vote of 29 to 12.[43]

Negro leaders feared that Drew's plan for election reform would result in disfranchisement of their race. The law which reached the floor on February 16 called for a reregistration of voters in order to eliminate the practice of "floaters" voting at several precincts. Despite the fact that no clause in the bill openly discriminated against the Negro or called for a literacy test, the small group of black senators fought bitterly to prevent its passage. John Wallace, who came to Florida as the schoolmaster on William D. Bloxham's plantation, predicted that the bill would prevent all persons from voting who could not read or write. Robert Meacham called the bill unjust, unfair, and unlawful. Fred Hill of Quincy saw it as an attempt to disfranchise one-third of the legal voters of the state, meaning of course the Negroes. Disregarding the slight opposition of the Negroes, the Democratic majority swiftly passed the bill, and on February 27 Governor Drew signed it.[44]

In his fight for economy, illustrated by his reluctance to spend money on the state prison, Drew followed a pattern laid down by previous Republican administrations. At the Chattahoochee institution, Warden Malachi Martin and Surgeon W. J. Scull held humanitarian views but were seriously handicapped by a lack of funds. Martin's chief complaint was that all prisoners ate at one table and were confined in one room at night. Perennially petitioning for improvements, he pointed out that by the erection of a few cells he could separate calloused prisoners from boys convicted of minor offenses. Stressing that better discipline could be enforced by kind treatment, he requested sufficient money for a school teacher and books. Dr. Scull's 1876 report caustically assailed the prison system of herding sick and well together. Warning that the loss of life in the event of a passing epidemic would be frightful, Scull expressed disgust with existing state prison facilities. He also termed the attitude of past legislatures toward the few insane persons confined at the prison heartless and indifferent. In spite of these poor prison conditions, under Warden Martin the death rate was remarkably low, only one death being recorded in 1875 and three in 1876, with an average of one hundred prisoners confined.[45]

Any hopes which the warden and surgeon held for Democratic-sponsored prison reforms were abruptly smashed when the joint committee on the state prison made its report on February 28. Ignoring the recommendations of the institution's officials, the committee displayed interest only in economy. It had discovered that Martin was working prisoners in his own vineyard without recompensing the state for their labor and that he could not account for five hundred crossties missing from the prison inventory. To remedy this, it recommended that the warden's accounts be settled before he received his salary. Then, without the slightest investigation of the ills of the convict lease system or the condition of the convicts at the prison, the committee endorsed Governor Drew's proposal that the convicts be leased upon the most advantageous terms obtainable.[46] Convict leasing was not a new proposal for Florida. It had supplemented prison operation by the Republicans during Reconstruction. In line with the leasing policy, carpetbagger Adjutant General John Varnum had sent seventy-two convicts under the supervision of the prison deputy warden to Lake Eustis in South Florida in the spring of 1876. There, in a virtual wilderness, they engaged in construction work for the St. Johns, Lake Eustis and Gulf Railroad Company. The political changeover was marked for these convicts only by a perfunctory trip to Lake Eustis by Adjutant General Dickison.[47] Apparently no legislator, Democrat or Republican, white or black, was sufficiently interested in the convict leasing proposal to make a similar visit to the convict labor camp. In the senate, only Negroes Josiah T. Walls and A. B. Osgood voted against convict leasing.[48]

Early in March Governor Drew signed a package of six bills changing the state prison into an insane asylum and establishing a convict hire system in its stead. The idea of a state insane asylum had been previously proposed by outgoing Republican comptroller C. A. Cowgill. It was obviously for the sake of economy alone, not humanitarianism, that the state opened its asylum. Heretofore, Florida insane had been boarded in other states' institutions at some expense to the state.[49] As a result of the new laws, Dickison was authorized to hire convicts out to private contractors for a minimum of two years. Provisions in the laws attempted superficially to protect the welfare of the prisoners, but no funds were allocated to enforce these safeguards, and no adequate system of state supervision was provided. The lowest bids for state cost submitted and accepted were those of Henry A. Wyse, a Live Oak merchant, and Green A. Chaires, a Leon County cotton planter and member of the antebellum aristocracy. The two jointly agreed to take the convicts for two years, thus relieving the state of the burden of confinement. In return, the state was to pay them $5,000 for the convicts' upkeep. The prisoners at the state prison went to Chaires, while those laboring on the St. Johns, Lake Eustis, and Gulf Railroad were leased to Wyse. The former immediately moved his group to his plantation, where he quartered them on the first floor of his residence, reserving the second floor for his family. Wyse, who had vague, speculative ideas on using convicts, allowed them to remain temporarily with the railroad.[50] A joint committee of the legislature later charged that when Wyse was given charge of the convicts, they were in good health.[51] This is doubtful.

Besides setting up the insane asylum and convict leasing, the legislature passed measures reducing fees, made changes in jury law, and cut down legislative expenses.[52] The Democrats were determined to balance the budget.

New railroad construction in Florida had been promoted earlier by territorial Whigs, antebellum state Democrats, and Reconstruction Republicans. No railroad construction of importance had taken place since the outbreak of the Civil War. Drew and the Redeemers were ready to try their hands at it. They were vitally concerned with Florida's serious lack of adequate transportation. The Vose Decree must be satisfied if the Internal Improvement Fund lands were to assist in the building of railroads.

There was now some question concerning the legal status of the Internal Improvement Fund, particularly in respect to the lands belonging to it. The fund was the most important inducement to future railroad promoters, since the original act granted land for railroad building and guaranteed at a rate of $10,000 per mile the interest on the bonds of railroads constructed in the state. Adding to the difficulties of the state in railroad building, the fund was never able to make good its guarantee of the interest on Florida antebellum railroad bonds. Taking advantage of this situation, Francis Vose and other bond-holding speculators substituted for dividends questionable political lobbying and shady financial practices. By 1877 the fund guaranteed payment of $500,000 in unpaid coupons. At the same time it still possessed nine million acres of land, worth considerably more than the amount in default but with no immediate buyers in prospect.[53] A court-ordered auction of fund lands for the purpose of paying the bondholders, mostly Northern speculators, would have resulted in their gaining possession of an empire in Florida for a trifling sum of money. The assembly committee on railroads, making its report on February 10, took a negative stand on the construction of a land grant railroad extending the length of Florida's Atlantic coast, from the St. Marys River to Key West. Committee chairman W. A. Hocker stated that the reservation of millions of acres for the Key West railroad might embarrass the Internal Improvement Fund Board in its efforts to extricate the fund from its indebtedness.[54] Hocker's recommendation killed the bill. But later in the session, disregarding the dormant state of the fund, the legislature passed two pet measures, the Gainesville, Ocala, and Charlotte Harbor Railroad and the West Florida Railroad bills.[55]

On March 2 the legislature adjourned.[56] Its main themes had been economy and pay-as-you-go. Taxes had not been reduced. Although Republicans obviously were pushed into the background, no organized effort was made to eliminate them from the political scene, the Democrats being content with the wholesale dismissal of Republican state and county officials. It had been a depression legislature, dominated by the yeoman farmer, the small town merchant, the county courthouse lawyer, all willing to operate within the existing framework and seeking to establish a government which would encourage the development of Florida at the least possible expense to the property holder. The politicians from the piney-wooded white counties had accepted Governor Drew's leadership, and close coordination had existed at almost all times between the legislature and the executive. Drew had surprised Duval county leader Wilk Call and others, who, expecting a weak, easily influenced governor, instead found an aggressive leader.[57]

3

A Period of Political and
Economic Uncertainty

The solidarity of the Democratic majority in the Redeemer legislature contrasted strongly with the factionalism of its Republican
majority predecessors. The poorer white counties of West and
South Florida dominated proceedings for the first time in Florida's
history. At the same time, railroad promoters and land speculators,
having to shift their lobbying efforts from the Radicals to the Redeemers, were further handicapped by the uncertainty following
the Vose Decree, which had severely reduced the availability of
capital for Florida railroad building. Yet with new railroad construction prospects almost nonexistent, the only two active railroad
promotional companies in the state, the Gainesville, Ocala, and
Charlotte Harbor, and the West Florida, were both successful in
getting their special bills through the legislature.[1] It was obvious
that conditions imposed by the Vose Decree would prevent any
generous land grant for either company, but the small town merchants, the Southern yeoman farmers, and the Northern immigrants
all wanted these railroads constructed. The Gainesville road would
open up the South Florida country west of the St. Johns River.
The West Florida railroad would provide much needed transportation for the isolated panhandle. No organized group, with the
possible exception of the Vose interests, would oppose land grants
for the building of these two railroads.

Possessing ties with neither the railroads nor the Vose interests,
Governor Drew scrutinized both bills carefully and consulted State
Senator William D. Barnes of Marianna, a leading proponent of

the West Florida road. By vetoing both, he then served notice on Florida's railroad promoters that future railroad building would depend on the settlement of the Vose Decree. [2] The *Weekly Floridian*, always strong for railroad construction, reversed itself to support the governor, pointing out that a major objection to the Gainesville road was its narrow gauge.[3]

Not only did the governor have to shoulder the burden of the Vose Decree; because of the Swepson-Littlefield fraud during Reconstruction, the control of existing railroads presented an immediate problem. Wildcat promoters, seeing profit in the litigation resulting from the fraud, further complicated the issue. One of these, Frank R. Sherwin, had entered into correspondence with the Dutch bondholders. Then, without bothering to obtain a power of attorney from the Hollanders, Sherwin had had the temerity to petition Governor Stearns to seize the Florida Central and the Jacksonville, Pensacola, and Mobile railroads in behalf of the Dutch bondholders. In one of his last acts, Stearns partially complied with this request and ordered the sale of the Florida Central Railroad. At the same time, litigation was commencing between the defrauded Dutch bondholders and the state of North Carolina, which sought to recover the money with which Swepson had absconded and which he had invested in Florida railroads. Governor Drew, in complete accord with his predecessor, arranged for proceeds of the Florida Central sale to go to the bondholders. However, on February 5 North Carolina gained a respite when State Circuit Judge Robert B. Archibald, a holdover Republican carpetbagger, halted the sale and directed the master, Joseph H. Durkee, to retain possession of the railroad until the final hearing of the case, which was set for April 12.[4]

Unwilling to accept Archibald's directive, Governor Drew had Attorney General George P. Raney serve an executive proclamation of seizure on the railroad. Drew then ordered Captain T. C. Spooner, general manager of the state-operated Jacksonville, Pensacola and Mobile Railroad, to commandeer the trains on the Florida Central road. Infuriated by these actions, Joseph B. Stewart, whose law firm represented the interests of North Carolina, wrote Edward M. L'Engle, president of the Florida Central, "We will be able to give the great railroad seizers Drew, Raney, and Company all the fun they want." Meanwhile, armed with a pistol, Captain Spooner attempted to take possession of the railroad but was frustrated by its officials. Adjutant General J. J. Dickison, coming to Spooner's assistance, ordered the sheriff of Columbia County to meet an incoming Florida Central train at Lake City with a posse. Freight shipments at the railroad's western terminal at Lake City were at a standstill as the railroad's officials grimly opposed efforts of the state government to take possession. On April 11 Governor Drew personally took charge of the state forces. Arriving at Lake City, a focal point of the clash, Drew conferred with the railroad's officials and agreed that the Florida Central would remain in the hands of Durkee until right of possession was settled by the courts.[5]

With two of Florida's three main railroads shackled by litigation, it was not surprising that Governor Drew became interested in a proposed cross-state canal. This canal was being promoted by a group of Northern capitalists headed by John H. Fry of New York, who planned to construct the waterway from the St. Marys River to the Gulf of Mexico via the Okefenokee Swamp. The projected route would parallel David L. Yulee's railroad and disrupt its monopoly on all goods shipped across the Florida peninsula. In June, anxious to get the canal started, Governor Drew wrote a circular letter to all Democratic legislators, sounding them out on the advisability of calling a special session for the company's incorporation.[6] News of the governor's canal activities reached Yulee in July. Disturbed by Drew's conduct, the veteran pro-railroad politician decided to block his attempt. In a strong letter to the governor he opposed the special session because the expense in "these very hard times" would add greatly to the burden of the people.[7] Whether or not this letter influenced Drew, he discarded plans to call the legislature and instead sought the help of Florida's Congressional delegation in obtaining a federal survey of the proposed route.[8] Sufficient financial support was lacking, however, for the canal company to begin operations.

During the summer, while Governor Drew was concentrating his attentions on canal building, the new state system of handling convicts ran into difficulty. The road contractors of the St. Johns, Lake Eustis and Gulf Railroad Company, who had been allowed by convict-lessee Henry A. Wyse to retain his charges temporarily, completely neglected to provide for the welfare of the prisoners. These unfortunate, forgotten men were housed in crude dirt-floored huts in a swamp; consequently they became accustomed to awakening in the morning half submerged in mud and slime. Sadistic guards maintained discipline by hanging up miscreants by their thumbs. The camp commissary became depleted, leaving the convicts starving. One prisoner existed for fourteen days on palmetto tops and a little salt.[9] A malaria epidemic in July finally forced Wyse to remove his prisoners from Lake Eustis to Live Oak in North Florida. There they arrived in such deplorable condition that their new guard commander, Captain J. C. Powell, was unable to tell white from Negro. Seeing that the twenty-seven men in the group were clothed in verminous rags, Powell ordered them bathed and their clothing burned. At first the new prison camp, appropriately named Padlock, resembled a hospital; in addition to the malaria, nineteen convicts were ill with chronic dysentery, and some of these also had typhoid fever. Two of the most seriously ill died within several days after arrival at Live Oak, and six more who had extreme cases of malaria expired a short time later.[10] Despite these shocking conditions, neither Governor Drew nor Adjutant General Dickison contemplated an investigation, though Drew, when he received a complaint from Nassau County prisoners later in the year, sharply took to task their custodian, Peter Cone.[11]

Wyse sent his few healthy convicts to the Santa Fe River Valley to range timber, and a short time later closed a contract with Dutton, Ruff and Jones, dealers in turpentine, rosin, and naval stores. By the terms of this agreement, the convicts were virtual slaves on the Dutton company's vast holdings in the Suwannee River Valley. Major Charles K. Dutton of New York City resorted to convict labor because turpentine culture was exhausting work, and it was difficult to obtain enough free labor for the proper cultivation of any great number of trees. Natives of Florida's piney woods would quickly abandon the work when any other type of livelihood became available.[12]

In addition to this rugged occupation, the Dutton-leased convicts underwent the severe servitude of the prison camp where the whip provided discipline. Overworked, their welfare neglected as a result of the new Democratic policy, the convicts died in increasing numbers: eighteen during the first year of the Drew administration, thirteen during the second year.[13] Ignoring these fatalities, Adjutant General Dickison reported in 1880 that turpentine culture was "a very healthy business" for these unfortunate people.[14]

Because of unfavorable publicity resulting from a yellow fever epidemic in Fernandina during the summer of 1877, rumors spread in Jacksonville that the fall tourist business would be seriously affected. To silence the pessimists, the Jacksonville *Evening Chronicle* observed that favorable business conditions existed in the North and West which would make possible a peak crowd of tourists and immigrants.[15] Actually, the North was in the throes of a panic. In November of the same year, the Board of Trustees for the new Florida Agricultural College met at Eau Gallie and voted seven to one to move the college.[16] The land and buildings reverted to William H. Gleason, who had donated the land.[17] With no college operating in Florida, students desiring higher education would continue to leave the state, to its economic disadvantage. With the state government functioning at a minimum of expense, Governor Drew lowered the mill rate of ad valorem taxes from twelve and a half to nine in December. At the same time he made it plain that there would be no extension of the time limit for the payment of these taxes.[18]

While the Redeemers were cementing their control of the state, the Republican party was still very much alive. As late as February 1877, ex-Governor Stearns was sounding out state Radical leaders on the possible continuance of the fight for the governorship. Writing ex-Senator Thomas W. Osborn, the Quincy carpetbagger suggested that State Senator Joseph H. Durkee and Edwin Higgins, both from Jacksonville, Chief Justice Randall's hometown, together with Dennis Eagan of Madison County, should contact Randall in an effort to sound him out. If Randall were receptive, Stearns thought that he could carry his case to the Florida Supreme Court. Financial backing for this project was to come from interested parties in Washington. No help was expected from Hayes, who, Stearns felt, would not support an existing Southern Republican government, much less help build new ones. He predicted that the new national administration would "warm and lovingly embrace the Southern whites." Inasmuch as Stearns's critical letter found its way into Hayes's file, it was unlikely that he received any support from Osborn.[19] Although Stearns failed in his effort to solicit support for a fight to recover the governorship, his visit to Washington was not entirely fruitless. President Hayes rewarded the ex-governor for his services by appointing him a commissioner of the Hot Springs Reservation, thus removing from the local

Florida scene one who might upset the presidential policy of conciliation.[20]

Florida Negro leaders were more hopeful than Stearns of receiving aid from the Hayes administration. Although Peter W. Bryant, leader of Hillsborough County's Negroes, accepted from Drew the office of justice of the peace, he saw the futility of battling the Democrats without federal assistance. In March 1877, together with state black leaders J. Willis Menard and William U. Saunders, Bryant journeyed to Washington and succeeded in gaining an interview with President Hayes. The assurance of this unofficial delegation that Florida Negroes fully endorsed the policy of reconciliation was met by President Hayes with the recognition that the Negro people were more interested in the success of his Southern policy than any other class and a promise that he would not forget that the Negro composed the Republican party in Florida.[21] In giving their approval to the President's Southern policy, black leaders were indirectly aligning themselves with the Drew administration.

To engender further support among Florida's Negro Republicans for Hayes's Southern policy, a black convention was held at Tallahassee in the early summer. Federal officeholders led by white carpetbagger Senator Simon B. Conover firmly controlled the meeting. Conover informed the meeting that public opinion in the North demanded that Hayes follow the course he was following. Conover hoped that the race issue in politics would disappear and that "throughout the South we shall now have peace, order, confidence, more tolerance of opinion than ever before, and better protection to life, liberty, and property. . . ."[22] Another Negro meeting was also held in the early summer. This meeting at Key West protested the killings of the Reverend Arthur St. Clair and Henry Loyd of Hernando County, by white men. St. Clair was murdered on his way to the Tallahassee Negro convention. The Key West Negro meeting censured their town's Democratic newspaper, the *Key of the Gulf,* for its comment relative to the murders that "There is sad intelligence from the main land. The blackberry crop is on the wane."[23]

Former Whigs and moderates were now more active politically in Florida than they had been since early in Johnson's administration. Almost immediately following President Hayes's inauguration, an ex-Union soldier engaged in railroad promotion in Gainesville found the new state of affairs a great improvement. Writing President Hayes, N. R. Gruelle practically credited him with bringing about a millennium in Florida. According to Gruelle, the old Southern-Whig element was fast springing into vitality and soon would become quite a formidable party.[24]

Encouraged by this activity, ex-Whig leader Wilkinson Call, who had regularly worked with the Democrats since the beginning of Reconstruction, made an effort to replace Radical federal officeholders with men who would follow Hayes's Southern policy. Writing Senator Stanley Matthews of Ohio and enclosing a letter to Hayes, Call suggested a complete new slate of appointees for Florida, including two former Whigs who supported Hayes in the 1876 election.[25] Probably because Call had been a Tilden elector, his suggestions were rejected; the Hayes administration showed no indications that it would turn Florida patronage over to the Whig wing of the Democratic party. Florida federal patronage continued to be in the hands of the old carpetbagger crowd. Southern ex-Whigs, including Call, remained in the Democratic party.

Appealing to the national administration and the North for sympathy and support, the scalawags and carpetbaggers continued vociferously to complain that Florida had been lost to the Republicans through cowardice, treachery, and the prostitution of the courts. Attempting to draw a dark picture of the aftermath of the Republican defeat, scalawag Samuel B. McLin in May wrote a friend that a graveyard peace existed in the state. He reported that Malachi Martin, chairman of the Republican state committee, had been physically attacked by a major Democratic politician as the "fires of political hate" were on the increase. Furthermore, an Iowa man who voted Republican in Alachua County had come to McLin requesting aid to leave the state because he had been proscribed and could not obtain employment in his trade as a carpenter. Also according to McLin, Negroes were being shot and driven from their homes, and the clink of the chain gang was heard in the streets of Tallahassee.[26]

Samuel N. Williams, residing near the Civil War battleground at Olustee, was another scalawag made uneasy by Hayes's Southern policy. In a letter to Secretary of the Treasury John Sherman on February 18, 1878, Williams warned that if the President did not take a firm stand, the "trials of 1860" would be repeated. In

Baker County, lying in North Florida's piney woods, the color
line was the political line, and Williams was the only white Republican.[27] Both McLin and Williams failed to mention the strong
opposition developing within Florida Republican ranks against the
old carpetbag-scalawag leadership.

Republican businessmen in Florida were seeing that for social
and economic as well as political reasons there must be a change
of party leadership, or successful elections would be things of the
past. In Alachua County the Hayes administration was faced with
the choice of supporting either a strong, predominantly Negro
political machine or a weak group of ex-Northern businessmen
adherents to the policy of reconciliation. N. R. Gruelle, one of
the businessmen, was very much agitated by the activities of
Leonard G. Dennis, carpetbagger political boss of Alachua. Writing President Hayes in May, Gruelle informed him that Dennis
and the carpetbaggers had brought the party to the verge of an-
nihilation. But if there were a housecleaning and the Republicans
got out and worked, he predicted that they would carry the state
in the next election by a two thousand vote majority and possibly
control the legislature.[28] At the same time, Dennis complained to
a *New York Times* reporter that it had become a crime to be
a Republican in the South. He also alleged that in the past decade
the Democrats had engaged in a campaign of terror against the
Republicans.[29] Because he had the backing of national Republicans
such as William E. Chandler of New Hampshire, he was able to
control local federal patronage. The appointment of Dennis's lieutenant, W. K. Cessna, as Gainesville's postmaster showed conclusively that federal support would continue for the carpetbaggers.[30]
Thus without federal support, the businessmen were unable to take
over the Republican party in Alachua County.[31]

Ruthlessly exploited by the carpetbagger and not wanted—
except for his vote—by the businessmen within the Republican
party, the Negro failed to find sanctuary in the Democratic party,
although Democratic Negro votes had made possible the election
of Governor Drew in 1876. John Wallace, Leon County Negro
state senator, was quick to capitalize on the prejudice shown his
race by the county's Democratic commissioners. In a letter to
Charles E. Dyke, Sr., which appeared in the March 5 issue of
the *Weekly Floridian,* Wallace reminded Dyke that the over four
hundred Negroes in Leon County who voted Democratic in 1876

had been promised by the Redeemer leaders—including Dyke, Bloxham, and Samuel Pasco, Democratic state chairman—the rights they had held under Republican rule. However, when the new grand and petit jury lists were published on March 2, not one Negro name appeared. Wallace denounced this action as "outrageous" and as against Hayes's policy of reconciliation. Dyke replied editorially that while he thought that none of the Negroes' rights would be less secure, it would have been better had the county commissioners not excluded them.[32]

With the Negroes possessing a sizable majority in Leon County, the Democrats now sought to compromise with them to the extent of having a fusion ticket of candidates for the legislature. Negroes were not to run on the Republican ticket if they accepted this proposal. At a mass meeting in Tallahassee on May 4, Leon County's Negroes decided to remain in the Republican party. In accordance with the decision the meeting passed resolutions stating that the Republicans were the best friends of the laboring man and were desirous of equal, exact justice for all men.[33]

In 1878 elections would be limited to the congressional and legislative races. The First District Republicans, hoping to stage a comeback, held their convention at Monticello in late July. The three candidates for Congress were all from the Black Belt. Major Edmund C. Weeks, an extreme Radical, and Robert Meacham, Jefferson County's Negro state senator, made strong appeals to the Negro vote. United States Senator Simon Conover, though a moderate, was also popular with the Negroes, who predominated in the convention. With certain defeat by the Redeemer legislature facing him in 1879, Conover was willing to step down to the House of Representatives. Despite the fact that less than half a dozen delegates were white and the convention was being held in Meacham's hometown, Conover won the nomination easily.[34] Major Weeks, claiming fraud in the convention, came out later as an independent Republican candidate for Congress. In the Second Congressional District, the Jacksonville businessmen allied with the patronage crowd continued in control as Horatio Bisbee, Jr., was renominated with only token opposition. [35]

East Florida Democrats were sharply divided on evaluating the strength of the Republicans, the majority thinking that the Radicals could easily be defeated. But the more shrewd Democratic observers soon realized that they were in for a hard fight. In this vein, Aaron Marvin, a Jacksonville lawyer, wrote President Edward M. L'Engle of the Florida Central Railroad that Bisbee would make a close race, because most people in Jacksonville felt that he would look after their interests more effectively than the Democratic candidate. If the apathy existing among the Democrats continued, Marvin warned, they would be badly beaten.[36]

First District Democrats renominated the incumbent R. H. M. Davidson by acclamation.[37] Because the Democrats were in firm control of most of the counties of the district, Davidson would be difficult to defeat. The rivalry existing between Fernandina and Jacksonville deprived the Second Congressional District of such unity and harmony, however. At a meeting in Palatka on July 25, the Jacksonville delegation led by Wilkinson Call seized control, to young Wickliffe Yulee's disgust. Lieutenant Governor Noble Hull was nominated for Congress, and a platform calling for the improvement of the St. Johns Bar, benefiting Jacksonville as an ocean port, was adopted. The Yulee candidate, J. H. Roper of Gainesville, was never in the running.[38]

Shortly after the conventions, the black Democrats of Leon County held a mass meeting at the courthouse to determine their future course. Resolutions were passed condemning the reduction of the school term from six to three months, the discrimination against their race in drawing juries, the refusal of the county commissioners to assist sick and infirm Negroes, and the increase in county taxes. Until the county officials responsible for these abuses were dismissed, the black Democrats announced, they were voting Republican.[39] The Democrats chose to ignore this revolt. Editor Dyke continued to be optimistic about thousands of Negro voters joining the Democratic party. His *Floridian,* clearly anti-Negro, repeatedly solicited their votes. To persuade Negroes that they were welcome in the Democratic party, black orator J. C. Williamson of Jacksonville stumped the state with white Democratic leaders, telling the black voters to forget the past sins of the Democrats, since the Republicans would leave the state after defeat. A political unknown, Williamson was of dubious value to the Democrats.

The Black Belt was seething with political unrest. Although in Leon the Negro Democrats were bolting, in Madison it was the Republicans who were having trouble. When J. C. Williamson spoke at Greenville, Joseph N. Stripling, scalawag member of the assembly, announced from the same platform that although he was still a Republican, he would vote the Democratic ticket.[40] White Republicans were scarce in Madison County, and Dennis Eagan, faced with the rising antagonism of whites toward his primarily Negro machine, could hardly afford the loss of Stripling. The Madison Negro community was exercising strong pressure to keep all Negroes in line. When J. G. Johnson, a Negro schoolteacher, made public his decision to be a Democrat, he was threatened with whipping by a mob of Negro women. His school enrollment dropped from fifty-four students to six, and two Negro school trustees complained to the county superintendent that he was a Democrat and they they didn't want him to teach their children. The superintendent answered, "You shall have no other teacher." But Johnson had had enough, and after his term expired he went to farming.[41] In Alachua, county judge J. C. Gardner of Gainesville reported that the Negroes were docile except in politics, when they acted more like demons than men.[42]

The Republicans appeared to have an edge in East Florida's port-city counties. Nassau County Democrats did not reflect the confidence of the other East Florida Democrats. Wickliffe Yulee wrote his father on August 9 advising him to compromise with the Republicans. Although Naylor Thompson, who served the Yulees faithfully in the assembly, was the Democratic candidate for the senate, the compromise plan was to let that position go to a Republican. The plan fell through, however, because the Democrats outside of Fernandina had been promised the two assembly seats and the compromise would leave the Fernandina Democrats without a single candidate for the legislature.[43]

In Duval County, Dr. James H. Paine of Jacksonville, campaign manager for Noble Hull, discovered to his dismay that Sherman Conant, carpetbagger United States marshal for the Northern District of Florida, planned to name an unusually large number of deputy marshals for service at the polls to offset the Democratic control of the election. When Paine protested to Conant, he was told: "By God, I'll appoint a million of them and not a damned one a Democrat." Paine also ran into difficulty in attempting to organize Duval Negroes for Hull. His two prospective club leaders, although dissatisfied with the Jacksonville Republican organization, informed him that they were afraid to come out in open opposition.[44]

Considering that Florida was still a frontier state in 1878, the election was rather quiet, particularly in the First Congressional District, where Davidson easily defeated Conover 11,532 to 8,301, as Gadsden deserted the Black Belt Republican ranks to go Democratic.[45] In the Second Congressional District, trouble occurred mainly in Madison County, where whites were becoming more and more unruly each election day and the Negroes, made aggressive by the strong leadership of ex-Union Army officer Dennis Eagan, were belligerently resisting any encroachments on their rights. Apparently welcoming trouble rather than trying to avert it, Democratic election officials in the town of Madison cut the number of polling places from four to one. Eagan, who had entered into an agreement with the Democrats to vote Republicans and Democrats alternately throughout the day, found in the late afternoon that the Democrats were stalling to hold the Republican vote down, and a number of Republicans would not have voted at sundown when the polls closed. By this time the atmosphere was tense. White members of the state militia had drawn their muskets and were in evidence near the polls. Eagan requested the inspectors to hold the polls open until the Negroes had voted and was refused. When the polls closed at sundown, the number of votes cast was approximately one-half that in 1876. Rather than send the blacks home without voting, Eagan, acting solely on his own initiative, opened a polling place in the nearby store of B. F. Tidwell, a former county judge. Irregular voting at Tidwell's store was carried out without registration lists, since these were in the possession of Democratic election officials who refused to surrender them. After dusk, 182 Negroes voted for Horatio Bisbee, Jr., at Eagan's impromptu polls.[46]

Out in the county at the Harmony Church polls where a majority cast their votes for Bisbee, Democratic inspector T. A. Jones was entrusted with bringing the ballot box to Madison in a buggy. At Mosely Hall he conveniently accepted an invitation for a drink of whiskey and returned to find the ballot box missing.[47] Before the smoke of battle cleared, county judge Robert Witherspoon and the sheriff had both been arrested by United States Marshal Conant and charged with election frauds.[48] Marion County had a strange change take place at the Whitesville polls, a strongly Negro precinct in Long Swamp. In the past, Democrats had always trailed by ninety votes, but the election count there showed

Hull leading Bisbee 134 to 41. During a brief recess of election officials, the Democrats had packed the ballot box.[49] In spite of these frauds both Marion and Madison went Republican.

With South Florida yet to be heard from, Hull trailed Bisbee by 941 votes. Orange and Volusia came in, cutting the Republican's majority to a little over 200. Brevard County was now Hull's last hope for victory, and it had cast only 169 votes in 1876, of which 58 were Republican. Hull requested Nat Poyntz, an Orlando merchant, to go to Brevard to see what could be done. Instead of going himself, Poyntz sent Major J. H. Allen, an Orange County lawyer, armed with $200 and the information that Hull must have a two-hundred-vote majority in Brevard or he was defeated.

Allen, accompanied by Eugene S. Gaulden, a former Brevard County official, journeyed to Lake View, the county seat. There Allen showed John M. Lee, clerk of the county court, Hull's letter to Poyntz. Hull had carried the county by a vote of 120 to 41, and Lee refused to alter the returns. In some precincts, instead of being put in boxes ballots were strung on a string, or deposited in a sealed beer bottle or a tea box. Allen then paid Lee $140, and Lee turned his office over to Gaulden, who raised Hull's vote from 120 to 310. The county canvassing board approved the altered returns, and Hull had his majority.[40]

The state canvassing board threw out the returns from both Brevard and Madison, but Hull still had a majority.[51] Bisbee appealed to the state supreme court, which ordered the Madison votes counted. This seemingly elected Bisbee, but Governor Drew issued the certificate of election to Hull.[52] Bisbee then contested Hull's seat, claiming Democratic frauds in Madison, Marion, Orange, and Brevard counties. Hull countered with claims of Republican frauds in Madison, Alachua, Nassau, St. Johns, Putnam, Volusia, Brevard, Suwannee, and Duval counties. His counsel accused the Republicans of never noticing irregularities during their administration of Florida and of having a new-born zeal to prosecute the few weak imitations of Republican frauds.[53] Finally, on January 22, 1880, after he had served almost one-half of the term, Hull was unseated and replaced by Bisbee.[54] The sheriff and judge of Madison County, the canvassing board members from Brevard County, and two election officials from Whitesville were tried for election frauds in the federal court at Jacksonville. All except Judge Witherspoon of Madison were found guilty.[55]

After the Brevard canvassing board members had been imprisoned a year, Governor Drew attempted to intercede with President Hayes to gain a pardon for two of their number. Ironically, J. H. Allen and Eugene S. Gaulden both turned state's evidence and were freed.[56]

The Democrats would control the new state senate by twenty-three to seven. The assembly would contain forty-six Democrats, twenty-eight Republicans, and one independent. Republicans gained one representative in Baker, two in Nassau, one in Hamilton, and one in Putnam. Losses of two representatives in Gadsden and one in Marion held Republican gains to two. Republican Reconstruction Governor Harrison Reed would return to Tallahassee to represent Duval in the assembly. A third party, the Greenback, which ran a Negro minister for state senator in Leon County, was easily defeated by the Republicans.[57]

The unscrupulous management of election machinery by the Democrats left no doubt that they would continue to use extreme measures to maintain their control of the state. While the Republicans were guilty of minor frauds in 1878, the onus was on the Democrats for refusing to allow a free election. Since the Democratic party was made up of autonomous county organizations, the burden of guilt was on those local units. As further indictment of the Democrats, the Brevard episode revealed that those close to Hull—if not Hull himself—desired victory at any price. Commenting on the election in an interview with the Boston Herald, ex-Governor Stearns stated that the majority of Floridians were Republicans and that the Negroes were solidly loyal to that party. Stearns felt that white Republicans were socially ostracized. He suggested that Negroes be protected in voting without a return to bayonet rule.[58] In the Hull-Bisbee elections hearings it was brought out that a white man who voted Republican was likely in certain communities to be called "white trash," while a Negro who attempted to vote Democratic was apt to have his ballot torn from his hand. One ominous question stood out: "Do you or [do you] not know that Democrats seek to destroy the Republican party?"[59]

4

Republican Intrigue and
Democratic Unrest

In early 1879 it was certain that Senator Simon B. Conover would not be reelected; the legislature was now predominantly Democratic. Adding to the precariousness of the Tallahassee carpetbagger's political future was his feud with ex-Governor Stearns. Since Conover splintered the Republican party in 1876 by running for governor as an independent Republican, Stearns's supporters were not predisposed to support him. Their campaign to prevent him from receiving federal support had opened in late December 1878, when John Tyler, Jr., former editor of the *Tallahassee Sentinel*, sent a bitter letter to John Sherman, secretary of the treasury. Tyler was particularly annoyed because Conover, after accepting a $3,000 bribe to withdraw from the 1876 gubernatorial race and support Stearns, had not, because of his deep personal hatred for the Quincy carpetbagger, lived up to his agreement. Furthermore, Tyler charged Conover with surrounding himself with unscrupulous men.[1] With the Tallahassee physician shorn of his senatorship, the fight for the leadership of state Republican party would be wide open.

There were only minor personnel changes in the legislature which met on January 7, 1879; however, Republicans would sit in the assembly from Hamilton, Putnam, and Suwannee—all East Florida, predominantly white counties. Democrats would be in the assembly from Gadsden and Marion—hitherto solid Republican Black Belt strongholds.[2] The legislature's first business was the election of a United States senator. State Senator Silas L. Nib-

lack of Columbia County and the Fernandina *Florida Mirror*
looked to the past for a candidate to end the Whig monopoly
of major offices, a monopoly dating from 1876.[3] Senator Charles
W. Jones, elected in 1875 and now the only non-Whig Democrat
in a major office, had been a compromise candidate with little political influence outside Escambia County. Niblack's and the *Mirror*'s nominee, David L. Yulee, was willing to accept a draft but
would not actively campaign. When the draft failed to materialize,
Yulee threw his support to ex-Governor David S. Walker.[4] Other
possible candidates included John A. Henderson, a Tallahassee
railroad lawyer, and Confederate brigadiers Jesse J. Finley of Lake
City and Robert Bullock of Ocala. But even before the legislature
met, it was obvious that the front runner was the leader of East
Florida's ex-Whigs, Wilkinson Call. Call's strength was coming
from the anti-railroad people in the white wiregrass counties, and
no candidate could be more displeasing to Yulee.[5]

Overtures were made by Alachua County carpetbag leader
Leonard C. Dennis to W. Naylor Thompson, state senator from
Fernandina, to swing twenty Negro votes to Yulee's candidate,
Walker. Although Thompson did not commit himself to Dennis,
he did relay the offer to Yulee. Within the Democratic ranks,
Thompson formed an anti-Call alliance with West Florida men
led by the pro-railroad Jackson County leader, General W. D.
Barnes. Thompson warned Yulee that the white county Democrats
were working for a constitutional convention, a move which he
was opposing since he believed that a convention at this time
would be in the hands of people prejudiced against railroads.[6]
In offering to make a deal with Thompson, Dennis was striving
to drive a wedge into the Democratic party, splitting the railroad-
Bourbon faction from the wiregrass men. This would give the
Republicans the balance of power, making them participants
rather than onlookers in the legislative proceedings. In trading with
the Republicans, however, the Bourbons would run the risk of
arousing the antagonism of the white yeoman farmers.

Yulee and the railroad faction had their first serious setback of
the session when the Democratic legislators decided to choose their
senatorial candidate in caucus, thus excluding the Republicans
from active participation in the selection. At the caucus, held on
the night of January 20, the railroad group failed to marshal sufficient strength to stop Wilkinson Call's nomination. The election of

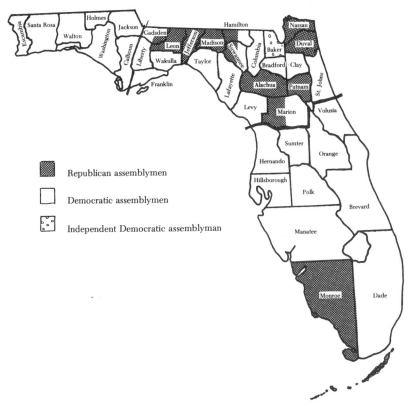

Republican assemblymen

Democratic assemblymen

Independent Democratic assemblyman

3. Party Representation in Florida Assembly by County, 1879. (Statistics from *Florida Assembly Journal*, 1879.)

the ex-Whig leader occurred on the nineteenth ballot, his nearest opponent being General Robert Bullock of Ocala.[7] The following day the legislature made Call's election official by a strict party vote.[8] Call would serve three terms in the Senate, where he was a continual thorn in the side of Florida Bourbons, who viewed him as a virulent demagogue. He was as strong for white supremacy as the Bourbons, and neither Independentism nor Populism could induce the ex-Whig to bolt the Democratic party. Opposition to railroad land grants was to be his major issue.

In his message at this session of the legislature, Governor Drew espoused a sliding rate for assessment. As a temporary expedient he suggested that the state rate of taxation remain at the eight mills set in August 1878. Instead, the legislators recklessly estimated the assessment of property at $35 million to $40 million, cut the rate to seven mills, and suspended the sinking fund tax for two years. The assessment actually came to only $30 million, forcing Drew to borrow money on his own and his cabinet's responsibility to meet interest on bonds. County commissioners were limited to a two-mill tax, about half what Drew thought they needed.[9] Both the governor and the state superintendent of public instruction advocated the limitation of free public instruction to grammar schools.[10] Their frugality was appreciated by the legislature, which slashed the county school tax maximum from five to two and one-half mills.[11] That this economy move had gone too far was apparent when it was protested by both the state and county superintendents of public instruction.[12]

In other actions, the legislature repealed the two-year-old game protection law, passed a joint resolution favoring the building of the Texas and Pacific Railroad (reversing the position of its predecessor), provided for city and county boards of health, established the Bureau of Immigration, and incorporated the Florida State Grange. A concurrent resolution provided for a vote on a new constitution in the 1880 election.[13] Turning to railroad building, the legislature approved three bills which would have approved railroad construction from the Chattahoochee River to Pensacola, from Gainesville to Charlotte Harbor, and from Tampa to Peace Creek and the St. Johns River. Because the land grants for these railroads would have taken 4,028,000 acres from the Internal Improvement Fund (which was already in receivership) in addition to the customary alternate sections six miles on each side of the railroad, Governor Drew vetoed the bills.[14] The railroad sponsors then conferred with Attorney General Raney and amended their proposals to conform with the governor's objections. The amended bills then passed both houses and received the governor's signature.[15]

Although the legislature was friendly to interests planning to build new railroads, it was decidedly hostile to those running existing ones. A bill specifically directed against David L. Yulee would have required the Internal Improvement Fund trustees to institute a suit to obtain possession of the Atlantic, Gulf, and West India Transit Company, the latest name for the Florida Railroad.[16] Thus the legislators from the white counties threatened to do at one stroke what a war and military occupation had not done—deprive Yulee of his railroad. While the other railroads in the state had fallen prey to carpetbaggers and unscrupulous promoters, Yulee had firmly held on to his road, although at times he had found it expedient to use the services of carpetbaggers. Fighting back against the wiregrass attacks, Yulee wrote Lieutenant Governor Hull asking for a full investigation and pointing out that the bill claimed the sale of the road in 1866 was illegal. This sale, according to the pioneer railroad promoter, had not been questioned before, and the railroad's operators had spent large sums of money for improvements and incurred serious obligations since that date.[17] Brushing Yulee's objections aside, the senate passed the bill twenty to five, four Republicans joining Thompson in opposition.[18] In the assembly the bill passed thirty-three to twenty-four, eight Democrats and sixteen Republicans opposing.[19] A similar bill against the Pensacola and Georgia Railroad Company which passed both houses with only nine votes cast against it revealed that Yulee was able to count on a large bloc of Republican votes in the hostile legislature.[20]

Reversing the anti-railroad stand he had previously taken in the Florida Central controversy, Governor Drew vetoed both bills because he thought that they would be injurious to the Internal Improvement Fund and the state.[21] Since tempers were rising in South Florida over Yulee's failure to extend his railroad to Tampa, the governor's veto was unpopular in that section of the state. Dr. J. P. Wall, editor of the Tampa *Sunland Tribune*, charged that Yulee was playing "dog in the manger" by not coming into Tampa and at the same time using his influence to prevent the construction of the long-awaited railroad by others. Tracing Yulee's past in state politics, Dr. Wall accused him of using ex-Governor David S. Walker as a particular tool in controlling the state administration since the Civil War. According to Dr. Wall, Walker had permitted the state to be swindled out of its interest in the Florida Railroad while he was governor, and further, had persuaded ex-Governor Harrison Reed, during the latter's term, to allow Francis Vose, also influenced by Yulee, to obtain an uncontested judgment that prevented the building of any more railroads. The Tampan termed Yulee a trickster.[22] Upset by this personal attack but sensing ulterior motives, Walker wrote Wall asking him the real cause of the complaint. Wall replied that while governor Walker had allowed Yulee to clip coupons from a large number of bonds which he had already surrendered to the Internal Improvement Fund, and that a large number of Internal Improvement Fund bonds deposited with the Department of the Interior in Washington had disappeared. Deeply injured by the accusation and anxious to clear himself of the charges, Walker wrote Yulee that he did not remember any coupon cutting or missing bonds.[23] Yulee then coldly informed Wall that since Wall had not been in a situation to have personal knowledge of the history of railroads in the state, he had relied on the false and untrue statements of others.[24]

Although convict leasing was a minor issue in comparison to the railroad construction, it too continued to plague the Drew administration. Disregarding the high mortality rate, severe treatment, and neglect of the convicts under Major Wyse, Adjutant General J. J. Dickison arranged a new lease with Wyse on January 2, 1879. Under the new agreement, Wyse was also to work the state convicts formerly employed by Green A. Chaires.[25] Quiet when the Democrats established the convict lease system, Republican legislators now began sniping. Joseph H. Durkee of the Jacksonville businessman faction of the Republican party called in the senate for a thorough overhaul of the convict lease system, pointing out that although only twenty-six prisoners died during the Republican administration of the state from 1869 to 1876, the Democratic record was eighteen deaths for the first year. Durkee proposed that the legislature investigate all phases of the system to determine whether the savings gained were made at the sacrifice of human life. His proposal fell on deaf ears as the legislators, pleased by the money-making attributes of the system, extended convict leasing to county prisoners.[26] During the legislative session, a mass jailbreak was attempted on the Chaires plantation, only a few miles from the capital. Led by trusty Joseph Alston, a member of a prominent antebellum Florida family, nine prisoners escaped to a swamp five miles distant. There they were overtaken by Chaires and his sons. When the convicts refused to surrender, the guards opened fire, killing one and wounding two. Alston, one of the wounded, was recaptured; two convicts escaped.[27]

While the Democrats were concentrating on organizing and consolidating their hold on the state and local governments of Florida, white Republicans, who for the past two years had looked in vain for help from the federal government to win state and local elections, were becoming increasingly unhappy over Hayes's policy of reconciliation. Former comptroller C. A. Cowgill of Orange Mills expressed their sentiments to William E. Chandler, a leading New Hampshire Republican: "I hope our next President if Republican will be a man of some nerve and may not entertain the opinion that all Southern Republicans are necessarily rascals in some form."[28] Negro postmaster W. G. Stewart of Tallahassee, hearing unpleasant rumors concerning the possibility of his dismissal, appealed to Chandler, "Please . . . look out for us poor colored people down here in the South." Stewart told Chandler that the only ground the Democrats would have for his removal was that he was a "black man." With Senator Conover, the "friend" of the Florida Negroes, gone from Washington, Stewart thought the Democrats would turn them out.[29] He was right; Governor Drew was at this time corresponding with Senator Charles W. Jones about getting complaints against the colored postmaster substantiated.[30] At the same time, Governor Drew was attempting to intercede in the fight for United States marshal for the Northern District of Florida. Drew's candidate was white Republican businessman Joseph H. Durkee, because the governor believed that his appointment would be better for the interests of the Democratic party. When Durkee received the appointment and resigned as state senator, Drew wrote him: "I have always admired your conservative course while Senator. . . . Our people have every reason congratulating themselves upon their present marshal."[31]

Disunity continued to plague the Republican party, a three-way fight developing for the appointment of collector of internal revenue at Jacksonville. The incumbent, A. A. Knight, had incurred the enmity of Congressman Horatio Bisbee, Jr., when he accepted a retainer to defend Lieutenant Governor Noble Hull in the 1878 election frauds. Dennis Eagan, who received the presidential nomination for the position, had his bond refused, leaving Knight temporarily in the office.[32] In early June, former Senator Simon B. Conover, whose previous attempts to obtain a federal position had been rebuffed by the Hayes administration, succeeded in having himself nominated for the position. Writing to Secretary of the Treasury John Sherman, carpetbagger Conover complained that the only opposition to his nomination came from a clique of men known as carpetbaggers. Ignoring his dubious role in the election of 1876, he self-righteously claimed that the sole cause of their animosity was his support of the Hayes administration. Foreseeing a Republican comeback in 1880, he thought that the old Whig and conservative elements in the state were becoming thoroughly dissatisfied with the Democratic party and would vote Republican because of their approval of Sherman's financial policy. Thoroughly understanding the volatile atmosphere in the Black Belt, the southern-domiciled Yankee warned that a "blood shirt" presidential campaign by the Republican party would lose Florida.[33]

When Eagan submitted a second bond, Conover's name was withdrawn. Disappointed, he impulsively telegraphed President Hayes that he was deeply hurt. But after careful consideration he apologized to the President and promised that he would cause no discord in Florida Republican ranks in the next election.[34] When Eagan's bond was again refused, Leonard G. Dennis warned William E. Chandler that Conover and Senator Wilkinson Call were working behind the scenes to place a Democrat in the office.[35] Eagan's bond was finally confirmed, and he remained in office until the national defeat of the Republicans in 1884.[36]

During the summer, Governor Drew continued to show interest in the proposed Florida ship canal. To gauge public opinion on the canal, he wrote a number of the state's prominent Democrats on the advisability of calling a special session of the legislature to give the canal company a charter. In August he was still undecided on the special session, though he had not run into any canal opposition.[37] Opposition to the governor arose from another source. The Monticello *Constitution* in July printed a bitter editorial against Drew and Northern people in general. It was plain that the extremist element of the Democratic party was already thinking in terms of overthrowing the moderate ex-Whig leadership in 1880. Coming to the governor's assistance, Wickliffe Yulee in a letter to his father took a stand against the editorial.[38] The Yulees, father and son, could see the importance of wealthy Northerners in the development of Florida. Ignoring the attacks of the Black Belt Democrats, Drew continued his fairminded course. When a Negro in the Madison jail for attempted rape was assaulted, he immediately ordered an investigation and announced his determination to prosecute the guilty and prevent similar offenses.[39]

Just as Democratic Ku Klux Klan–like elements resented Governor Drew's restraining arm, Republican radicals held grievances against President Hayes. Appointment of Democrats to federal offices under the policy of reconciliation gave great dissatisfaction to James T. Magbee, scalawag editor of the *Tampa Guardian*, who had held the position of state circuit judge during Reconstruction and now aspired to the leadership of the West Coast Republicans. Inclined to heavy drink and extremely partisan on the bench, he had incurred the hatred of the white citizens of Tampa.[50] Returning this hatred, Magbee resented having to share the federal patronage with his political enemies. In a letter to John Sherman in January 1880, he complained that a Democratic member of the legislature was keeping the lighthouse at Egmont Key at the mouth of Tampa Bay, that the inspector of customs at Manatee was highly critical of Hayes's administration, that custom officials at Key West, Cedar Key, and St. Marks were Democrats, and that except in Cedar Key, Tampa, and Key West, the west coast postmasters were also Democrats. Magbee informed Sherman that he had been born and raised in the South and that Hayes did not understand Southerners.[41] On the basis of this complaint, Sherman ordered an investigation, later writing to Magbee concerning the sending of an agent to probe the charges. The editor's wife replied in his absence that with proper management, Florida could be carried by the Republican party in the next election.[42]

Encouraged by Sherman's support, Magbee attempted to build up the woefully weak, white wing of the Republican party on the west coast. In *Guardian* editorials he argued that while the Republican party operated for the good of the whole people, the Democratic party was a band of aristocrats. He also maintained that the Republican party was no more a Negro party than the Democratic party but warned that "this old enemy to human rights [the Democratic Party] will tell the poor white man that if he votes the Republican ticket . . . he belongs to the negro party."[43] In another editorial, Magbee maintained that there were good men in all parties, but the Democratic party protected the rich only.[44]

In Pensacola, ice merchant S. C. Cobb was making plans to be an early rider on John Sherman's presidential bandwagon. Describing himself as a Sherman supporter, Cobb told treasury official George C. Tichnor at New Orleans that he was confident the Republicans could carry Florida. Cobb modestly credited himself with having assisted with the establishment of harmony among Republican factions in Escambia County. He counseled Tichnor that national convention delegates should be chosen in district conventions to avoid jealousies.[45]

Because the newspapers published in Pensacola and most of those in the rest of the state were Democratic, R. W. Ruter of nearby Ferry Pass was anxious to establish a Republican journal. In a letter to Collector of Customs F. C. Humphreys of Pensacola he also made known his desire to run for a minor office. Ruter felt that Ferry Pass, Molino, and Bluff Springs would all go Republican in the coming election.[46] Ruter's plan for a newspaper received early support from S. H. Welch, Negro clerk of customs at Pensacola.[47] Humphreys, however, was more concerned with promoting the presidential candidacy of his superior, Secretary of the Treasury Sherman, than he was with building up the strength of the Republican party. To gain Negro support for Sherman outside of Pensacola, Humphreys acquired the services of the Rev. H. Call, a Negro circuit rider.[48] The enthusiasm which Humphreys was displaying for Sherman might partly have been caused by the feud the Pensacola Republicans were having with their fellow townsman Senator Charles W. Jones. Since Humphreys's son had been dismissed from the federal payroll while Jones's brother was retained, it would seem that the senator was getting the better of the feud. As a member of the Senate Naval Committee, Jones was pushing a bill to appropriate $50,000 to rebuild the Pensacola Naval Yard. Fearful that this might mean a number of jobs for Democrats at election time and a source of campaign funds for the Democratic party, Pensacola Republicans were quietly opposing the rebuilding of the navy yard until after the election. One of their number, George E. Wentworth, wrote John Sherman that he favored the delay since there was a chance of electing a Republican legislature and defeating Jones. Wentworth suggested that Republicans replace Democrats in jobs at the navy yard but that the present commandant, a quiescent Democrat, be kept.[49]

Most Republican attention in the state was now centered on a visit to Florida of ex-President U. S. Grant. George Wentworth told George C. Tichnor that Grant's visit to Jacksonville had not created a great amount of enthusiasm and that Florida's Republican National Convention delegation would be evenly divided between Sherman and Blaine.[50] The views of Black Belt leader Malachi Martin conflicted sharply with those held by Wentworth. Martin, who was in a better position to evaluate the situation, thought that Grant had a strong hold on the masses. Having talked with Wentworth at the Republican state executive committee meeting in Jacksonville, Martin considered him a Blaine man. Martin also reported that although ex-Senator Conover was working for Sherman, there was little enthusiasm for him outside of federal officeholders. Horatio Bisbee, Jr., was leading the Blaine forces, and his coalition had been labeled the Jacksonville "Ring" by its opposition.[51]

Pre-election Republican hopes continued bright. T. M. Davey, traveling through Florida in the interest of Sherman's candidacy, found reason to foresee a Republican victory in the coming election. He thought that the undisguised frauds, the general bad management of state affairs, the proscriptive, intolerant spirit of extremists, and the inadequate tax levy for schools had demoralized the Democratic party and alienated from it the more liberal and intelligent element in the state.[52] On the other hand, he found Florida's Negro leaders intelligent and capable of holding any federal office. Davey hurt Sherman's chances in Key West when he became involved in a party dispute between the Allen and Wicker factions. George Allen, with whom Davey sided, was state senator, while Frank N. Wicker was collector of customs.[53] Obviously from Davey's reports to Sherman, he spoke only with Republicans.

In spite of the aggressive Sherman campaign in Florida, it was apparent by early March that the tide had swung definitely to Grant. Discouraged, ex-Collector of Internal Revenue A. A. Knight wrote ex-Senator Conover that there was no further use in working for Sherman in Duval County, which was certain to go for Grant.[54] A Western tourist, ex-Senator Jerome B. Chaffee of Colorado, saw Florida in Grant's column.[55]

Carpetbagger Leonard G. Dennis of Alachua County stood in the main aloof from the delegate contest. Dennis was bitter because he felt that President Hayes regarded his election as a personal rather than a party victory. The Alachua carpetbagger had very actively helped in carrying Florida for the President, and he felt that he had not received proper recognition. What little action he was taking was in behalf of Blaine.[56]

The strong movement to oust Conover from the nominal leadership of the state Republican party continued to gather strength. On March 6 Collector of Customs Humphreys, in a letter to General W. M. Bateman of Washington, D.C., seriously questioned the Leon County carpetbagger's leadership. Estimating that out of twenty-three thousand Republican voters in the state twenty thousand were Negro, Humphreys thought that Conover's vote for the seating of South Carolina Democrat Matthew C. Butler in the United States Senate in preference to his Republican opponent had lost him the confidence of Florida's colored men. The voting, according to Humphreys, was so close that if Conover had voted the other way, Butler would not have been seated. Humphreys qualified his criticism of Conover by saying that he was speaking only for West Florida.[57] Though it was true that the relatively well-educated Negro working at the custom house was aware of political activities in Washington, the rank and file of Negroes making up the county machines had no knowledge of Conover's activities in the nation's capital. The Negro did not vote as an independent. Conover's leadership was based on support received from Republican county leaders rather than his vote on seating Butler.

In the Black Belt, Malachi Martin was busy promoting Blaine for president and Martin for Florida surveyor general, a federal patronage position. Florida Secretary of State William D. Bloxham raised Martin's hopes by informing him that he had the inside track to the job. That Northern help would be appreciated was delicately hinted when Martin sent Mrs. William E. Chandler a box of orange blossoms.[58] But Blaine support was lacking, and Martin came to the opinion in late March that the Florida delegation should go to the national convention unpledged. Jesse D.

Cole, white Republican leader in Jefferson County, agreed with Martin. Martin expected opposition from ex-Congressman William J. Purman, armed with Grant money, and ex-Senator Simon B. Conover, with Sherman money. While not requesting financial assistance, the ex-warden subtly informed Chandler that he knew honest and good men who were willing to work for Blaine but could not afford to leave their jobs.[59] To combat Grant's popularity, he requested Blaine pictures and literature, particularly the Maine senator's speech on Hayes's Southern policy when "he calls on God praying that his right hand might wither and his tongue cleave to his mouth when he forgets or deserts the Reps [sic] of the South."[60]

In South Florida, Editor James T. Magbee beat the drums for a Republican party based on white votes. A letter in his *Tampa Guardian* mentioned old-line Whigs at Fort Ogden joining the radical ranks. Judge N. H. DeCoster, writing to the *Guardian* from Charlotte Harbor, reported a new crop of Republicans springing up in Manatee County. One of this variety was a heavily taxed ex-Democrat who was now on the county Republican executive committee.[61]

By the middle of April, politicians were thinking in terms of attendance at the various conventions. Both party state meetings were to be held at Gainesville. Because of the distance and the lack of a West Florida railroad, transportation was a serious problem to the Escambia delegations. Writing General B. D. Fearing, Collector Humphreys requested that arrangements be made for the federal ship *Seward* to cruise as far east as Cedar Key and remain there until the convention was over. The pro-Sherman delegates who would ride in her would pay for their food at the contract price of twenty cents a ration. Humphreys thought that Captain Weldon, commanding the ship, might refuse to make the trip since he had not been as far east as Apalachicola. Humphreys warned Fearing that a rumor was circulating that Conover was playing Sherman false and had made a deal with the Jacksonville Ring. He thought that the rumor might be true, since he considered that the ex-Senator would not hesitate to sell out Sherman's interest.[62] A letter from S. C. Cobb to John Sherman on April 16 confirmed the rumor of Conover's desertion. Cobb also mentioned that opposition was developing in West Florida to a third term for Grant; but he thought this intra-party dispute could be contained and would not disturb hopes of success.[63] A Pensacola ice merchant not dependent on political patronage, Cobb now seemed more concerned with maintaining the two-party system within the state than getting on the Republican presidential bandwagon.

Late in the spring, county conventions of both parties began electing delegates to state and district conventions. A reporter for the *Weekly Floridian,* seeking admission to the Leon County Republican Convention, was informed "dat none sabe dose who spo'ts a delicate ticket can enter here." One speaker at the meeting, ex-Marshal Sherman Conant—no Hayes supporter—told the Negro delegates that the only three friends they ever had among the white men were "Jesus Christ, Abraham Lincoln and General Grant." Negro Tallahassee postmaster W. G. Stewart warned the convention that there must be no more selling of votes for a little whiskey, a little meat, a new pair of shoes, or a new coat. Cautioning the gathering that men boasted they controlled the Negro vote with a few gallons of whiskey, he stated, "I'm talking about Democrats now." The postmaster told the members of his race to quit the cornfield, the cottonfield, the store, and every other place, and come to the polls for victory or death. At the last election in Leon County, he recalled, the white man would slip in through the throng of Negroes, drop his little ticket in the box, and slip meekly out again.[64]

Stewart had seen the Democrats in 1876 cut sizably into the majority that the blacks gave Republican candidates. He was also aware that in certain other counties in the Black Belt apathy on the part of blacks and intimidation by Democrats had reduced the Republicans to the minority party. Despite the large Negro majority in Jackson, there was no sign of Republican vigor there. Its Republican county convention met without enthusiasm. Only one white man was present.[65] Although the Negroes in Jackson were strongly for Grant, one county leader hopefully requested Sherman to send $200 to provide the Jackson delegation transportation to the state convention.[66] Despite the fact that in earlier days Jackson had sent two of its carpetbagger leaders to Congress, its Republican leaders were now obscure men with their hats in their hands.[67]

The Republican First Congressional District Convention held at Tallahassee was refused the use of Gallie's Hall, traditional meeting

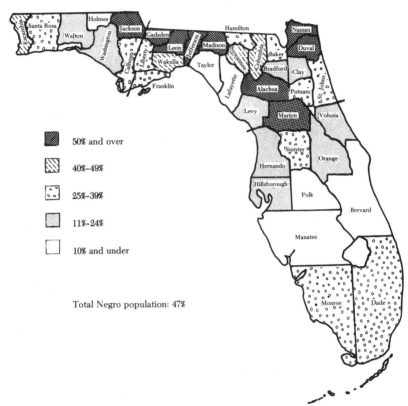

Santa Rosa
Holmes
Jackson
Gadsden
Hamilton
Nassau
Walton
Escambia
Washington
Leon
Jefferson
Madison
Duval
Calhoun
Liberty
Wakulla
Taylor
Suwannee
Columbia
Baker
Bradford
Clay
St. Johns
Franklin
Lafayette
Alachua
Putnam
Levy
Marion
Volusia
Sumter
Orange
Hernando
Hillsborough
Polk
Brevard
Manatee
Monroe
Dade

50% and over

40%–49%

25%–39%

11%–24%

10% and under

Total Negro population: 47%

4. Ratio of Negro Distribution by County, 1880. (Statistics from U.S. Census Office, Tenth Census, 1880.)

place of Florida's political parties. Adjourning to the courthouse, the convention opened with lines quickly drawn between the Negro and carpetbag groups, with the Negro as usual in the majority. Postmaster Stewart, continuing to favor strong aggressive Negro leadership for the party, nominated the colorful Jefferson County Negro orator, George Washington Witherspoon, for Congress. The carpetbag element had as its candidate ex-Warden Malachi Martin. Playing a lone hand and bidding for Negro support at the forthcoming state gubernatorial convention, ex-Senator Simon B. Conover advocated the candidacy of Witherspoon. On the third ballot the flamboyant Negro orator led by two votes. Faced with this crisis, the carpetbaggers moved to adjourn the convention. The Negro leaders refused, one telling the delegates, "Stick to him right now if you want to elect a colored man. If you wait till morning you'll never get him in the world." The balloting continued and Witherspoon was nominated. After endorsing ex-President Grant and Judge Thomas Settle as presidential and vice-presidential candidates, the convention adjourned.[68]

West Florida's Democrats renominated the incumbent, R. H. M. Davidson. In the Second Congressional District the Democrats nominated General J. J. Finley, and the Republicans again selected Horatio Bisbee, Jr.[69] Preliminary political skirmishes over, both parties were busy making final preparations for their state conventions.

The Republican state convention would determine whether the Negro faction with white candidate Simon B. Conover, the Jacksonville Ring with its strong businessman element, or the Black Belt carpetbaggers would control the party. On May 12 the convention assembled at the lower Black Belt town of Gainesville. Again the majority of delegates were Negroes. The major item on the agenda was the selection of gubernatorial candidates and delegates to the national convention. Strong delegations arrived from the periphery; however, Collectors of Customs Humphreys of Escambia and Wicker of Monroe failed to obtain federal transportation for their pro-Sherman delegations. Traveling costs were nearly $800 for the Pensacola group and $600 for the Key West contingent.[70] To complicate matters further, the Allen faction from Monroe sent a contesting delegation. There were also contesting groups from Marion and Franklin counties.[71]

On the evening after the opening of the convention, a partisan crowd assembled at Leonard Dennis's large Arlington House to hear Republican oratory. The gathering first listened to Negro leader J. Willis Menard state that whenever a Democratic victory was proclaimed in the North, "some Bourbon Democrat in the South would go gunning for a nigger." Menard also denounced the Democrats for robbing Negro children of the advantages of education and for trying to enact laws detrimental to Negroes. One such proposed law, he said, would make it a penitentiary offense to steal chickens and pigs. He thought this theft justified because it was a habit born of necessity during slavery. Success in the coming election, he predicted, would depend on the Northern element in the St. Johns River valley and the Cuban vote at Key West. H. S. Harmon, Negro secretary of the state executive committee, charged that the Democrats, acting in defiance of laws, had taken schools away from the Negroes and robbed thousands of Republicans of the right to vote.[72]

The gubernatorial nomination race the following day was at first a three-cornered affair. The Ring was backing Jacksonville scalawag William Ledwith; Negroes were generally supporting Conover; and the Black Belt carpetbaggers were advocating the nomination of Dennis Eagan of Madison.[73] Since no faction had a clear majority, the balance of power was held by the two delegations from the periphery. Controlling federal patronage at Pensacola and Key West respectively, Wicker and Humphreys were at the convention solely to gain an endorsement for the presidential candidacy of John Sherman. Expected enthusiasm for Sherman was failing to materialize. A large majority of the delegates were solidly for Grant, with the Jacksonville Ring pro-Blaine.

Confronted with this unfavorable situation, Sherman representative A. E. Bateman, though neither a delegate nor even a resident of the state, assumed command of the customhouse groups and entered into an alliance with the Conover-Negro faction. Under the terms agreed upon, Bateman threw the twenty-eight votes of the Sherman delegates to Conover. The Negro faction was to see that Sherman received a complimentary vote when the convention endorsed Grant. Furthermore, Humphreys and a strong contingent of Sherman supporters were to be named to the national convention delegation, of which Sherman was to be second choice. No Blaine supporters were to be delegates. With the Sherman people swinging behind him, Conover gained the nomination on

the fifth ballot. To promote unity within the party and placate
the Ring, Ledwith was nominated for lieutenant governor. Despite
Conover's victory, the Negro faction was unable to carry out its
part of the agreement—the endorsing of Sherman—when Blaine's
supporters, resenting the unnatural alliance against them, served
notice that they would fight any pro-Sherman resolution to the
bitter end.[74]

In their platform, the Republicans reminded the voters of Florida that they had established the school system in Florida. Various
planks favored civil rights, railroad building, and Cuban rebels.
Other planks opposed a constitutional convention, condemned the
treatment of convicts by the Drew administration, and castigated
the registration act of 1877 which removed five thousand Negro
voters from the election lists. Completing their platform, the Republicans charged: "That the Democratic party in this state has,
from the first, through many of its leading business men, adopted
a system of business ostracism against men who cooperate with
the Republican party; that as long as a Northern man lives among
them, voting with them or not voting at all, he is tolerated, but
when he asserts his independence, and votes and co-operates with
the Republican party, he is marked by the leaders of the Democratic party for ostracism and informed that if he advocates Republicanism or acts with the Republican party, his business and
social standing will be injured."[75]

Bourbon editor Charles E. Dyke, Sr., evaluated the Republican
ticket as mediocre but cautioned *Floridian* readers that the Negro
would support it; and if Conover should be victorious, the ordeal
of Reconstruction would return.[76] The Tampa *Sunland Tribune*
saw Conover's nomination as a payoff for his many acts of kindness
to Negro leaders and his support of Witherspoon's candidacy for
Congress.[77]

The main issue before the Democratic state convention, held
in Gainesville in June, was the renomination of Governor Drew.
While the Ellaville lumberman was desirous of a second term,
he would not actively seek one, feeling that on the basis of his
record a draft should be accorded. He thought his most likely
opponent, Secretary of State William D. Bloxham, had given him
definite assurance that he too would be an inactive candidate.
Meanwhile, Charles E. Dyke, Sr., was astutely managing an under-
cover campaign to gain a large Bloxham delegation at the con-

vention. The autonomous county leaders, particularly the Bourbons, were doubtful of giving the independently minded governor
a second term and were falling in behind their old Reconstruction
leaders. Both Drew and Bloxham were nominated in the convention, but while Drew received the thanks of the delegates for an
able and successful administration, Bloxham received the nomination. Feeling that his secretary of state was guilty of ingratitude,
Drew bitterly awaited the outcome in a sideline role.[78] To reward
South Florida's large Democratic majority, the convention nominated Livingston W. Bethel, little known outside of Key West,
for lieutenant governor.[79] The platform of the Democrats
advocated equal protection of all persons regardless of race,
economy in government, the disencumberment of the Internal
Improvement Fund, and the building of railroads in South and
West Florida.[80]

For the second time since the beginning of Radical Reconstruction, Florida voters in the gubernatorial race would choose between a Southern Democrat and a Northern Republican, between
a Deep South Bourbon planter and a Yankee carpetbagger. Both
Bloxham and Conover were amiable, personable men, kind to and
generally liked by Negroes. Bloxham viewed the Negro with the
concept of noblesse oblige. Although unwilling to grant him equality, he did not approve of racial extremism. On the other hand,
Conover was willing to support Negroes for major offices in the
state. Ex-Confederate generals John B. Gordon of Georgia and
John T. Morgan of Alabama arrived in Florida to invoke memories
of the Lost Cause and emphasize strongly that the Democratic
party continued the fight for the South.[81]

Although Democrats were firmly united behind Bloxham, white
Republicans not dependent on federal patronage were discouraged by the victory of the Negro faction of the party. R. W. Ruter,
writing from Pensacola, thought that the Republican ticket was
the weakest possible. His opinion was that an independent would
have a good chance of election in the First Congressional District
race.[82] East Florida white Republicans were equally discouraged.
Edward M. Cheney, a prominent member of the Jacksonville
Ring, stated in the *Telephone*: "I am satisfied that the election
of the present Republican State ticket would be a curse to the
State and a death blow to the Republican party of Florida."[83]
In South Florida, James T. Magbee was up in arms over the nomi-

nation of Conover and Witherspoon. Still hoping that the Republican national ticket could carry Florida, the *Guardian*'s editor complained to John Sherman that the antics of the Black Belt carpetbaggers had driven the Southern Republicans and the better class of Northern settlers into a state of poltical neutrality, with many of these formerly active party members believing that Republicanism in the South meant Negro domination. Castigating Witherspoon's nomination, the ex-judge thought that Conover would make the most ignorant colored man think himself fit for Congress.[84]

Magbee and other disgruntled Republicans hoped to persuade Witherspoon and Conover to withdraw. Then a new convention could be held and other candidates nominated. This hope vanished when Governor Drew, whose name was mentioned as a possible independent candidate for governor, quickly came out with a statement that he had no intention of running and planned to retire from politics at the end of his term.[85] His chances of success considerably lessened by the division in his party and meager newspaper support, Conover nevertheless stumped the state, using a treasury cutter for transportation in South Florida.[86] Financial support for the campaign came from wealthy Northerners who were solicited by Henry S. Sanford.[87] But the state Republican executive committee found Hayes's reconciliation policy a stumbling block in its statewide money-raising campaign. When asked for a ten dollar contribution, D. M. Blue, Keysville postmaster, replied that since he was a Democrat he would not contribute.[88]

Although the Democratic party was able to reconcile its differences after the various conventions and go into the election united, the Republican county machines began to show signs of disintegration. In Alachua County, a Republican stronghold since 1868, the party split into Walls and Dennis factions, each running its own slate of candidates for the legislature. Because "Little Giant" Dennis had spent much time outside the county during the preceding four years because of having been involved in the Alachua frauds of 1876, and because he lost out to Bisbee for nomination as Congressional candidate, leadership of the regular county machine passed to Josiah T. Walls. While Walls regulars supported Bisbee, Dennis and his insurgents displayed little enthusiasm for the Jacksonville congressman. Feelings became so bitter that at a political meeting held outside the Federal Land Office in Gainesville, Walls supporters tore down the platform to prevent Dennis from speaking.[89]

Duval County Republicans also divided into two factions. A reform movement was led by Jacksonville businessman Jonathan C. Greeley, ex-Governor Harrison Reed, and Emanuel Fortune, one of the Negro Republicans forced to leave Jackson County a decade previously.[90] Both factions supported the state and national tickets of their party. But the solidarity of the Negro community in Jacksonville was broken, enabling the Democrats to form a black Bloxham and Finley club.[91] Additional help for the Democrats came from the Jacksonville *Daily Florida Union*, whose new owners switched the paper's politics. The state's only daily reminded the Negro voters that Bloxham's first act after the Civil War was to build a black schoolhouse on his plantation, a school still in operation.[92]

Editor Dyke of Tallahassee alternately attacked the Negro voter and urged him to vote Democratic. A typical Dyke device was to print in the *Floridian* an obviously spurious letter from a colored man who claimed that he was going to vote for Bloxham on the basis that Democrats owned the land and did not mistreat the Negro.[93] A Tallahassee Negro politician, suggesting an alliance between the black people and the poor whites, stated: "If we could just get these poor white tackies yoked in with the colored folks we could carry this election like a flash and if I was a white man I could scare them into it, for they ain't got as much sense as a darkey." Dyke countered that the "poor white tackies" were the white laboring class, and that they had "intelligence enough not to be 'yoked' in with a mass of ignorant blacks for the purpose of hoisting into power a horde of adventurous dead-beats to disgrace the state again."[94]

Considering that the election machinery was firmly in the hands of the Democrats, that Bloxham was making a strong appeal for Negro votes, and that the Republican party was badly split, a *New York Times* report of a possible Republican victory was extremely unrealistic. The *New York Times* relied for its information on a reporter's tour of Florida. The reporter claimed to have discovered more than three hundred active Republican clubs in Florida. He had also been informed that prominent Democrats were flocking to the Republican banner. His accounts, oddly enough, did not specifically mention one prominent Democrat.[95] To assist the state Republicans the national party sent two Massachusetts politicians into Florida. Apparently without any particular knowledge of Southern politics, Charles J. Noyes, speaker of the Massachusetts House, and E. B. Callender, a member of that legislative body, toured Florida without major incident or effect on the outcome of the election. The two reported that no Democrats attended the Republican meetings where they spoke. They did report that the black people of the South were determined to maintain their right to vote by all means in their power.[96]

A little rain fell in East Florida on Election Day 1880. It was rather quiet contrasted with 1876; but the time had not yet arrived when Florida could have a free, honest election. On the Republican side the Negro community continued to use intimidation to keep its vote solid. The Democrats won the prize for fraud. Particularly in the Black Belt, Democratic election officials resorted to a systematic scheme of stuffing the ballot box. Tissue paper ballots folded inside regular Democratic tickets were cast. When the excess ballots were destroyed after the election in accordance with the law, Republican ballots only were drawn out of the box by officials who could feel the difference in texture of the paper. Then the tissue paper ballots were counted. Only in Madison County was there serious violence as Negroes were intimidated by armed white Democrats. Open frauds were condoned by Democratic election officials who clearly counted the Republicans out. In Hamilton County there was a small disturbance caused by Democrats furnishing liquor to Negroes voting for Bloxham.[97]

The statewide result of the election was a complete Democratic victory, Bloxham defeating Conover 28,378 to 23,297. Bethel and the Democratic nominees for Congress also had what seemed to be safe majorities. A resolution calling for a constitutional convention was defeated by a large majority. Much of the opposition to a constitutional convention came from Black Belt whites who feared that a return to home rule would turn their counties back over to the Negroes. While the Republican margin in the Black Belt counties was cut considerably, white South Florida rolled up tremendous Democratic majorities. In Manatee County, Witherspoon trailed the remainder of the ticket badly, indicating that Northern settlers would not vote for Negroes. Gadsden joined

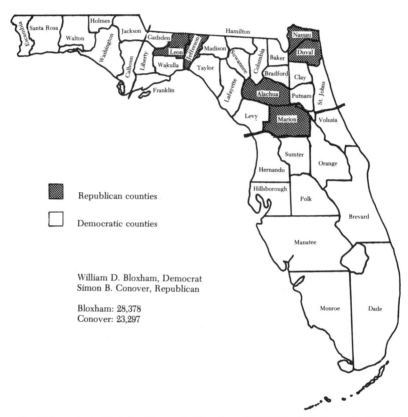

Republican counties

Democratic counties

William D. Bloxham, Democrat
Simon B. Conover, Republican

Bloxham: 28,378
Conover: 23,297

5. Gubernatorial Vote by County in Election of 1880. (Statistics from the Official Certificate of the Board of State Canvassers of the General Election held November 2, 1880, published in the Tallahassee *Weekly Floridian*, December 28, 1880.)

Madison in voting Democratic in a gubernatorial election for the first time since the start of Reconstruction. Alachua, because of the Republican split, elected Democratic legislators.[98]

But the victory was open to question as Governor Drew heard cries of fraud and irregularities from many parts of the state. The old Unionist, trying to be fair to the end of his administration, called for the protection of the voter in the preparing and casting of his ballot.[99] It was the consensus among white Republicans that the Democrats had used extreme measures to keep the state from going Republican. Both Bisbee and Witherspoon, having recourse on the federal level, began to contest the election of their opponents. Conover, after making a weak protest, acquiesced in the outcome.[100] Ex-Warden Malachi Martin, defeated for the assembly, complained that Gadsden County commissioners appointed "God-Daring men" on the Democratic side and illiterate, incompetent men to represent the Republicans at the polls. According to Martin, many Negroes who had previously been convicted of petty larceny were not permitted to vote. He further accused the Democrats of trimming the constitutional convention vote from tickets which were folded inside regular tickets. The ballot box was then thoroughly shaken to separate the folded tickets. Writing William E. Chandler, Martin requested a job outside Florida, claiming that on election day he was threatened by men in shirt sleeves carrying knives but was saved by a group of Negro friends. Told in an ominous manner by Democrats that they would have no trouble controlling the Negroes if he left, Martin feared for his life. No longer farming, he sublet his land to Negro tenants and employed a nightwatchman with dogs to guard his house. Socially ostracized by the Chattahoochee community—only one of the Stearns brothers had been to see him and no one called on his wife— Martin pleaded to Chandler: "I want to leave here. I am alone in the woods and know the danger well."[101]

5

Land, Politics, and Lynchings

Before the end of the Civil War, five of the six state governors were Democrats from the planter aristocracy of the Black Belt. From 1865 to 1880, Florida's six governors represented every shade of political coloring—except Democratic planters. With the inauguration of William D. Bloxham on January 4, 1881, the clock was turned back and a Democratic planter was again governor. The main theme of Bloxham's speech was an open invitation to railroad promoters and land developers. It was evident that Northern and foreign capitalists would receive warm Southern hospitality from the new Bourbon-dominated administration. Insofar as race relations were concerned, Bloxham had always been kindly disposed toward the Negroes. He now assured them that they would continue to have equal rights and justice.[1]

More like a vestige from Reconstruction than an aggressive second party, the state Republican organization would have fewer representatives in the legislature: only five senators and seventeen assemblymen. The senate would be filled with powerful Democratic county leaders. Senators such as John H. McKinne of Jackson, Stephen R. Mallory, the Younger,* of Pensacola, and John B. Dell of Alachua were the oligarchy of the Democratic party. Without their support, the governor's program would be meaningless.[2] In the assembly, matters were different; in fact, veteran

*Stephen R. Mallory, the Elder, died November, 1873. *Biographical Directory of the American Congress 1774-1927*, p. 1284.

70

assemblyman Charles Dougherty found confusion there, with most members as green as grass.[3]

To emphasize to the legislators a continuance of status quo and implying a closeness which did not exist, Bloxham submitted Drew's outgoing message to the legislature on January 3 instead of formulating a program of his own. Because of the overeagerness of the 1879 legislature to cut taxes, Governor Drew left office with a deficit of $100,000 in the treasury. Nevertheless, a frugal spending policy during his administration reduced the floating debt carried over from Republican rule from $250,000 to $50,000, state bonds rose to par, and the financial integrity of the state was partially restored. Recommending that the legislature raise taxes, the outgoing governor stated: "At the present valuation of property and rate of taxation, the State cannot be kept at a cash basis and the interest on the public debt paid." To overcome the lack of industry in Florida, Drew suggested a law exempting new industries from taxes for five to ten years. Florida Seminole War claims against the federal government amounted to over $300,000. Drew notified the legislators that he had obtained the services of lobbyist Colonel Sydney I. Wailes of Washington, wise in the ways the federal government operated, to investigate for a mere 15 per cent —$45,000—the collection of the Indian war claims.[4] A mysterious figure in Florida public land operations, Wailes was already representing the state before the Federal Land Office in cases which involved the antebellum selection of public lands. His commission in these cases was 20 per cent.[5] To provide Bloxham with sufficient revenue to administer the state government, the legislature refused ex-Senator David L. Yulee's request that taxes be reduced. The new tax bill raised the ad valorem levy from seven to eight mills.[6]

After caucusing, Florida's Democrats voted in a bloc to reelect the innocuous Charles W. Jones to the United States Senate. An East Florida boom for General William Wing Loring, Fereeh Pasha in the Egyptian army following the collapse of the Confederacy, failed to materialize.[7] In the only disputed election, Jonathan C. Greeley, reform Republican and Jacksonville businessman, contested the seat from the Eighteenth District—Duval County—of Joseph E. Lee, Negro party regular. John H. McKinne, chairman of the Committee on Privileges and Elections, held that the testimony submitted by Greeley was so vague, indefinite, and unsatisfactory that his committee could not reach a decision. Therefore, Lee kept his seat.[8] Despite this ruling, McKinne was no believer in equal rights for Negroes. During the session he introduced Senate Bill 53, the first clearly anti-Negro proposal before the Florida legislature since the redemption of the state. This measure made marriage of a white and a Negro—anyone with one-eighth Negro blood—a felony. McKinne's bill passed both houses on a strictly party vote and was signed on February 9 by Bloxham.[9]

Strong grass roots opposition from the rural white counties continued to stand against special privileges for railroads. Most of the railroads had been claiming exemption from taxation under the Internal Improvement Act of 1855. Refuting this claim, the legislature held that only roads actually constructed under the 1855 act could claim exemption; the others were to be taxed.[10] High freight rates, which were a severe hardship to farmers, generated the first organized anti-railroad sentiment in the grass roots of North Florida. Columbia County vegetable growers held an indignation meeting in March to protest a sixty per cent tariff increase by the Southern Express Company. In resolutions angrily framed at the meeting, the farmers asked for the immediate and active cooperation of all Florida market gardeners in order to bring about reasonable rates for service to the northern and western markets.[11]

Governor Bloxham, although a charter member of the grange in Leon County, ignored the discontented rumblings of the farmers. The first objective of his administration was to encourage new capital into the state. A crisis was near as the indebtedness of the Internal Improvement Fund approached $1 million. Drew had been satisfied to delegate the responsibility of bringing about the sale of the fund lands to the state's capable land agent, Samuel A. Swann. Bloxham now personally took charge. Meanwhile Swann, unaware that he now had the governor as a competing land agent, attempted to interest an English syndicate in the purchase of several million acres. Other possible buyers included a New York group supported by a German banking house, several Boston capitalists, a London syndicate headed by Henry S. Sanford, and John H. Fry—the Florida ship canal promoter.[12] With all of Florida's public domain in jeopardy in the event the Vose estate forced an auction, State Land Commissioner Hugh A. Corley reconsidered his earlier opinion that the people would growl at the sale of a large portion of the state lands. He was now satisfied that such a sale would be received with approbation because the granting of the remaining lands would bring new railroads.[13]

Since Reconstruction, the ally of the new Northern capitalists seeking investments in Florida had been the businessman wing of the state Republican party. Although a few Democrats, notably David L. Yulee and John A. Henderson, engaged in economic activities which crossed party and sectional lines, the yeoman farmer and small town businessman who formed the rank and file of the Democratic party were wary of such dealings. But believing that the state's future lay in attracting outside capital, Bloxham married his administration and the Democratic party to the land promoters and railroad builders: absentee ownership was solicited to fill the vacuum caused by the decline of the plantation aristocracy and the building of inefficient railroads. The keystone of the alliance between Florida Bourbon and Yankee capitalist was the Disston Sale.

Nouveau riche Philadelphia society clubman Hamilton Disston at thirty-six headed the Keystone Saw, Tool, Steel and File Works. A self-educated man, his formal training had ended with grammar school. Counter to his father's belief that he should devote himself to the steady and reliable business of sawmaking, Hamilton had many and varied interests, including Philadelphia politics, Atlantic City real estate, and western mining property. Independent and strong-willed, he was described by a Quaker City newspaper in 1875 as "not dickering worth a cent, wanting nothing, owing nothing, and playing his own hand all the time." In national politics he was a loyal supporter of the Republican administration and, conditioned by the competition of the British saw industry, a whole-hearted believer in the encouragement of domestic industries by means of the protective tariff. This firm Republicanism on a national level, however, did not prevent him in 1876 from bolting the corrupt Philadelphia gashouse machine and supporting Democratic reform candidates for city offices.[14]

Disston first visited Florida in the role of a tourist and sportsman in 1877. Its undeveloped southlands attracted his interest, and momentarily forgetting fishing, he envisaged a sugar empire in the wilderness of the Everglades. After returning to Philadelphia, he decided to translate his dream into reality. On February 26, 1881, he made an agreement with the Internal Improvement Fund trustees to engage in a drainage project in the Everglades, his remuneration to be alternate sections of the reclaimed land. Capitalizing on Disston's interest in the development of the peninsula, Governor Bloxham in the late spring visited Philadelphia and secretly conferred with him on a sale of four million acres of the public domain. They then reached an agreement. Returning to Tallahassee on May 30, Bloxham announced to the Internal Improvement Fund trustees that he had accepted Disston's offer of $1 million for the four million acres. The trustees unanimously approved Bloxham's action.[15]

Under the contract drawn up by Attorney General George P. Raney, Disston agreed to make a down payment of $200,000. Ninety days later a payment of $300,000 was due, 150 days later a payment of $250,000, and the remaining $250,000 was to be paid before January 1, 1882. The first payment was to be made in lawful money, and obligations or indebtedness of the Internal Improvement Fund would be accepted for the later payments. The trustees agreed to allow Disston to select his first 3.5 million acres in ten-thousand-acre lots, the remaining half million acres to be chosen in smaller bodies. If Disston defaulted on any payment after the first, the contract allowed him to retain such lands as he had paid for.[16] The first payment marked the end of the long drought of large Northern investments in Florida which had existed since the promotional activities of David L. Yulee on the eve of the Civil War.

Meanwhile, Samuel A. Swann, the board's bypassed land agent, was negotiating at his own expense with James Hastings of London. In the early part of May, Swann made a business trip to New York, discovering there that capitalists in that city and Philadelphia were making overtures directly to the trustees for the purchase of the Internal Improvement Fund land. He also ascertained that the Vose claimants, who now held $750,000 in fund debts, proposed to acquire most of Florida's public domain in settlement of their lien. On May 16, Hastings cabled Swann that he had been successful in forming a British syndicate to sell Florida lands. Swann forwarded this telegram to the trustees but received no reply. Then on May 27, Swann telegraphed the trustees that he had received a binder of $110,000 from one William Little for one million acres at forty cents an acre, Little to pay the remainder at a later date. Land Commissioner Hugh A. Corley replied to his former partner on May 31 that a $1 million contract with Philadelphia parties had already been accepted. This abrupt termination of his services without notice came as a staggering shock to Swann. For five years, almost to the exclusion of other business, he had devoted his time and limited resources to effecting a sale. The following month, being informed that the Disston Sale might not be completed, Swann brought before the trustees an offer from C. D. Willard, attorney for the Sir Edward J. Reed interests, of twenty-six cents an acre for four million acres. Swann said he would waive his commission if this offer was accepted. Since the contract had been signed for the Disston Sale, the trustees refused Swann's final offer. On July 11 Swann presented a bill for his services as land agent. When the trustees refused to honor it, he brought suit in the federal court at Jacksonville. The trustees then compromised with him, settling his claim for $20,000.[17]

The *Philadelphia Press* announced that Disston was now the largest land proprietor in the world.[18] Further adding to his original purchase, the Philadelphian eventually obtained 1.5 million acres from the Everglades drainage operations of the Atlantic and Gulf Coast Canal and Okeechobee Land Company.[19] The citizens of Florida, barely escaping the clutches of the Vose claimants, were understandably leery of the motives of those who sold millions of acres at twenty-five cents an acre to a virtually unknown Yankee. Scholarly, conservative George R. Fairbanks, editorializing in the June 18 issue of the Fernandina *Florida Mirror,* condemned the secrecy of the transaction and the fact that public opinion had not been sampled before so large a sale had been consummated. Fairbanks had recently returned to Florida after devoting fifteen years to the rebuilding of the University of the South. In northwestern states, he pointed out, universities were endowed, schools liberally supported, and public works built from the invested income from public lands. He was not prepared to throw up his hat when the state sold its lands at twenty-five cents an acre. He summarized the sale as being caused by the poverty of Florida, which compelled it to sacrifice the future to present necessities or past misfortunes or improvidence.[20]

Three days later, the administration's faithful spokesman answered Fairbanks in the columns of the Tallahassee *Weekly Floridian.* Haste in the sale was necessary, Charles E. Dyke, Sr., explained, because it was an open secret that the creditors of the

Internal Improvement Fund would have moved at the next term of the federal court to have the entire fund taken from the trustees and placed under their own control, and as an alternative would have asked for a sufficient quantity of land set aside at twenty cents an acre to cover their claims. Without explaining his reasoning, the *Floridian* editor declared that the sale was the most important transaction for the welfare of Florida since Reconstruction: a progressive movement which meant future progress and development.[21]

The Jacksonville *Daily Florida Union* rejoiced that live businessmen had now become interested in Florida.[22] The DeLand *Florida Agriculturist*, catering to new immigrants to the peninsula, and the Titusville *Florida Star*, the first paper to be established in the Indian River country, both approved the sale.[23] Opposition came from Editor J. B. Wall of the Tampa *Sunland Tribune*, who feared that Disston would select all the public domain in Hillsborough County. If Disston did this, it would seriously injure Tampa's chances to obtain a land grant railroad—a project in which Wall was vitally interested. He bitterly called the Disston Sale a sellout of the southern counties.[24] The reaction of the grass roots Democrats of the northern white counties and the Republicans was yet to be heard.

Arbitrarily classified swamp and overflow lands in order to conform with the Internal Improvement Fund Act of 1850, most of the land selected by the Disston companies was dry. Disston was not interested in the old settled part of the state where the best lands had long since passed into private hands. The Everglades and the Kissimmee River Valley, populated by a few cowboys and Seminoles, were to be the heartland of his empire. Transportation would be supplied by steamboats from Key West, the only city in southernmost Florida, going up the Caloosahatchee River through a canal dredged by Disston into Lake Okeechobee and north through the lake to the Kissimmee River and upstream to Kissimmee City—the empire capital. North of Kissimmee City the South Florida Railway, under construction from Sanford, would transport the expected flood of immigrants. To allow Henry S. Sanford and its other backers to capitalize on the expected increase in the value of land due to the coming of the railroad, Disston agreed in July to relinquish alternate sections along its right of way to the South Florida Railway.[25]

Florida land sales, particularly in Orange and Sumter counties, enjoyed an immediate boom.[26] Samuel A. Swann, returning to his private land development business, expressed approval of the Disston Sale and felt that it would benefit the state.[27] Before the summer was over, Disston announced that a colony of 250 New York families which was in the process of organization would settle in Orange County near Orlando during September. At first the Disston companies placed their real estate—costing twenty-five cents an acre—on the market at prices ranging from $1.25 (the Federal Land Office price) to $5.00 an acre.[28] The large increase in price was made partly to offset the worthlessness of swampland included in the purchase and partly to pay expenses of promotional activities and return a profit to Disston and his associates. Later, business lots in Kissimmee City were advertised from $200 to $600, suburban lots from $200 to $500, and Kissimmee Valley farm land from $2.50 to $20.00 an acre.[29]

By September 1, Disston had paid $500,000 on the purchase price, all in currency except $15,000 in coupons guaranteed by the state. On December 17 he announced to the trustees that he had accepted an offer from Sir Edward J. Reed to complete the payments in return for two million acres. Reed agreed to select his acreage after Disston had chosen 1.5 million acres.[30] Disston gave Reed $100,000 for assuming one-half of the contract. This meant that Disston paid for his land thirty cents an acre, Reed, twenty cents an acre.[31] At approximately the same time, Reed bought control of the Atlantic, Gulf, and West India Transit Company—the Yulee road—renaming it the Florida Transit Railroad.[32] Although he paid irregularly and exceeded the time limit set by the trustees, the British capitalist was able to complete payment on December 26, 1882. Of Reed's total payments only one-third was in obligations of the fund, the remainder being in legal currency.[33]

Despite the fact that he was now the largest landowner in the state and was investing his private fortune in its development, Disston continued to maintain a "hands off" attitude in regard to its politics. While the Democratic party staked its future on the Disston Sale, the Philadelphia Republican capitalist quietly organized the Florida Land and Improvement Company and the Lake Butler Villa Company. As a rule, only immigrants who were able to purchase land were encouraged by the Disston companies to come

to Florida.[34] Disston failed to divert the flow of immigration southward, partly because of the old reason that climate and abundant
land did not have the same attraction as the minerals of the West
and partly because Florida shared the stigma of being a Southern
state; immigrants continued to prefer the North and the West.[35]
In a day of robber barons, land pirates, and political vassalage
in the South to absentee economic interests, Disston's forbearance
was unique and commendable. Typical of the high-minded manner in which he operated was the opportunity squatters and
homesteaders were given to purchase their land at the state price
of $1.25 an acre from the state, Disston to select an equal amount
of land elsewhere.[36] Though he lost a good part of his fortune
in his Florida investments, his activities enabled others, most of
whom did not have his exemplary ethics, to make fortunes. The
interest excited by the Disston Sale and the freeing of the Internal
Improvement Fund lands gave a great impetus to the opening
up of the peninsula.[37]

Eagerly taking advantage of this freeing of the Internal Improvement Fund lands and the resumption of grants, ten railroads made
plans for construction. The two giants among these were the Plant
system and the Louisville and Nashville Railroad Company. Self-
made Yankee tycoon Henry B. Plant was a native of Connecticut
and a longtime resident of Georgia. Emerging from the wreckage
of the war as president of the Southern Express Company, Plant
branched out into the carrier field, buying several bankrupt railroads to form the Savannah, Florida, and Western. A branch of
this road from Dupont, Georgia, to Live Oak, Florida, gave him
his first railroad holding in the state. Later he made a second connection—from Waycross, Georgia, to Jacksonville, Florida. Shortly
after the Disston Sale, Plant bought the controlling interest in the
South Florida Railway and became the major provider of transportation for Disston's empire.[38] The canal route through Lake Okeechobee, though opened, was never satisfactory. On March 21,
1882, the South Florida Railway was completed to Kissimmee,
and construction was then begun to extend it to Tampa.[39] Land
grants resulting from railroad building in Florida eventually made
Plant the owner of several million acres.[40] Whereas President
Milton H. Smith of the Louisville and Nashville Railroad Company
held a stranglehold for many years on Alabama, Plant, who was
as important to Florida's economy as Smith was to Alabama's,

exerted a less powerful influence. Florida's representative of the Louisville and Nashville would, however, attempt to emulate Smith.

Although the transportation boom centered in South Florida, the Louisville and Nashville decided to extend its railroad east from Pensacola, giving the panhandle its long-awaited railroad. William D. Chipley, a native of Georgia and manager of the L & N interests in Florida and southern Alabama, anticipating the freeing of the fund, obtained a charter for the Pensacola and Atlantic Railroad Company from the 1881 legislature. The projected one hundred sixty mile route received the customary grant of alternate sections six miles on each side of its track plus a special grant of twenty thousand acres for each mile completed, making a total of 3,860,-619 acres. Of this grant, 2,830,065 acres were actually delivered. Much of the land selected was in South Florida. From Marianna to Milton the route of the railroad bypassed all existing towns. The new railroad townsites bore the names of P & A officials: Chipley, Bonifay, DeFuniak.[41] Chipley considered that his railroad had a vested interest in Florida's public domain, and he vigorously censured Governor Bloxham for transferring Everglades land to Disston's Atlantic and Gulf Coast Canal and Okeechobee Land Company as a reward for reclamation. It was obvious from a Chipley letter to Bloxham that he did not consider the lands which his railroad desired to select in South Florida to be swamp and overflow.[42] Chipley's energy, cold-blooded business methods, and aggressiveness contrasted strongly with the free and easy manner of his political rival for control of Escambia County, fellow townsman Stephen R. Mallory, the Younger. A graduate of Transylvania University, Chipley had served with distinction on the Confederate side as a lieutenant colonel with Kentucky troops. A combat veteran of western campaigns, he had been wounded at Shiloh and Chickamauga and captured at Peachtree Creek. He had ended the war in the Federal prison on Johnson's Island. After the war he had married, engaged in the mercantile business at Columbus, Georgia, and entered politics as the first chairman of the Democratic executive committee of Muscogee County.

The fighting spirit that Chipley displayed as a soldier carried over into his political activities. In 1867 he was arrested and jailed by the occupation forces as a ringleader of the mob which lynched G. W. Ashburn, a scalawag ex-member of the Georgia Constitutional Convention. Despite strong efforts to obtain a conviction by General George G. Meade, military commander in Georgia, evidence was not forthcoming, and Chipley and the alleged mob members were freed. Suffering financial losses because of his imprisonment and the failure of a firm with which he had been associated, in 1873 he entered the employment of the Baltimore and Ohio Railroad Company. In 1876 he moved to Pensacola to assume the management of the Pensacola Railroad Company, which shortly afterward became part of the Louisville and Nashville system. Chipley began the construction of the Pensacola and Atlantic in June 1881, and as there was little heavy grading required, the railroad was completed at a rapid pace, reaching the Apalachicola River in January 1883.[43]

While West Florida's apostle of the New South was building his railroad and a small boom was showing signs of beginning in the southern counties, the Black Belt was still smoldering from the 1880 election. Possessing the largest Negro following of any Democrat, Bloxham had repeatedly emphasized Negro rights. A series of events in Madison County made it clear that if he followed this policy he would estrange himself from the Bourbon leaders of the Black Belt counties. The first incident occurred at Madison on February 3, 1881, when two election officials, William T. Forrester, a white Democrat, and Augustus Crosby, a Negro Republican, engaged in a bloody fight. Several Negroes had previously testified before a federal jury at Jacksonville that Forrester stuffed the ballot box during the election. He in turn blamed Crosby for this charge and accosted him. Though Forrester was the aggressor, he was released with a three-dollar fine, while Crosby was assessed seventeen dollars. County Judge Robert M. Witherspoon then placed the Negro under a $300 peace bond. Deciding to avoid further violence, four of Madison's Negro leaders—Crosby, Charles Savage, John G. Gambia, and Howard James—took the evening train to Jacksonville.[44]

This seemingly minor disturbance had robbed Republican county boss Dennis Eagan of his lieutenants. Intimidation and coercion, two weapons which ten years previously had eliminated Negro leadership in Jackson County, were being successfully used in Madison. Eagan, however, was not ready to concede defeat. He held the collectorship of internal revenue at Jacksonville, one of the juiciest federal patronage plums in the state. Now his prestige as a leader in the party was at stake. To bolster his crumbling machine and keep the county Republican, the Irish-born carpet-bagger made arrangements for hearings in early February on the disputed congressional election between General J. J. Finley and Horatio Bisbee, Jr. On objection of S. Y. Finley, attorney for his father, the hearings were transferred from Eagan's plantation, two miles from town, to the courthouse at Madison.[45]

Eagan then persuaded Savage and James to return from Jacksonville to testify at the hearings. Upon arrival, Savage—armed and in a reckless mood—confided to friends that he expected to be "ku-kluxed" or killed.[46] On February 7, the first day of the hearings, Savage, who was the defeated Republican candidate for the assembly, testified that two prominent Madison Democrats were guilty of election frauds. He accused Colonel Carraway Smith, Confederate hero at the Battle of Olustee, of stuffing the ballot box, and Frank Patterson, young law partner of Mayor Frank W. Pope, of challenging Republican voters on unlawful grounds and handing out ballots with other ballots secretly folded inside them. Clearly showing that he intended to conduct the hearings on a partisan basis, Eagan then appointed Savage bailiff.[57]

The following day Frank Patterson, angered by Savage's accusation, accosted him at the hearing. In the altercation Savage assaulted Patterson and then shot him. James moved to Savage's assistance as the hearing ended in chaos. A. R. Spradley, an eye-witness to the shooting, later testified that he thought that he heard Eagan call "Shoot him again."[48] As tension mounted, a Negro woman, Vine Stephens, told a crowd of Negroes who had gathered outside the courthouse to be men and not cowards. Sheriff Theodore Willard, a strong leader in the Democratic party, quickly took action to restore order. Gathering a posse he entered the courtroom and arrested both Savage and James. Several members of the posse threatened to kill Eagan but were restrained by the sheriff. Eagan adjourned the hearings to his plantation, and the white citizens of Madison began to arm themselves. The group of Negroes outside the courthouse quickly dispersed, a few going with Eagan.[49]

Patterson died almost immediately following the shooting. A feeling of intense excitement now prevailed in Madison. Resistance was gone from the town's Negro population, who—fearing mob action—were in a state of terror. Public sentiment directed against

Eagan held him responsible for the death of the young, well-liked lawyer. Informed that Sheriff Willard was riding toward his plantation with a warrant for his arrest, Eagan fled during the night on foot through the woods to seek sanctuary in Georgia, twelve miles distant. Arrested later at Albany, he was returned to Florida and set free on a writ of habeus corpus by the state supreme court. Because of the hatred manifested toward him there, it was now unsafe for Eagan to return to his Madison County plantation.[50] Leaving the county's large Republican majority leaderless, he moved his residence to Jacksonville.[51]

A fair trial being impossible in Madison, a change of venue was granted, transferring the Savage-James case to Jasper, county seat of Hamilton, a predominantly white area adjoining Madison on the east. Circuit Judge Enoch J. Vann would preside. Mayor Frank W. Pope was appointed to assist state attorney B. B. Blackwell with the prosecution. The political aspect of the case was emphasized when two prominent Republican lawyers, ex-Judge A. A. Knight of Jacksonville and Joseph N. Stripling of Madison, arrived in Jasper to defend the accused.[52] Dennis Eagan was paying their counsel fees of $1,500 and writing party friends soliciting contributions.[53] Leading Democrats also viewed the murder as a political incident. To Senator Wilk Call it was evidence of the malign influence of Horatio Bisbee, Jr.[54] However, despite the setback which the hearings received at Madison, Bisbee was able to complete his case. Accepting his version that the Patterson murder was caused by rioting Democrats, the House of Representatives seated him 141 to 9.[55]

An all-white jury, in spite of the stout defense put up by Stripling and Knight, sentenced the two Negroes to death.[56] Appealing the verdict to the state supreme court and charging that they were not allowed to cross-examine a key witness, the two lawyers were able to gain a writ of error on August 20 from Judge B. B. Van Vaukenbaugh, a Republican.[57] Jacksonville Republicans, continuing to consider the case a political issue, formed a committee which solicited contributions for the retrial.[58]

Not all of Florida's Republicans, however, blamed the Democrats for the Madison County disturbance. General Henry S. Sanford, a wealthy Northern capitalist who was now a resident of Orange County, wrote President Chester A. Arthur in November that Dennis Eagan was a reckless and unprincipled demagogue who encouraged Negroes to resort to violence. A former minister to Belgium, called by the New Haven *Palladium* a carpetbagger who took his trunk to Florida, Sanford had successfully developed an extensive area in Orange County. The town bearing his name on Lake Monroe was the southern terminal of the major steamship lines plying the St. Johns. As the expected Northern settlers came into South Florida and the war became more of a distant memory, Sanford envisioned a white Republican party with a dormant Negro wing. Such hopes would be frustrated, he told the President, by the actions of Eagan and other carpetbaggers which arrayed the two races against each other in the Black Belt, making the Democratic party a compact union of Southern whites. If further racial outbreaks could be avoided, he reasoned, with the wave of prosperity passing over Florida, Independent tickets would appear in every county, and the Democratic party would begin to disintegrate.[59]

Sanford's hope for a splintering of the Democratic party in Florida probably stemmed from the sudden bolting of David S. Walker, Jr., son of the ex-governor. Along with other idealistic young Floridians, Walker was highly dissatisfied with the rule of the party's dominant Bourbon wing. By the Bourbons he obviously meant Bloxham, Dyke, Chipley, and the conservative county leaders. But he did not desire to affiliate himself with the carpetbagger leadership of the Republican party. In October the youthful Tallahassee lawyer published a pamphlet calling for a new political party. Shocked by this political heresy, Editor Charles E. Dyke, Sr., denounced it, but at the same time he agreed with its call for the destruction of the Republican party.[60] However, little other interest was shown in the new movement, and as late as March 17, 1882, Governor Bloxham thought that there were few indications of Independentism in Florida.[61] A month later, Daniel L. McKinnon, state's attorney for the West Florida circuit, staged a one-man revolt against the Jackson County Democratic political machine. Announcing his candidacy for Congress, the young Marianna lawyer stated that Democratic county leaders had destroyed the purity of the ballot box by bold and audacious violations of the law, justifying their tricks by saying, "The Republicans taught us." He described the courts as powerless against this flouting of justice. He claimed that Independentism would remove the sectional distrust growing out of the Civil War which was being kept alive by politicians.[62] These accusations substantiated the outgoing statement by Governor Drew concerning election frauds. Since both Jackson and nearby Gadsden contained large Negro majorities, it seemed hardly possible that in a free election either would have been carried by decidedly anti-Negro Bourbons. The attitude of noblesse oblige shown by Bloxham toward the freedmen did not exist to any extent among the planters in the two counties.

Although McKinnon's outburst caught the Democrats by surprise, few joined him.[63] Even the anti-administration Pensacola *Commercial,* leaning further toward Independentism than any other Democratic newspaper in Florida, intimated that McKinnon was a latter-day scalawag who planned to lead the Negro voters.[64] It reported that his only strength was coming from Robert Meacham, Jefferson County Republican Negro leader.[65] Meacham's interest in Independentism was the first indication that Negro leaders were becoming dissatisfied with the Republican party, to which they had been shackled by the anti-Negro bias of most Democratic leaders in the Black Belt. This bias was evidenced by the growing sentiment for a poll tax among white property holders. The Monticello *Constitution* complained that while taxation and representation should be inseparable, in Jefferson County the ignorant rabble elected the legislators, depriving taxpayers, some of whom paid as much as $1,000 for a voice in their government. Agreeing with the *Constitution,* the Gainesville *Bee* maintained that no man was justly entitled to the elective franchise who did not contribute to the government.[66] Port city Democrats were also biased against Negro participation in government. Ex-Senator David L. Yulee, with large holdings in Fernandina, was particularly unhappy about the government of that municipality. Protesting that the Negroes who controlled the city government were not property holders, the elder statesman of the Democrats wrote Senator W. Naylor Thompson that property owners were a town's only permanent inhabitants and they should have protection for their interests and an effective voice in the local government.[67]

Leon and Jefferson County Negroes, meeting at Miccosuki late in May, countered Yulee's views with the declaration that it was by their labor that all classes were enabled to pay their taxes. Strong pro-Independent sentiment was shown by those in attendance. Faced by the danger of the Negroes' making a mass exodus from the faltering Republican party, ex-Senator Simon B. Conover addressed the gathering. While he announced his support of Mc-Kinnon, the carpetbagger pleaded with the Negroes not to break ranks. Loyalty to the party of Abraham Lincoln reached a low ebb among Black Belt Negroes when the meeting voted to join with the ex-Democrats in the Independent movement.[68] Led by State Senator John Wallace, Leon County's Negroes continued to move closer to an alignment with the Independents. When the party's county executive committee met at Gallie's Hall in Talla-hassee on June 17, Wallace warned the group that, judging from the sentiment expressed by the Democratic press, the Democratic party would virtually disfranchise the entire Negro population in order to restore harmony within its ranks. Conover, however, again spoke against alignment with the Independents. Taking one of the first stands of the state Republican party on the Disston Sale and the policies of the administration, the meeting went on record as opposing large land grants and existing railroad rates. A railroad commission was endorsed, and the legislature was petitioned to approve a land grant railroad from Thomasville, Georgia, via Tallahassee to Carabelle, Florida. The committee also voted to endorse the Independent movement.[69] In East Florida, Frank W. Pope, mayor of Madison and scion of an old planter family, was among the first young Democrats to espouse the cause of Inde-pendentism by becoming its candidate for the state senate. In a case similar to Walker's and McKinnon's, Pope risked a promising political career in making a stand against his county's Bourbons.[70]

McKinnon continued to draw his main support from Black Belt Republicans. On August 21 a group of these Radicals, mostly carpetbaggers, met at Quincy to determine their future course of action. Among those present were the Stearns brothers of Gads-den, George Washington Witherspoon and Jesse D. Cole of Jeffer-son, and ex-Senator Simon B. Conover of Leon. Conover ostensibly withdrew his opposition to Independentism, and a resolution favoring the endorsement of McKinnon passed without opposi-tion. Opinion was generally expressed in Quincy after the meeting that McKinnon would be the coalition candidate, the Republicans and Independents combining behind him. Some citizens of Quincy were predicting that McKinnon would easily defeat their fellow townsman Robert H. M. Davidson.[71]

While Republicans and Independents planned with increasing hopes to defeat the Bourbon-dominated Democrats in the approaching congressional and legislative elections, the state prepared to try Charles Savage and Howard James a second time. On August 25 Sheriff Sampson Altman of Hamilton County and a guard of four men started by rail to return Savage and James from Tallahassee, where they had been held awaiting the outcome of their appeal, to Jasper via Madison. Taking special precautions for the prisoners' safety en route, Altman had contacted newly appointed Sheriff S. M. Hankins of Madison. Hankins assured him that there would be no trouble if the prisoners were routed through his county. Instead, news mysteriously leaked out that Savage and James were departing from the Leon County jail, and a mob of one hundred men gathered at the Madison station to await the arrival of the train bearing them. Sheriff Hankins neither made an effort to disperse the mob, many of whom were armed, nor attempted to notify Altman of the danger. Further, wires were cut to Greenville to prevent the Madison station agent from warning the Hamilton County law officer. When the freight train bearing Savage and James arrived at Madison, the mob immediately uncoupled the two passenger coaches. Armed men entered the car containing the prisoners. Courageously and without any aid from Madison County law officials, Sheriff Altman fought to protect his charges, only to be quickly overrun by force of numbers. Both prisoners were riddled with bullets. One guard was wounded slightly.[72]

News of the lynching electrified the state. Outraged by vigilante-type "justice," Governor Bloxham telegraphed Sheriff Hankins, ordering him to arrest the guilty parties.[73] Later Bloxham offered a reward of $5,000 for their arrest.[74] Editor Dyke in the Tallahassee *Weekly Floridian* demanded the arrest and punishment of the murderers, being chiefly concerned with the injury to the reputation of the county and state which the brutal act inflicted.[75] The Jacksonville *Daily Florida Union* denounced the killing of Savage and James as a cold-blooded, premeditated murder which deserved the reprobation of law-abiding citizens.[76] George R. Fairbanks in the Fernandina *Florida Mirror* lamented that the majesty of the law had been defiled and trampled.[77] The *New York Times* described the lynching as "a piece of daring brutality" by ruffians.[78] It seemed that instead of being punished as criminals for their misdeed, Savage and James were now becoming martyrs to their political principles. It was said they were shot because they were black and Republicans.[79] In Madison County opinion was sharply divided. In the town of Madison, Mayor Pope called a mass meeting of whites and Negroes to be held at the courthouse. Judge Vann, who presided, asked the world not to "judge us by the crimes of a few desperadoes." Several of the town's ministers publicly denounced the crime as a gross and bloodthirsty act by irresponsible persons.[80]

Whether the lynchings would be punished depended on the findings of the coroner's jury. Savage's widow and another Negro claimed to be eyewitnesses to the murders and named Hugh Patterson, brother of Frank Patterson, and four others as members of the mob that did the shooting. Nonetheless, a partisan jury brought in the verdict that Savage and James came to their deaths at the hands of unknown parties.[81] To Malachi Martin, carpetbag leader of the Republicans in the Black Belt, the failure to bring in an indictment was a "case in point." Writing to D. B. Henderson, secretary of the National Republican Congressional Committee, Martin complained that often after fraud and ballot box stuffing investigations, Negroes who had given evidence were ruthlessly murdered. No jury, however, would even be impaneled to punish the assassins. The continuance of such a state of affairs, Martin felt, meant the end of the Black Belt Republican party. "Unless we can get some of the southern white men with us," he bluntly stated, "elections in the South are worse than a farce."[82]

Governor Bloxham made another effort to bring the mob members to trial. He promised State Attorney Blackwell "hearty and vigorous" cooperation and Circuit Judge Vann a military guard for his court if one was needed. It would not do, the governor asserted, for it to be stated that Florida could not protect witnesses.[83] From Bloxham's statement and the failure of the jury to indict, it is obvious that the mob members were in a strong position in the county. It is also apparent from the evidence that Sheriff Hankins was guilty of dereliction of duty and perhaps of complicity in the lynching. That the governor did not remove him suggests that Bloxham, despite his outrage, was unwilling to interfere with local police powers where white public opinion was against punishment of the lynchers. This had been his attitude following the lynching of a white man in Leesburg in the summer prior to the lynching of Savage and James. Leesburg was the county seat of Sumter, a predominantly white South Florida county with a sizable minority of Northern settlers. J. J. Dickison, Jr., son of Florida's famed guerrilla commander, had been arrested for assault.[84] He was taken by a mob from the Sumter jail on July 15 and lynched. His father, ex-Adjutant General J. J. Dickison, conducted his own investigation of the crime and as a result demanded immediate removal of the sheriff and trial of the guilty.[85] Governor Bloxham handled this lynching as he later handled the lynching of Savage and James—as a matter for local law enforcement officials. Writing General Dickison, he described Judge James B. Dawkins and State Attorney W. O. Hocker as men of such high character "that no stone would be left untouched in the line of official duty." Since he did not believe that he had the power to remove the sheriff, he informed Dickison that he was leaving it to the court to decide whether a coroner or an elisor should be appointed to replace that wayward official.[86] No action was taken.

Scholarly George Fairbanks editorialized in his Fernandina *Florida Mirror* that the Madison lynching was of far greater importance than just the race issue; it was a question of which would prevail, "law or anarchy."[87] With Bloxham's refusal to take any further action, the initiative rested with Madison police officials. It was their decision to let the matter rest and not to press for a trial. Their rejection of Bloxham's demand for law and order, together with his refusal to appoint new county officials or a special prosecutor, left the lynching of the two Negro Republicans an unpunished crime. The state's Democratic press failed to censure Madison officials for their blatant dereliction of duty. Truly, a Negro could say of Madison, "there is no part of justice in the court there for colored people."[88] On the other hand, when State Senator John B. Dell of Alachua County requested the removal of Sheriff J. W. Turner, Bloxham promptly complied.[89] His policy regarding law enforcement strongly indicated that he had given carte blanche to the Democratic county leaders. It seems that, regardless of the race of the victim, Bloxham would not move to bring the perpetrators of a lynching to trial without the support of the local Democratic leaders.

With the collapse of the Madison machine, the rejuvenation of the state Republican party was a major task. Ex-Governor Harrison

Reed, seeing an opportunity to make a comeback from political oblivion, had in April requested that Secretary of the Navy William E. Chandler, serving as administration liaison man with the Southern Republicans, obtain for him complete control of federal patronage within the state.[90] Although Chandler had persuaded the President to abandon the remnants of the Negro-carpetbag-Straightouts in Virginia in favor of General William Mahone's Readjusters,[91] Reed's request was refused and the Straightouts in Florida remained in full control of the patronage. Head of the Straightouts in the First Congressional District, Collector of Customs John M. Tarble, who was also mayor of Pensacola, opposed any compromise with the Independents. His candidate for Congress was Emory Fiske Skinner, a wealthy ex-Wisconsin lumberman with political ambitions. Owner of large holdings of virgin timber in Santa Rosa County, Skinner had lived in Florida eight years. A Douglas Democrat before the Civil War, he was making his first bid for office. Except for the appellation "Damn Yankee," he would have been more at home among the Democrats. However, despite three straight Democratic victories in the district, Tarble somehow had persuaded him that the majority of voters were Republicans.[92]

As the Escambia delegation was leaving Pensacola, the town was declared under quarantine for yellow fever. Using the quarantine as subterfuge to bar the Straightouts from the Republican District One Convention at the Gadsden County courthouse in Quincy, ex-Governor Marcellus L. Stearns attempted to stifle the opposition to Independentism. This maneuver failed, and by a narrow majority the Straightouts organized the convention, electing as chairman John Eagan of Pensacola, a brother of the ex-Madison County leader. The only dispute in delegations came from Leon County, where the regular group led by Postmaster W. G. Stewart was opposed by insurgents headed by ex-Senator Simon B. Conover. Although Conover had deserted McKinnon for Skinner, the convention recognized the Stewart delegation which was clearly entitled to be seated. A second serious defection from the ranks of the McKinnon supporters occurred when George Washington Witherspoon attempted to become a candidate, and failing, affiliated himself with the Straightouts. S. C. Cobb, a Pensacola businessman, told the convention that the National Republicans wanted a Straightout ticket rather than an alliance with

Independents. Even more effective in keeping the Negroes Republican, Collector Tarble passed out silver dollars for meals to hungry Negro delegates. In the contest between McKinnon and Skinner, the Straightout won by three votes.[93] After chairman Eagan announced that the Yankee lumberman was the victor, a surprised Negro delegate remarked that he had never heard of Skinner before. Rather than accept certain defeat with the political unknown from the periphery, disgruntled delegates from the Middle Florida counties of Gadsden, Leon, Liberty, Calhoun, Franklin, Jackson, and Jefferson met in a rump convention. After denouncing federal officeholders, particularly Collector Tarble, and accusing Skinner's backers of using money to influence delegates, the dissenters endorsed McKinnon.[94]

The outcome of the Quincy Convention showed conclusively that the Pensacola Straightout faction would continue to oppose any compromises necessary for working with the Independents. It was more important to the former to retain control of Republican party machinery and federal patronage than to win elections. The convention was but another in a long series where the Negro was the pawn of a few patronizing, scheming white Republicans. The Pensacola businessmen showed even less interest in Negro welfare than the Black Belt carpetbaggers. An unsigned letter printed in the October 24 issue of the Tallahassee *Weekly Floridian* accused Skinner of running a company store at his "second hand" sawmill and paying his employees only one-half their wages in cash, charging for the remainder prices between 35 and 40 per cent above those in Pensacola, just nine miles away.[95] By his own admission Skinner considered Negroes very shrewd and unscrupulous in politics.[96] Neither Skinner nor Tarble, living in the small affluent Northern colony at Pensacola, was aware of the critical condition of the Republican party in the Black Belt. Both confidently expected Florida to remain a two-party state indefinitely.

Ignoring the fact that the Straightouts opposed the Independents with as much vigor as the Democrats, Editor Dyke in the *Floridian* maintained that Independentism and Republicanism were one and the same and "Mack quit the Democratic party because it would not give him what he wanted."[97] Aloof from the Independent-Republican fireworks, the Democrats quietly renominated by a unanimous vote Robert H. M. Davidson.[98]

Skinner toured the district, conducting an aggressive campaign.

He was best able of the three candidates to finance his activity, and his expenses, which included supporting a Republican newspaper in Tallahassee, amounted to $5,000. To appeal to the Negro voter, George Washington Witherspoon traveled with Skinner and spoke on the same platforms. Bitterest opposition came not from the Democrats but from ex-Governor Stearns and the Independents. The yellow fever epidemic in Pensacola further added to Skinner's handicap.[99]

Although in other Southern states Secretary of the Navy Chandler had become disillusioned with Straightout combinations and had sought alliances with white Independents, this was not to be in the First District. The decision was made contrary to information supplied Chandler by J. Willis Menard, editor of the Key West *News*. Menard informed Chandler that all Negro leaders in Florida were supporting the Independent movement and only two white carpetbag leaders, Malachi Martin and ex-Governor Stearns, were opposing it.[100] Menard was wrong about Stearns; he was the only carpetbagger in the First District effectively helping the Independent movement.

In the Second District both Horatio Bisbee, Jr., and General J. J. Finley were renominated by their parties.[101] Independent support went to Bisbee, the Republican carpetbagger. In Madison County the Negro vote was solicited by Frank W. Pope, the Independent candidate for the state senate. The Bourbon-oriented *Madison Recorder* warned its white readers that the Republicans in the county backed Pope and the Independents so that two years hence the latter, being indebted, would support the former.[102]

The election of 1882 was the freest and fairest since the start of Reconstruction. In the First District, ex-Whig Davidson outpolled the combined vote of Skinner and McKinnon. Davidson had 11,246 votes, Skinner 7,029 and McKinnon trailed with 3,547. Stearns carried Gadsden for McKinnon, but elsewhere in the district's Black Belt the Negroes, continuing to vote Republican, supported Skinner. John Wallace, relinquishing his leadership of the regular Negro Republicans in Leon County to lead the Independents there, ran a poor third for the state senate. Jackson, McKinnon's home county, gave him only 362 votes to 1,368 for Davidson and 604 for Skinner. In South Florida, Hernando, Hillsborough, Manatee, and Polk counties cast a total of five votes for the Independent ticket, showing conclusively that Northern settlers in the

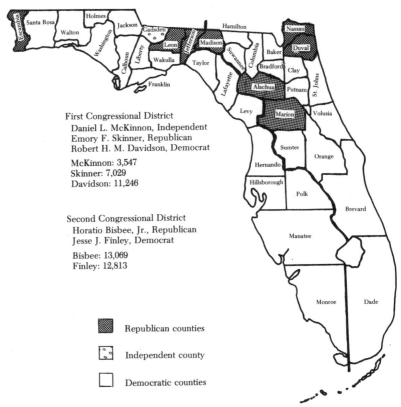

First Congressional District
Daniel L. McKinnon, Independent
Emory F. Skinner, Republican
Robert H. M. Davidson, Democrat

McKinnon: 3,547
Skinner: 7,029
Davidson: 11,246

Second Congressional District
Horatio Bisbee, Jr., Republican
Jesse J. Finley, Democrat

Bisbee: 13,069
Finley: 12,813

▓ Republican counties

▒ Independent county

☐ Democratic counties

6. Congressional Vote in Election of 1882. (Statistics from the Official Certificate of the Board of State Canvassers of the General Election held November 7, 1882, published in the Tallahassee *Weekly Floridian*, December 19, 1882.)

district, outside of the Black Belt carpetbaggers, had not the slightest interest in the Independent movement.[103]

Unity provided a different story in the Second District. There for the first time in the history of the party, Republicans reconciled their differences, combined with the Independents, and dealt the Democrats a setback, Bisbee leading Finley 13,069 to 12,813. Madison County (where—despite the Savage-James lynching—the Negro got out and voted) provided Bisbee's margin of victory. The Negro-Independent coalition here also elected its ticket headed by Frank W. Pope to the legislature. Elsewhere in the district white counties voted Democratic and Negro counties went Republican, four of the five South Florida counties in the district voting better than two to one Democratic. However, Volusia, possibly showing the influence of a fresh crop of Republican-oriented Northern settlers, voted for Finley by the narrow margin of 484 to 404.[104]

Although a few Independents would make their appearance in the legislature, local elections went Democratic in most white counties. The trend of Black Belt counties to go Democratic was temporarily halted as Alachua switched back to the Republican column while Gadsden and Madison went Independent. All port city counties would for the first time since the end of Reconstruction be represented by Republicans.

Pleased by the Democratic victories in the recent state election and by the new prosperity within the state, Governor Bloxham fairly glowed with enthusiasm in his message to the legislature on January 2, 1883. The Bourbon governor asserted that the Disston Sale was the only alternative to the destruction of the Internal Improvement Fund and that more miles of railroad had been constructed in the past two years than in the entire history of the state. The budget had been balanced, and state bonds were selling at a premium price. Though progress had been made in public education, he advised the legislators that Florida's resources were insufficient to support the two-school system, and federal assistance should be requested. Ignoring continuing fatalities, he declared that the improved condition of the convicts showed that they had been properly taken care of by the East Florida Railway Company. The governor also stated that he favored revising the state constitution.[105]

Showing the effects of the railroad and other promotional activity following in the wake of the Disston Sale, the legislature was more Bourbon than its predecessors. The strength of the autonomous Democratic county leaders was at a new high. The Republican opposition was as usual since 1876: ineffectual and weak. The railroad promoters showed their strength in the passage of eighteen railroad bills, and the senate committee on railroads and telegraphs reported unfavorably on a bill for a railroad commission. The majority report, signed by five members including one Independent and one Republican, stated that railroad commissions were established to correct two evils: unjust and unreasonable rates, and unjust discriminations for the benefit of favored persons or localities. Since these evils did not exist in Florida, no remedy was needed. Furthermore, the report stated that Florida should invite and not repel capital. Dissenting State Senator John H. McKinne, representing the Third District in West Florida, stated that unjust rates and discrimination were a common complaint, and he failed to see how a commission could hurt or how transportation could be slower than it was. Firing the first shot in the legislature against the heart of Bloxham's policy, he attacked the policy of devoting the vast landed domain of Florida to railroad enterprises and the giving of special privileges to railroads.[106] When the issue came to a vote, only four Democrats and one Republican voted with McKinne in favor of his minority report.[107]

Sentiment had been growing stronger for a constitutional convention. On January 16, the senate passed a bill calling for the convention by a vote of twenty-eight to eight. Three Democrats joined with five Republicans to oppose the bill.[108] The assembly also passed the bill, and once again Florida's citizens would decide whether they wanted to revise the constitution.[109]

On February 7 a committee from the legislature visited the state convict camp and returned with a favorable report. It found punishment very light, since no more than fifteen lashes with a leather strap were given for an offense.[110]

Though the Independents made only a weak showing in the legislature, they continued to make plans to organize the state in preparation for the 1884 elections. In early April, the Tallahassee *Weekly Floridian* reported the organization of an Independent state executive committee.[111] Their hopes for the future were expressed by the Tallahassee *Economist*: "The Independents were 'kinder-gartens' in 1882, but rest assured they will be giants in

1884 and that 'old and unreliable firm Dyke, Bloxham, Conover & Co.' will be sent [so] far up salt river that they will never be heard from anymore."[112] While carpetbagger Conover was not an open political ally of Bloxham and Dyke, it was becoming obvious to the Independents that control of the state Republican party was more important to him than the continuation of the two-party system in the state. Thus he was accused of playing ball with the Bourbons.

6

The Independent Revolt

Unsuccessful in 1882 in wresting control of the Republican party from the Pensacola Straightouts in the First Congressional District, and not venturing a contest at that time with the Jacksonville Ring in the Second District, by 1884 the majority of Florida's black leaders were extremely dissatisfied with their party's white, largely patronage-oriented, carpetbag leadership. Four consecutive state-side defeats multiplied their discontent. While concerned white Republican politicians watched anxiously from the sidelines on February 5, a group of influential Negro leaders met at Gainesville to plan future action in national and state politics.[1] Although Joseph E. Lee, deputy port collector of Jacksonville, was present to protect Ring interests, the exceptionally capable ex-Congressman Josiah T. Walls dominated the gathering. Walls favored a coalition of the Negroes with the independent Democrats. Among his supporters were J. Willis Menard and James Dean, a federal officeholder in Washington, from Key West. Dean was keeping Secretary of the Navy Chandler informed on Florida Negro political activities. The Gainesville participants brushed aside Lee's objections and called for Florida's Negroes to support an independent Democrat for Governor. Their meeting resolutions also advocated civil rights, protested against unjust disfranchisement, asked for a fair amount of the patronage, and requested equal rights and accommodation privileges in public places, railroad cars, and steamers.[2]

Reform-minded white Republicans hoped that the Gainesville

Negro meeting would encourage the Arthur administration to abandon its support of the old-line, carpetbag-scalawag, patronage-oriented Republicans who were engaged in political horse-trading with Bourbon Democrats.[3] They saw the possibility that the national Republican candidate could carry Florida in the event of a coalition with the independent Democrats, inasmuch as the latter concentrated on state offices, leaving the support of national electors open to bargaining. To retain the Negro vote, so effectively influenced in the past by Eagan and himself, Congressman Horatio Bisbee, Jr., the last of the old carpetbaggers to retain a major elective office in Florida, had been responsible for several appointments of Negroes, particularly that of the influential Lee to the deputy collectorship.[4] The partisan Tallahassee *Weekly Floridian* charged that the Gainesville meeting proved the Independent movement to be largely Negro activated. Veteran editor Charles E. Dyke, Sr., had retired July 11, 1883, but successor J. W. Door was carrying on the same pro-Bourbon policy of not dividing the Democratic vote.[5] Actually, the hard core of Independentism was a small number of highly dissatisfied young white Democrats.

Meanwhile, the Jacksonville *Florida Weekly Times* discovered that the past Democratic legislature had granted railroads 22,360,000 acres although only 14,831,739 acres were in the public domain.[6] Fortunately, the railroads had to fulfill certain conditions of construction before receiving their grants; thus this overage was not an immediate problem. In a more pressing matter, Bloxham refused an attempted compromise settlement of the state's long-standing Seminole War claims. Real estate developer and congressional lobbyist Sydney I. Wailes, who had been retained by the Drew administration to present the claim, had been promised fifteen per cent of the total. The compromise proposed by Senator Wade Hampton of South Carolina would have given Florida $92,000 cash and $356,000 in bonds. Since fifteen per cent of the total for Wailes would have left only $24,800 in the cash settlement for Florida, Bloxham advised Senator Charles W. Jones to allow the bill to expire.[7]

Despite his moderate policies and mild disposition, Bloxham as governor had been unable to harmonize the various factions of the Democratic Party, a failure which contrasted sharply with the success he had enjoyed as a statewide Reconstruction leader. Instead of being placated by the governor's act of relinquishing the power of patronage to them, a number of county leaders showed increased signs of dissatisfaction. That this dissatisfaction went as high as Lieutenant Governor Livingston Bethel was indicated by Bloxham in a letter to a Key West citizen blaming Bethel for attempting to dictate Monroe County patronage. To solve this vexatious problem the governor recommended a new constitution that would provide for the election of county officials, taking the power of appointment from the governor.[8] Feeling that the increasing rate of attacks on his administration by fellow Democrats was largely caused by second term opposition together with suspicion that he had profited from the railroad building boom, Bloxham wrote General John B. Gordon in May to request that the Georgia railroad builder deny that Bloxham would become president of Gordon's projected road in Florida.[9] Bloxham had scrupulously avoided profiting from the Disston Sale and railroad building. Furthermore, as governor he had neglected his farming interests to the extent that he had been forced to sell his plantation to meet expenses.[10]

In addition to the dissatisfaction of the Negro Republican leaders, the feud between white Ring members and reformers prevented the Republicans from taking advantage of dissension within Democratic ranks and becoming once again a viable political party. Florida's Republicans had been faction-plagued since early Reconstruction. This time General Henry S. Sanford and ex-Governor Harrison Reed led the reformer revolt against the Jacksonville Ring's control of party machinery and federal patronage. Reed's enmity towards Bisbee went back to 1868.[11] The feud had been rekindled in 1881 when Reed accused Bisbee of surrendering the Duval County Republican convention to an irresponsible Negro mob, causing him to lose the confidence of the more intelligent Republican voters.[12] Reed had feared that Bisbee would influence the outcome of the Gainesville meeting, and he had been corresponding with Sanford relative to defeating Bisbee since early 1883.

Reed felt that the Florida Republican party should become an adjunct of the national party, attuned to the protective tariff, nationalism, and the end of violence and fraud in state elections. Instead of being dominated by patronage-hungry carpetbaggers such as Bisbee, Dennis Eagan, and Martin, it would then become an aggressive second party. The feisty ex-governor perceived that if Martin were replaced as surveyor general, ex-Whig Congressman Davidson could control federal patronage in the First District and would become "a potent ally in restoring the state." In enlisting Sanford's help, Reed played on his ego by informing him that for the reform movement to be successful it might be necessary to run him for governor.[13] Since at this time Secretary of the Navy Chandler was relying on Bisbee and Martin for advice on Florida patronage, it is apparent that Sanford decided to bypass Chandler and appeal directly to the President. Senator Joseph R. Hawley, a Connecticut Republican, acted as Sanford's spokesman in a conference with Arthur. Hawley later reported to Sanford that he had a "long and pleasant talk with the President." Arthur indicated good will toward Sanford but did not see how he could "ostracise" any leading Republican in Florida or do otherwise than encourage all to do their best.[14] This decision, heavily favoring the Jacksonville Ring, was a severe setback for Sanford's plan for a reformed Florida Republican party.

Reed had been hopeful that the aristocratic Sanford could replace the parvenu Bisbee as the Second Congressional District's federal patronage czar. Reed correctly saw that the Ring type of Republicanism for patronage only was a major cause of the growing Negro dissatisfaction. To eliminate the Ring he advised Sanford to persuade the Republican National Committee to withhold funds from its candidates. He warned the South Florida citrus grower that if no better alternative was offered the Negroes, they would abandon the Republican party and join the Independent movement. For reform Republicanism to become effective among the Negroes, he suggested that Bishop John M. Brown of the African Methodist Episcopal Church be induced to return to Florida to campaign. Bishop Brown had had a stabilizing effect among the state's Negroes during Reconstruction while Reed was governor.[15] Brown not only declined to come to Florida, however, but bolted to the Democrats during the campaign and supported Cleveland.[16]

Despite Arthur's refusal to place him in charge of Florida's federal patronage, Sanford determinedly proceeded with his plan to reform the state Republican organization and restore the two-party system. Reed and he agreed that a Republican newspaper, preferably a daily, should be established immediately. Then, since in their opinion Bisbee was through as a political leader, he should

be denied renomination. The peppery ex-governor was to be Sanford's chief lieutenant in the reform effort since he, "while not
all *I* would like, has nevertheless a knowledge of men and politics
in the State as few possess." His position was to be twofold—
editor of the paper and postal agent. As postal agent he could
travel within the state without personal cost. It was hoped that
Bishop Brown could be appointed a special agent in the Treasury
Department.[17] Obviously Sanford expected Arthur to reverse his
original decision of a hands-off policy when the reform movement
had sufficient momentum.

From the standpoint of Reed's age and political reputation in
Florida, the heavy reliance Sanford placed on him was highly
questionable. Reed was now seventy, and for the past decade he
had been in both political oblivion and dire financial straits. Furthermore, as governor he had faced impeachment proceedings on
four different occasions. The most serious charge involved the
Swepson-Littlefield railroad frauds wherein Reed had allowed the
issuance of state bonds without proper security. He had thus left
the governorship under a cloud. Since that time he had operated
an orange grove near Jacksonville and had published the *Semi-
Tropical*, a tourist periodical that collapsed after three years.[18] In
the spring of 1884 he was also in the real estate business, opening
up the new subdivision of South Jacksonville.[19] All in all, though
Reed was a dedicated reformer with respectable contacts in the
state,[20] his limited financial capabilities were to be more of a burden than Sanford was willing to assume.

To establish their new Republican newspaper in Jacksonville,
Sanford and Reed decided to purchase the independent *Putnam
County Journal* and move it from Palatka to Jacksonville. Its pub-
lisher, Solon A. Adams, agreed to become business manager with
financial support from Sanford, Reed, and interested Florida businessmen. Plans proceeded slowly, however, because of the reluctance of Sanford and Jacksonville businessmen to support the
paper generously.[21]

In building the reform movement in West Florida, Reed contacted S. C. Cobb, president of the Pensacola Ice Company.
Cobb, an ex-Whig, expected to run for Congress and modestly
predicted that he would carry the First District by two thousand
votes. He felt that the protective tariff was a major issue and
looked forward to taking on the free trade Bourbons.[22] Earlier

in the year, Pensacola reform Republican leader R. W. Ruter had been optimistic that the state could be won under the Independent banner. Ruter was particularly interested in defeating the Pensacola alliance of Republican Collector of Customs John M. Tarble and Democratic Senator Charles W. Jones. He called this bipartisan alliance a ring of thieves.[23]

Meanwhile, the Jacksonville Ring appeared in early 1884 to be controlling conventions from county to state level as well as federal patronage, thus insuring domination of the state Republican party. In late April Reed complained to Sanford that a recent Duval County convention under the influence of Deputy Collector Joseph E. Lee had been a "colored mob." He recommended that the Arthur administration admonish Lee.[24] Reed obviously felt that the Negroes were being badly exploited by the Ring, and there is ample proof that he was right. That he did not attempt a coalition with Josiah T. Walls, the outstanding black leader and a man of intelligence and integrity, is difficult to understand.

Before the St. Augustine Republican state convention was held to elect delegates to the national convention, Postmaster William Ledwith, together with a few Ring members, used the back room of the Jacksonville post office to serve liquor to Negro delegates. Free railroad tickets to St. Augustine were then provided those attending. Ledwith hoped to be named a delegate to the national convention. At St. Augustine, Bisbee and other Ring members blocked Ledwith's election, sending Joseph E. Lee to Chicago in his place. In effecting this coup, Bisbee used strong-arm tactics in theatening the convention's presiding officer, W. G. Stewart, Negro postmaster at Tallahassee. Although Florida's capital was not in Bisbee's congressional district, he told Stewart that he would have him removed if he did not support Lee's election.[25] The majority of the delegates elected were pledged to Arthur.[26] Lee, selected delegation leader, wrote Secretary Chandler that the Ring was supporting Arthur's renomination. He also suggested that Chandler defray the expenses of the Negro delegates to Chicago.[27]

Veteran Black Belt white Republican leaders, faced with the dual problem of Negroes being prevented from voting and the need for a fair count, attempted to bring up Independentism at the St. Augustine meeting. These leaders included a Stearns brother, Surveyor General Malachi Martin of Gadsden County, and one of the Gosses from Marion County. Stearns and Martin were carpetbaggers, Goss was a scalawag. Stearns and Martin suggested that a coalition of the Republicans and independent Democrats support either ex-Governor David S. Walker or Dr. George T. Maxwell for governor. These men were highly respected, independent-minded political veterans, although ex-Governor Reed strongly disapproved of both, calling them "irretrievable Bourbons."[28] The Black Belt white leaders were encouraged by the success of the Independent movement in Madison County in 1882 and desired to make it a statewide effort. For the Negro vote to be effective it needed to be counted; this required the support of respectable citizens who previously had been Democrats. Negroes did continue to go to the polls in all Black Belt counties, but in several they had become a minority in voting although they remained a majority in population.

With plans for the Republican newspaper well on the way, Reed now turned his attention to grass roots organizing. His chief proposal was the formation of a white Union League which would "bring together the intelligent and conservative who will not affiliate with or patronize negro mobs for office."[29] This was undoubtedly an effort to get Northern settlers to vote Republican in local and state elections. The first issue of the Jacksonville *Florida Journal* finally made its appearance in late May. Editor Reed affirmed that the paper's policy would be independent Republican. He hoped to attract support from the business community. He also vigorously attacked the concept of Florida's being part of the one party "solid South," which prevented the discussion of certain issues. The existing carpetbag constitution of the state Reed defended as protecting the rights of whites in the Black Belt and of Negroes in sparsely settled white counties. He saw Southerners becoming reconciled to Negro voting. The *Times-Union* evaluated the newspaper as divisive rather than ameliorative and foresaw that General Sanford would come to rue his political ambitions.[30]

The movement toward coalition of the reform Republicans and the independent Democrats was accelerated by a conference held at Jacksonville late in May. *The Florida Journal* warned the conferees that it would not support any advocate of free trade and direct taxation. Candidates would have to be for "home, labor and American industry."[31] Editor Reed was quite optimistic of the chances of success of those who opposed both the Bourbons

and the Republican patronage crowd.[32] With the device of pseud-
onymous letters, Reed began his campaign against Bisbee's renomination to Congress. "Anti-Ring" accused Bisbee of being
controlled by a small band of officeholders. "Business" affirmed
that there would be no packed convention in 1884. "X" stated
that nineteen out of twenty Republicans in the Second District
were in favor of the Independent movement.[33] "X" did not mention how this figure had been reached.

Early in June, a small advertisement indicated that the Disston
land company was giving very limited support to the newspaper.[34]
When Hamilton Disston had declined Sanford's request to purchase shares in the paper, he had agreed to have his Jacksonville
land agent advertise in *The Florida Journal*.[35] Significantly, a few
days before the advertisement appeared, the Disston company offered to donate $1,000 for the Florida display at the New Orleans
Cotton Centennial Exposition of 1885 after a total of $50,000 had
been subscribed.[36] Such an exhibit would propagandize the at-
tractiveness of Florida for tourists, settlers, and investors. Having
rapport with the Bourbons, Disston would not actively advocate
the reform Republican movement in Florida. At the same time,
the Jacksonville business community was failing to rally behind
the new paper in the manner that Business Manager Adams had
hoped. Adams complained to Sanford that three specific businessmen had failed to place advertisements and that "they ought to
help us out. . . ."[37] *The Florida Journal* first sniped at specific
Democrats on June 16, when Reed accused Governor Bloxham
of refusing to review a "company of colored militia." Bloxham
had always prided himself on his rapport with the Negroes. Three
days later Reed castigated the eight years of Bourbon rule. He
particularly emphasized the non-payment of the antebellum state
debt, the conversion of the state penitentiary into a "lunatic
asylum," and the farming out of prisoners on speculation. He also
criticized the Democrats for being unable to reduce taxation.[38]

The reform movement received a minor setback when the
Ring's chief Negro opponent, ex-Congressman Josiah T. Walls, was
defeated at the national convention in his bid to become Florida's
national committeeman. Four Negro votes were cast against him.
Judge John G. Long, a white delegate, blamed Lee for Walls's
defeat.[39] Walls appeared to be a possible rival to Bisbee for the
congressional nomination, which probably contributed to his

defeat. Lee claimed that Long's charge was selfishly motivated and that "the colored men do not intend to fight over fish-bones and slops, while such men as Long run away with the substance."[40]

Three political factions—reform white Republicans, Negro Republicans, and independent Democrats—were represented at the Independent state convention at Live Oak on June 18. Included among the one hundred delegates from twenty-seven counties were ex-Democrats Miles Mountien of Washington, Dr. George Troup Maxwell of Marion, Daniel L. McKinnon of Jackson, and Frank W. Pope of Madison. Sampson Altman, the courageous sheriff who had attempted to prevent the Savage-James lynching in 1882, was one of the delegates from Hamilton; Solon A. Adams from Putnam represented the reform Republicans. The large number of Negro delegates remained in the background, not attempting to play the same prominent role that they had had in past Republican gatherings.[41]

As the anti-Bourbon coalition became the state's second party, a behind-the-scenes agreement gave the independent Democrats the first place on the ticket and the reform Republicans second place.[42] This left the Negroes, who were to furnish a majority of the votes, without a candidate of their own unless they could obtain one of the congressional nominations later. The balloting for the gubernatorial nomination pitted two youthful politicians against each other. Both Daniel L. McKinnon and Frank W. Pope had given up promising careers within the Democratic party to protest against the white supremacy extremists of the Black Belt. Neither possessed a large following outside his home county. On the fourth ballot, Pope, the better orator of the two, was selected. Reform Republican Jonathan C. Greeley, a state senator from Duval, was nominated unanimously for lieutenant governor after Dr. Maxwell declined the nomination and George W. Allen, young Key West reform Republican, withdrew.[43]

The Independent platform charged the Republicans with eight years of corruption, racial prejudice, and election frauds. It accused the Bourbons—regular Democrats—of using state patronage and manipulating legislators to prevent the revision of an autocratic constitution. It underlined the fact that settlers were charged $1.25 an acre, and Disston, a wealthy speculator, only 25 cents. It accused certain unnamed Bourbon politicians of buying depreciated state bonds, realizing on them at par in the purchase and then sharing the profit with Disston. The platform also charged the Bourbons with defrauding the taxpayers of thousands of dollars in not requiring railroad corporations to share in the internal improvement indebtedness. The Bourbons were pictured as fostering and encouraging party hate and antagonism, making political campaigns seasons of dread and elections occasions of fear. To correct these abuses, the Independents called for a free ballot, a full vote, and a fair count. They also favored a railroad commission and a local option prohibition bill. All unearned land grants should be forfeited and other grants investigated. Their platform closed with the statement that the Independent movement was the "dawning of a better day in which political asperities would be softened, party animosities lose their intensity and prejudices their gall of bitterness, enabling a man to identify himself with his chosen party without fear."[44]

Pope, accepting the nomination, accused the Bourbons of using the black phantom of Negro supremacy to still the conscience of the people. The result of this generating of extreme party spirit was fraud and bloodshed. On the other side, Pope stated, the Radical Republicans had persuaded the Negro that the preservation of his rights depended upon the bloc vote. Independentism, he promised, would raise the voice of reason above the clamor of prejudice. Ultimately there would be a realignment on the basis of true Democracy and honest Republicanism. In his acceptance speech Jonathan C. Greeley supported local option on liquor, a free ballot, a full vote, and a fair count. His philosophy of government he described as "the greatest good to the largest number."[45] Greeley, a former Confederate soldier, had been in business in Jacksonville since the war. He was one of the early members of the state's Republican party and had served as major and alderman of Jacksonville. Formerly a railroad president he now headed the Florida Savings Bank and Real Estate Exchange.[46]

In nominating Pope, the Independents demonstrated their basic weakness, the lack of a strong leader with a state-wide following. Since Pope was running as a reform candidate, the Independents thought it necessary to make a frank admission of a tragic episode in his life. In 1867 the sixteen-year-old Pope had been severely whipped and assaulted with a heavy chair by his teacher. In self-defense Pope had then shot and killed him.[47] The explanation did not make clear why a schoolboy was carrying a revolver. Pope

had then fled west from Madison and tried his hand at mining.
He returned to Madison in 1877 and engaged in the practice of
law. Pope never came to trial for the murder, but the shooting
episode was obviously his Achilles' Heel.[48]

Of the state's newspapers, fifty-seven claimed to be Democratic,
four Republican, and four independent.[49] Two of the four independents, those with the largest circulations, the Jacksonville
Florida Times-Union and Pensacola *Commercial*, announced support of the Democratic party. Instead of assailing the Independent
platform, the Democratic press largely attacked Pope personally.
The Tallahassee *Land of Flowers*, an ultra-Bourbon weekly edited
by Don McLeod, labeled Pope a "harum-scarum-devil-take-the-
hindmost young hotspur." McLeod described Greeley, with supris-
ing candor, as an honest and upright man, who should have been
the gubernatorial candidate. He warned the Democrats that a poor
nomination might result in an Independent victory.[50] A second
Tallahassee newspaper, the *Weekly Floridian*, ignoring the fact
that the Democrats had run a political unknown eight years before,
satirized Pope's nomination as that of some insignificant young
man.[51]

Sturdily defending the Independents, Editor Reed accused the
Democratic press and the "old fogies" of binding the Solid South
to the lost cause. He envisioned the young Independents moving
into a new era which had been opened up by the overthrow of
slavery.[52] Reed very probably injected the issue of slavery because
of the sizable number of freedmen who had bolted to the Democrats in both 1876 and 1880. He also brought the issue of treatment
of convicts into the campaign. A letter to *The Florida Journal*
from Palatka mentioned the brutal whipping of a convict as
"prima-facie evidence" of the way Bourbon Democracy served
Negroes.[53] In addition, Reed uncovered disgraceful conditions in
mental health care. He quoted a special legislative committee
report on conditions at the asylum at Chattahoochee which found
the rooms for the mentally ill in bad condition, the bedding
thoroughly rotten, and the odor so bad that one could scarcely
stay in any of the rooms. The committee did find the food good
and sufficient.[54]

Meanwhile, the regular Democrats were badly split. The cause
of this breach was not the splintering off of the Independents but
a personal quarrel between two party titans, ex-Governor Drew

and Governor Bloxham. With county leaders throughout the state urging Bloxham's renomination, Drew, now a Jacksonville businessman, reentered the political arena in a frank interview with a *Florida Times-Union* reporter. Since the retirement of Charles Dyke, Sr., the *Times-Union*, ably edited by Charles H. Jones, had become the state's most influential newspaper. Drew threatened to bolt the Democratic party if Bloxham were renominated. His opposition stemmed from the old disappointment engendered when Bloxham defeated his bid for renomination.[55] Had Drew joined the Independents they would have had their first leader with a large state-wide white following and an unimpeachable personal record.

With the Bloxham boom effectively halted by Drew's bitter opposition, several dark horses became serious candidates. These included "Farmer" Austin S. Mann, a young Hernando County citrus grower with a Northern background, and General Edward Aylesworth Perry, formerly commander of the Florida Brigade which served with General Robert E. Lee in the Army of Virginia. Also Northern-born, Perry was now a successful Pensacola lawyer. Although a close friend of the ultra-Bourbon railroader William D. Chipley, Perry had won popular support when he represented the state in a tax case against the railroads. Pre-election alignments indicated that Drew would be the strongest candidate at the convention, but because of his feud with Bloxham, strong sentiment was developing against nominating either.[56]

The threatened showdown between the two was kept off the convention floor as county leaders meeting in Pensacola on June 25 strove for harmony. However, the appearance of Chipley as temporary chairman indicated the strong power that the pro-railroad Bourbon element wielded at the convention.[57] Despite the tax case, they were solidly behind General Perry. Reed reported in *The Florida Journal* that Colonel Francis P. Fleming of Jacksonville nominated Perry in a speech that fired Southern hearts and awakened the rebel yell from the delegates and the spectators in the galleries of an "elegant theatre" constructed by Northern capital. He also commented that there were no Negro delegates.[58] In the early balloting Perry led, although party moderates supported Black Belter Samuel Pasco, Monticello lawyer and chairman of the state executive committee since 1876. The candidacy of Mann failed to materialize. When on the sixth ballot Perry had

177 votes out of a total of 292, Pasco, seeing that his own candidacy was hopeless, withdrew and moved that Perry be nominated by unanimous vote.[59]

Since Perry was without political experience on a state level, the county leaders, in the loose coalition that constituted the Democratic party, were returning to the strategy they had used in 1876. This time a special appeal was made not to the moderate group or the Negroes but to the proponents of Southernism who would be strongly attracted by Perry's Civil War record. It was ironic that the Democrats had as their candidate a New England Yankee while his opponent was a young Southerner "to the manner born."

The Democratic platform advocated federal internal improvements and a constitutional convention. All other controversial issues were carefully avoided. Both Bloxham and Drew received a meaningless complimentary vote. Since Perry was from North Florida, the convention followed precedent and selected a South Florida man for lieutenant governor. Its candidate was ex-Mississippian Milton H. Mabry, junior law partner of Sumter County's political leader, W. A. Hocker.[60]

Dissatisfied with the nomination of the old Confederate war hero, ex-Governor Drew withheld comment until he had consulted with his friends.[61] Bloxham stated to a friend that Drew was not a Democrat and would accept the Independent nomination if it were offered to him.[62] Nevertheless, hints from Independent sources that Pope would withdraw if Drew would enter the race as the Independent standard-bearer failed to entice him.[63] After a short hesitation, Drew announced in lukewarm fashion his support of Perry.[64] He was not active in the campaign, while most other leading politicians spoke both in the heat of the summer noon and the cool of the evening in the contest between the Independents and Democrats. The vote on holding a constitutional convention became almost a forgotten issue, with both sides favoring its call.

Republican leaders viewed Perry's nomination with mixed feelings. Dennis Eagan observed that it was too late for the Democrats to run a war hero and that the ticket was a blow to liberalism. However, he thought Perry to be stronger than Pope. Ex-Judge R. B. Archibald, another white Republican, evaluated the Massachusetts-born ex-Confederate general as not too popular with Northern settlers. But, Judge Archibald went on to warn, if the

Ring put up a ticket, the split of Perry's opposition would elect him. Leader of the Ring's Negro faction, Joseph E. Lee, regarded the nomination as weak and easily defeated. Reed viewed Perry as a representative of the rebel element in control of the Democratic party and of those who glory in the shame of having sought to destroy the Union to perpetuate slavery.[65] *The Florida Journal* editor's emotional attack was obviously aimed at persuading the Northern and Western settlers with Unionist sentiments to abandon their alliance with the Bourbons insofar as state politics was concerned.

The key objective of the reform Republican movement generated by Sanford and Reed was to prevent Bisbee's renomination and thus to terminate his leadership. Reform had received a serious setback when Arthur refused to strip Bisbee of patronage. In fact, Dennis Eagan's nomination to the customs post[66] at Key West in the First District indicated that Bisbee was recommending federal appointees for the entire state. When the Second District Republican convention convened at Fernandina on July 9, federal officeholders obligated to Bisbee quickly assumed control. Seeing no possibility of an open contest, General Walls walked out and was nominated as an independent by a rump convention of delegates from six counties. Since the district was evenly divided between the two parties, Democratic victory was certain unless either Walls or Bisbee withdrew. Nevertheless, Bisbee accepted the Republican nomination. He also pledged his support of the Independent gubernatorial ticket.[67] With Bisbee attaching himself to the Independent movement it would be difficult for Pope to woo the white Southerner, and a great deal of enthusiasm of reform Republicans would be lost.

The reform Republicans were in for a second blow when it was announced at approximately the same time as Bisbee's renomination that General Sanford would take an extended European trip. Reed quickly denied a rumor in the Jacksonville *Herald* that Sanford was withdrawing from Florida politics and disposing of his share in *The Florida Journal*. The ex-governor maintained that Sanford was retaining his interest in Florida politics and continued to support the protective tariff.[68] An earlier letter from Adams to Sanford had indicated that *The Florida Journal* lacked local support. Adams hoped that Sanford would come up with additional funds.[69] But the wealthy settler had been turned down by President Arthur on patronage and had failed to attract support from wealthy fellow Northerners (such as Hamilton Disston) with investments in Florida.[70] Without the strong political and economic support that he felt was necessary, Sanford withdrew from the campaign, leaving the reform Republicans both leaderless and open to strong reprisals from the Jacksonville Ring. At their district congressional convention for East Florida, meeting at Palatka, the Democrats selected Charles Dougherty, youthful speaker of the state assembly and a resident of the Halifax River region in Volusia County. Some violence erupted at the District Two meeting when Charles L. Fildes, an Alachua County delegate who was a cousin of Pope and editor of the Gainesville *Weekly Bee*, attempted to make a speech in support of the Independent state ticket. He was physically ejected from the convention. His right to be a delegate was challenged by *Times-Union* Editor Charles H. Jones, a staunch partisan of Perry. Fildes then encountered Jones in the Carleton Hotel and assaulted him.[71] In the First District conditions were more placid as the Democrats renominated Congressman Robert H. M. Davidson of Quincy, and the Republicans selected as his opponent a Key West reformer, Eugene O. Locke.[72]

Reed evaluated the nomination of Dougherty as evidence that the Democrats were turning to a more progressive policy. The "old fogies" had been set aside and a young, progressive, liberal Democrat nominated. Reed commended the Volusia legislator for his conduct as speaker, particularly his respect for Negro legislators as contrasted with the intolerance and proscription of other Democratic leaders. He also praised Dougherty's views on industry.[73] Then two weeks later *The Florida Journal* lambasted Dougherty for making a racist speech in Jacksonville. Reed now thought that in comparison with Bisbee Dougherty sank to the insignificance of a pygmy.[74]

The spirited manner in which the campaign was starting contrasted strongly with the lackluster 1880 race between Bloxham and Conover. In answer to Pope's theme "the rascals must go," the friends of Perry waved the rebel flag and refurbished memories of the sacred cause.[75] Editor George R. Fairbanks of the Fernandina *Florida Mirror,* recovering from his disappointment over the Disston Sale, sacrificed his opposition to Bloxham's liberal land policy and his hope of reform on the altar of party regularity. Influenced no doubt by Bisbee's support of Independentism, Fairbanks predicted that the third party people would end up with the Republicans. To him they were dissatisfied men who blended prohibition with the railroad commission issue.[76] An editor of high principles and intelligence, Fairbanks would stop just short of being a reformer. He made a strong effort to persuade Negroes to vote Democratic because since 1876 they had been treated as equal citizens with all their rights protected. Schools had been established statewide for their children. Furthermore, their true interest lay in cooperating with the conservative Democrats, their employers, whose interests were identical with their own. He disparaged the Independents as office seekers using the Negro voter.[77]

The Macon (Georgia) *Telegraph* evaluated the Florida election as being extremely close. Considerable factional multiplicity existed, with the Democrats divided between regulars and Independents and between liberal Northern and Western elements and the proscriptive Southern element. The Independents numbered from two to three thousand young Democrats who were unhappy with the Bloxham administration, the Disston Sale and the public office monopoly held by Southern-born men and ex-Confederate army veterans.[78] Besides Northern and Western settlers there was a sizable assemblage of settlers from other Southern states; Georgia alone contributed twenty-four thousand. The recent settlers plus the small Cuban minority in Key West could well decide the outcome. The Northerners, according to the *Telegraph*, were prone to support the Republican presidential candidate but to split their ballots and vote for Democrats for state offices. The *Telegraph* classified native Floridians as Bourbons, crackers, and Negroes. The crackers were unhappy with the Disston Sale since it encroached on their long-established custom of pasturing cattle on public lands. The *Telegraph* warned its readers that if a strong, well-financed leader united the native white Republicans with the Northern, Western, Cuban, and Negro voters, he could win. To combat this dire eventuality the Democrats must display "unselfishness and patriotism."[79]

There were two leaders in the state who fitted the qualifications described in the *Telegraph*, General Sanford and ex-Governor Drew. To be effective, Sanford would have to get down to the level of grass roots politics, and Drew, now president of Jacksonville's Board of Trade,[80] would have to end his political isolation and run for governor, replacing Pope as the Independent.

Two key Ring members took the extremely ambiguous position
of fighting the third party movement and at the same time supporting Bisbee's reelection. Dennis Eagan, newly appointed collector
of customs at Key West, restricted his opposition to a personal
vendetta with Pope. Eagan was described by Fairbanks in the
Fernandina *Mirror* as the ablest man in the state Republican party
and its best public official.[81] His opposition was a serious threat
to Pope's success. Eagan's feud with Pope was a direct result of
Madison County politics. So bitter were Eagan's feelings that
he utilized a reporter of the staunchly pro-Perry *Florida Times-
Union* to describe Pope as an unprincipled Klan-type politician.
According to his story, when he arrived Pope was absent from
the county as an aftermath of shooting the schoolteacher. After
the return to power of the Democrats with the election of Drew
in 1876, Pope returned and as a Democrat engaged in a bitter
and unscrupulous manner in the 1878 election. The faction to
which he belonged used tissue ballots and committed outrageous
frauds. Then in 1880 Pope and other Democrats appeared at the
polls armed with rifles. When Frank Patterson, Pope's law partner,
was killed following this election, Pope volunteered his services to
prosecute the two Negroes accused of the crime, Savage and
James. He then—according to Eagan—made violent speeches
during the trial to incite a mob to violence in the event that the
men were acquitted; furthermore, both Negroes were murdered
because of the high feelings of Madison whites encouraged by
Pope. When in 1882 Pope failed to receive the Democratic nomination in Madison County for the state senate, he pressured the
Republicans into endorsing him as an independent candidate.
Faced with the threat of being counted out, the Republicans were
forced to accept the one place allotted them by the Independents
in a coalition. Eagan asserted that whether or not the Republican
party endorsed Pope, he would work for Pope's defeat.[82] In attacking Pope, Eagan made mention neither of his own involvement
in the Patterson murder nor of the utilization of the Independent
movement in 1882 to reelect Congressman Bisbee. Furthermore,
according to Harrison Reed, because Eagan exerted such a strong
influence on Negroes, had he so chosen in 1882 he could have
nipped the Independent movement in the bud.[83]

Besides having a personal bias against Pope which undoubtedly
influenced his attack, Eagan was fighting for his political life. The

coalition of reform Republicans with Independents had caused him to be passed over as a candidate for governor in 1884. Sanford and Reed would strip him of the power of patronage from the national administration. Pope and the Independents would replace him as a white leader of Negro voters. His change of residence from Madison to Jacksonville to Key West in a short period had weakened his influence in the Black Belt. His obvious objective was to alienate Negroes from the Independent movement by labeling Pope an extreme partisan of white supremacy. Throughout the campaign he would continue to fight Pope.[84]

Although Eagan gave lip service support to Independents other than Pope, another powerful Florida Republican leader totally repudiated the Republican-Independent coalition. In the middle of July, Edward M. Cheney, chairman of the Republican state executive committee, issued a statement opposing all Independent party candidates. Number three in the Jacksonville Ring behind Bisbee and Eagan, Cheney was also United States attorney for the district of South Florida. He reasoned that since Pope was a Democrat who had never shown any sympathy or respect for Republicans or their principles, he should neither claim nor receive Republican support in preference to any other Democrat. Furthermore, defeat would be preferable to alignment with the Independents since a third party made up of the worst elements of the other two was no improvement. Cheney optimistically maintained that the Republican party was constantly growing in numbers, influence, and respectability, and if it did not win in 1884, it would in 1888.

Cheney revealed a break in Ring ranks over support of the Independents. He admitted that United States Marshal Joseph H. Durkee and one or two other federal officeholders were backing the Independents. The "seeming" unanimity among the Negro voters in favor of the third party had been worked up by Josiah T. Walls, John Wallace, J. Willis Menard, and W. G. Stewart. Cheney predicted that this feeling, which he claimed was not genuine, would weaken later.[85] He failed to mention that both Congressman Bisbee and the chief Negro lieutenant of the Ring, Joseph E. Lee, were supporting the Independent party.[86] There is some evidence that Cheney vacillated before coming to the decision to oppose the third party.[87]

A leading Black Belt white Republican, Joseph N. Stripling, took issue with both Eagan and Cheney. Formerly a Madison County lieutenant of Eagan and now chairman of the Independent executive committee, Stripling labeled Eagan a personal enemy of Pope. He also pointed out that since Eagan had resided the last several years in Jacksonville he had lost touch with Madison politics. Insofar as the 1880 rifle incident was concerned, Pope, then mayor of Madison, had attempted to quell a disturbance between Democrats and Republicans. Cheney had refused to press charges at this time. Stripling strongly denied that Pope was "the bold bad man that the Bourbons and a few of his personal enemies would have us believe."[88]

The final public showdown on Independentism between white carpetbaggers and the Negro leadership occurred at the Republican state convention in Gallie's Hall at Tallahassee late in July. When carpetbag diehard Leonard G. Dennis of Alachua County declared that he would not consent to surrender by twenty thousand Republican voters to a little handful of men, he was shouted down by angry blacks. As earlier in the year at Gainesville, ex-Congressman Walls dominated the proceedings. Walls advised the delegates not to endorse Pope and Greeley by a call of counties, the traditional way, because if they did the Independents would be labeled Republicans by the Democrats. It was obvious by this statement that Walls believed that a sizable number of white voters would vote Independent but not Republican. Apprehension that these white voters might be alienated by too much Negro political action was shown by John Wallace's advice that Negroes remain in the background during the campaign. In a speech to the delegates Frank Pope informed them that he "would as soon trust this government to the ignorant people as the educated . . . we shall rout the plundering Democrats from yonder Capital in next November."[89] The Fernandina *Mirror* commented that ex-Senator "Simple Simon" Conover attended the convention with the hope that an Independent-controlled legislature would elect him to the Senate in place of Wilk Call.[90]

The Independent dilemma became more apparent as the campaign wore on. The Independents needed the support of Negroes to win, yet by accepting that support they alienated white voters who were still on the fence. This was particularly true in West Florida.[91] Secondly, the financial situation added to the predicament. Stripling attempted to alleviate this by an appeal for subscriptions to friends of the movement throughout the state, stating frankly that Pope was not a wealthy man.[92] It was obvious that the national Republican party was withholding contributions to the Independents, and wealthy Northerners with business interests in Florida were not giving substantial financial support. A third factor, the schoolteacher homicide, continued to crop up. The *Madison Recorder* published an account by an eyewitness who stated that Pope shot his teacher in retaliation for a whipping with a chinquapin switch.[93] Reed charged in *The Florida Journal* that Democrats were horror-stricken because a boy had "killed a school master to save his own brains" from being beaten out. Yet these same Democrats glorified a civil war that killed ten thousand schoolmasters and murdered millions of fellow countrymen, all because the people had elected Lincoln President. Reed's editorial was obviously aimed at Northern settlers in Florida, as he worked diligently to drive a breach between them and their Southern neighbors. He claimed that Northerners were "still boycotted in business, ignored in social life, held in abeyance in religious circles, and proscribed by the crackers." Only when they championed Bourbonism were they accepted.[94]

Democratic newspapers praised General Perry's Civil War record and gentlemanly qualities as contrasted to Pope's "harum scarum" youth.[95] Actually, Pope was thirty-four years old.[96] Sounding the bugle call for Perry, the Palatka *Herald* carried the story of an old veteran who became sick on the march and was placed by the general on his own horse while the general walked.[97] *The Florida Journal* countered with the tale of another veteran of the Florida Brigade. This ex-Confederate claimed that because he was starving, he helped himself to a little corn intended for the general's horse. Perry made him replace it, although the horse had plenty; therefore, he would not vote for him.[98] The Madison *New Era*, Pope's newspaper, mildly attacked Perry as a clever, genial old gentleman whom the Democratic party had spoon-fed for nearly twenty years and whom fortune had always favored with a gold spoon and padded chair. The *New Era* stated fairly, however, that Perry had unquestionably earned his laurels on the field of battle.[99]

Elated over the nomination of fellow resident Charles Dougherty for Congress, citizens of the newly settled Halifax River country held a fifty-horse procession in his honor.[100] Ex-Secretary of State (Florida) George J. Alden, the region's most prominent Republican, announced that he was supporting the Democratic ticket.[101] Later Dougherty campaigned along the Indian River, spending a night working his passage through the Haulover near the ruins of old Fort Anne at the northern end of the river. Speaking at Titusville in the evening of August 9, Dougherty told his audience that he would not promise a lighthouse every ten miles on the coast or make navigable every mud creek where water was not deep enough to float a mullet, but he would work to advance the interests of the district.[102]

The two opponents of Dougherty were ignoring him in their private battle. To bring the dispute with Walls to a head, early in August Bisbee invited the ex-congressman to stump the district with him and "to assign one single reason why any Republican should not vote for nor support me."[103] General Walls accepted, stating that "the methods that you use to perpetuate your official arrogance have driven from you a large majority of your former friends, and the manner in which you have ignored my people, who have heretofore formed a large majority of your supporters, are some among the many reasons why you should not be elected to the Forty-ninth Congress."[104]

In the gubernatorial race, Pope proved a powerful and tireless adversary on the stump. At Lake City, with an audience of about four hundred persons braving the midday heat on July 30, Pope attacked the Disston Sale and discussed the proposed constitutional convention. He appealed to his hearers to vote for him not as Democrats or Republicans but as honest men. Pope told Negroes present that his party and not the Democrats would give them their rights. Parson Thompson, a Negro preacher, followed Pope on the platform and advised members of his race to give up the carpetbaggers, Cheney and Eagan, and support Pope.[105] According to *The Florida Journal,* while Pope was speaking the Baya and Master engine works whistle blew five times at 12:00 P.M. and twenty times at 1:00 P.M. in an effort to disrupt the meeting.[106]

The following evening the Independents held a rally at the St. James Hotel in Jacksonville. Attacking both the state Democratic position in favor of white supremacy and the Ring leadership of the Negroes, Dr. George Troup Maxwell asked why the kindly feeling between the freed Negroes and the old slaveholder class had disappeared. Maxwell endorsed both Pope and the Democratic national ticket. This blow to the reform Republicans indicated the quandary that the independent Democrats found themselves in as part of the coalition. Pope assailed the state's Democratic party for misrule and corruption in both the public printing laws and land sales. He called for justice in the courts and for the end of election frauds. He censured the Bloxham administration for selling the state's domain to land speculators for 25 cents an acre when actual settlers were charged $1.25. He accused the state of paying land agent Swann $20,000 in hush money for his having been bypassed by Bloxham in the Disston Sale. Pope attacked the *Times-Union* and reasserted his belief in democracy, declaring that "the people, whether educated or ignorant, could and should be trusted." He also claimed that his campaign was doing well in the strongly cracker North Florida counties of Taylor, Baker, Columbia, and Lafayette.[107] In commenting on Dr. Maxwell's visit to Jacksonville, Reed recalled that Maxwell was the first to suggest that the Democrats abolish race distinction. At that time carpetbagger Senator Thomas W. Osborn had become alarmed that in following Maxwell's counsel the Democrats would take the lead and steal the thunder from the Republicans. In *The Florida Journal* Reed described Maxwell as a most eloquent and accomplished gentleman.[108] This favorable public comment differed somewhat from his earlier, private letter labeling Maxwell a Bourbon.[109]

Middle August found the Independent speakers at the deep water harbor of Fernandina. On the rostrum of the Lyceum Hall were Pope, Greeley, McKinnon, and Maxwell.[110] From there Pope went to Palatka, claiming to his audience at the St. Johns River town that according to history no political organization could reform itself. He acknowledged that the state lands must be sold; nevertheless, he did not think that they should be sold wholesale to a rich man. Instead they should have been sold in small quantities to actual settlers at twenty-five or fifty cents an acre.[111] Also in August, James R. Challen, a Northern businessman who had been connected with a company operating a line of refrigerator cars for carrying fruits and perishable goods, commented on the forthcoming election. Challen called Pope an active, vigilant, courageous, honest Democrat who had become disgusted with the outrageous frauds. He also informed a Cincinnati *Commercial-Gazette* reporter that the Independents supported the right of

Negroes to vote, and the Republicans hoped to carry the state. Concerning his own business, he saw strong support in Florida for a protective tariff on oranges.[112]

Despite seeming chaos, the strategy of Ring members Eagan and Cheney was clear: first, not to alienate Independent support for Bisbee; second, to defeat Pope regardless of the cost; third, to destroy the reform Republican movement. One of the major weapons against Pope was the Jacksonville *People's Journal.* Although its Negro editor had been a delegate to the Independent state convention, he withdrew Pope's name from his masthead because the "best" Republicans would not support the Independent gubernatorial candidate. The motive behind this action by Editor J. W. Thompson might have been revealed when he mentioned Eagan among the "best" Republicans. Without giving any proof, the *People's Journal* called Pope a "pitiful Negro-killing Democrat." Thompson also announced his support of Josiah T. Walls for Congress.[113] Since Bisbee was the Ring nominee, there was a possibility that Democrats were supporting Thompson. A large number of Negro votes for Walls would elect Dougherty instead of Bisbee. This Eagan would not have favored.

The attacks by the *People's Journal* were followed by a circular issued by Eagan, Cheney, and twenty-one other Republicans who refused to join the coalition with the independent Democrats. Eagan was now opposing the Independent movement instead of only Pope. The circular condemned the action of the Republican state convention in supporting the Independents. Besides repudiating Republican support of the Independent movement, the circular complained that the independent Democrats were supporting the Democratic candidate for President.[114]

At the same time that Bisbee was advocating Independentism, his friends and he were earnestly striving to crush the reform Republicans and bolting Negroes. In his opening campaign speech in Jacksonville, he affirmed that it was the duty of all Republicans to support the verdict of the conventions. He also mentioned that the major issues were federal aid to education, a protective tariff, civil service, and river and harbor improvement. "Soreheads," particularly the "venomous" Harrison Reed, were attempting to defeat him, and he advised fellow Republicans not to read *The Florida Journal* or contribute to its support.[115] The effectiveness of the attack of Bisbee and his allies caused *The Florida Journal's* business manager to urgently request additional funds, because Bisbee had "managed to kill off most of the Republicans in Jacksonville who were helping the *Journal*." Adams also informed Sanford that Walls was providing strong competition for Bisbee, and if those supporting the *Journal* could be provided with sufficient funds, they could defeat the Jacksonville carpetbag congressman.[116]

Disregarding the tremendous odds facing him, caused partly by the splintering of the anti-Democratic forces and partly by the Democratic control of the ballot box, in the last of August Pope stumped Central Florida with vigor. He was now in the heartland of the so-called liberal Northern and Western settlers. His most enthusiastic supporter here was James E. Alexander, editor of the Enterprise *Herald*.[117] Speaking across Lake Monroe from Enterprise at General Sanford's hometown, Pope mentioned a rumor that the "Democracy would count him out."[118] This was an appeal to the fairness of the settlers to assure a fair count. At Bartow he announced that he would vote for the Democratic national ticket of Cleveland and Hendricks. This destroyed the last hope of the reform Republicans that the Independents would support the Republican national ticket. Although South Florida was predominantly white, Pope made it clear here that he would appoint qualified Negroes to office,[119] once again making an appeal to the fairness of the liberal settlers. Farther north in the cracker territory of Taylor County, Pope and Stripling failed to arouse enough enthusiasm to organize a county Independent club,[120] a strong indication of which way the crackers would vote.

The Lake City *Columbia Star* reported that "Governor" Perry was meeting enthusiastic receptions, and his opponents could find nothing in his career through which to attack him.[121] At Sumterville, accompanied by Colonel Sydney I. Wailes, state lobbyist and land commissioner of the Florida Railroad and Navigation Company, Perry spoke favoring a new constitution. He also stated that Northern Republicans were becoming conservative Democrats upon moving to Florida, and he urged the Negro voter to accept the Democratic offer of good government. What more could the Negros want, he queried, than good schools, good government, low taxes, and ample protection for themselves and their families? Milton Mabry spoke next, assailing the Republicans. Jacksonville *Herald* editor John Temple Graves, Sr., addressed the crowd on national issues. Moving next to Ocala, Perry's party was reinforced by the addition of "Farmer" Austin S. Mann, the colorful Hernando County leader.[122]

A report from South Florida in early September indicated a number of Republicans present at Perry's Deland speech.[123] To carry the state the Independents needed a significant number of South Florida Republican votes. Earlier, State Comptroller W. D. Barnes had accompanied Perry through a number of South Florida counties, including Hillsborough, Manatee, Polk, Hernando, Sumter and Marion. From Northern settlers there Barnes gained the information that they would vote for Blaine and Logan nationally and for the Democrats in the state races. They gave as their reasons lower taxes, better credit, and prosperity. The only problem seems to have been the unpopularity of the Disston Sale.[124] Apparently the Disston Sale also needed to be explained at a meeting of the Palatka Cleveland and Perry Club.[125]

Hurt by criticism of his administration and heartbroken by the death of his only daughter in the fall of 1883, Governor Bloxham at first determined to retire from public life.[126] However, motivated by sharp attacks on his administration that he considered unjust, he vigorously entered the campaign to give strong and effective support to General Perry. At the Park Theatre in Jacksonville on August 26, Bloxham made a major speech labeling Independentism "the thinnest gauze thrown around the profligate carcass of Florida Radicalism." To prove his economy, he cited the paying off of both the state and Internal Improvement debts. He then launched into an explanation of the Disston Sale, recalling that when he took office the Internal Improvement Fund was saddled with a debt of over $1 million at 6 per cent interest. The only feasible solution was the sale of a large acreage. Disston paid cash for the four million acres at twenty-five cents an acre, except for $14,000 worth of coupon indebtedness which cost him ninety cents on the dollar. Defending himself against the charge of allowing special privileges for land speculators and not for settlers, Bloxham pointed out that the state law offering homesteads could not be in effect as long as the Internal Improvement Fund was controlled by the court. In comparison to his selling land to Disston, Bloxham mentioned that a Republican Reconstruction administration had deeded ex-Lieutenant Governor William H. Gleason 1.3 million acres of public domain without any consideration previously performed. As proof of the success of the Disston Sale in stimulating the development of Florida, he asserted that from seven to eight hundred miles of railroad had been constructed during his administration.

Then, abandoning statistics and marshaling the emotional appeal of white supremacy in order to hold dissatisfied Democrats under Bourbon leadership, he warned: "It is an insult to our patriotism and common sense to say that another night of gloom and despair, such as we suffered from 1868 until 1877, shall again cast its dark mantle over our fair state, and we stand silent witnesses of her degradation and dishonor, amid the hellish orgies of an ignorant and ruthless fanaticism."[127]

Following the pattern set by Bloxham of charging that the Independent party was actually the old Republican element, General Perry spoke in the Lyceum Hall at Fernandina in early September, telling his audience that he was determined that the state should henceforth be controlled by the conservative intelligence of the people and not go back again into the hands of ignorant Radicalism. According to his arithmetic, the Democrats had nine-tenths of the intelligence and virtue of the state, the Republicans one-tenth. The Republican party, he maintained, was built on the Negro vote, led by designing men who would bring back Reconstruction. Because of out-of-state capital now coming into Florida, the colored man could now make $1.25 to $1.75 per day instead of 50 to 65 cents, and one poor white's land had risen in value from $400 to $8,000 because of the coming of a railroad. Attacking the presumption of young men in forming the Independent party, he called them soreheads who contrasted unfavorably with the grey-headed old men of the Democratic party, who, devoted to the service of Florida, asked no return.[128] In describing his party's dissidents as soreheads, Perry used the identical term with which Bisbee earlier had characterized Republican dissenters.

Despite the strong white supremacy position taken by Bloxham and Perry, the Democratic party as in 1876 and 1880 appealed to the Negro voter for support. Along this vein the *Palatka Daily News* printed a letter from T. L. McCoy, a freedman, favoring the status quo and mentioning that the sole dependence of the Negro for his daily bread was upon the moneyed men of the South. McCoy accused the Republican leaders of being more prejudiced against the Negro than were the liberal-minded Southerners.[129]

The Bourbon hopes of Democratic Negro votes were dealt a severe blow by the anti-Negro speech of R. C. Long, Democratic candidate for presidential elector, at Madison in early September. The Tallahassee *Land of Flowers* carried an editorial favoring his stand and indicting the Negro for having drawn the color line, voting in a solid phalanx against every interest of his white neighbor. It described him as a political slave who voted automatically. The majority of whites, the editorial stated, had nothing against a Negro; however, they should cease trying to make him a Democrat. They should vote him down at the polls, and give him a far better government than he was capable of giving himself.[130] The *Floridian*, editorializing on Long's speech, mentioned the fairness of Democratic control in dealing with the education of Negroes, and complained that no black leader had attempted to break the color line. Leon County Negroes, according to the *Floridian*, were showing only an apathetic interest in the Independent movement.[131] It was obvious that the Democrats were disappointed in not receiving the support of the Negroes who in 1876 and 1880 had bolted the Republican party and supported Drew and Bloxham. General Perry did not have the same record of friendliness toward the Negroes, and those Negroes such as Walls who were displeased with the continued white carpetbag domination of the Republican party could now vote Independent. Samuel Pasco, chairman of the Democratic State Executive Committee, was unwilling to countenance Long's speech. Accepting his resignation as a candidate for elector, he stated that "the Conservative Democratic party of Florida has maintained the constitutional right of the colored man and has faithfully carried out and built up the public school system since its advent to power."[132]

General Walls at Jacksonville on September 18 called on Negroes to stand together. He warned them that the Democrats were threatening to deprive them of certain rights in the forthcoming constitutional convention. For proof he offered Long's Madison speech. On the other hand, Pope promised to deal fairly with white and black alike. Walls attacked Bisbee in his hometown as no longer a resident of Florida. Editor Charles H. Jones of the *Times-Union* admonished Walls, "so strong and sensible a person," for giving credence to the stories of Republican demagogues of the Reed stripe, who were trying to foment trouble between whites and blacks in Florida. Further, the Democratic party had "no desire nor intention to injure the colored people, but on the contrary" was "their best and truest friend" and would "always treat them with due consideration."[133]

Editor J. Willis Menard of the Key West *News*, attacking the Democratic attempts to woo Negro voters, charged that the "studied and polished hypocrisy which the Bourbon leaders have displayed toward the colored people since the war has been and is remarkable only for its transparency." Don McLeod of the *Land of Flowers* retorted that it was a question of whether the white man or the Negro with a handful of whites should rule the state.[134] Bloxham, drawn into the racial controversy and attempting to take a moderate position, stated in a speech at Fernandina: "I would scorn any man who would trample upon the rights of another on account of his color."[135]

To the end of the campaign, the Disston Sale continued to be an issue. On August 31 Comptroller William D. Barnes wrote Samuel A. Swann for a statement proving that the $20,000 which the Internal Improvement Fund Trustees had paid him was not "hush" money.[136] Promptly answering Barnes's letter, Swann asserted that the money was payment to him for services rendered under contract.[137]

As the election drew near newspapers of varying shades of opinion were busy discrediting Independentism. The Democratic Tavares *Herald* accused Pope and the Independents of being the violent and lawless element among the Democrats, those who were Ku Kluxers and dealt in tissue ballots and Negro slaying.[138] The black-edited Jacksonville *People's Journal* asserted that Pope had headed the mob which lynched Savage and James.[139] Pope's appeal to the ex-Northerners in South Florida was apparently affected by this barrage of slander. Although the Republicans in Brevard County decided to support the Independent ticket, in Dade County there were three tickets in the field.[140] To insure victory, the Nassau County Democratic leaders decided to hold a preferential vote on all important county offices, those with the highest vote to be suggested to the governor for nomination. It was announced that only those who voted for Perry and the Democratic legislative ticket would be allowed to participate in this election; voting for the national Democratic electoral ticket was not requisite.[141] On the eve of the election the *Times-Union* reported a forged letter making the rounds signed E. A. P.—General Perry's initials—addressed to Samuel Pasco, urging the Democratic state chairman to do all in his power to prevent Negroes and poor whites from voting.[142] Pope in turn was accused of being a thief as a youth. The Madison *New Era* refuted this charge by printing a denial by the man from whom Pope allegedly stole.[143]

The vigorous campaign Pope waged raised the hopes of Independents and their reform Republican allies. Even though the Tampa *Tribune* reported that the Cubans would not bloc vote for him,[144] Eugene O. Locke was optimistic in his congressional race. Stressing that he had a good chance of election, Locke wrote Secretary of the Navy Chandler, asking him to withdraw his support from the Ring and to stop interfering in Florida patronage matters.[145] It was obvious that Jacksonville Ring politicians such as Eagan, who did not normally operate in the First Congressional District, were interfering with Locke's campaign by bitterly fighting the Independent movement. By supporting the Ring Republicans, Chandler was contributing to a Democratic victory and the defeat of Blaine in Florida.

With a close election in prospect, into the state came General Alfred H. Colquitt, commander of the forward battlefield elements of the Confederate army at Olustee, where a Union invasion force attempting to capture Tallahassee had been sent reeling back to Jacksonville. Colquitt would refurbish memories of the Lost Cause. Now a Georgia United States senator with conservative views, Colquitt was accompanied by other prominent Southern Democrats in an eleventh hour effort to bolster the Bourbon ranks.[146]

The election went off quietly in most counties, although a murder was committed the night of the election at the Titus House in Titusville. A Democrat was killed in a knife fight by one who had been a bystander in the political argument which preceded the altercation.[147] In Madison County, ballot boxes were stolen in the town of Madison, at Cherry Lake, and at Hamburg in an apparent effort to defeat Pope and the Independents.[148] Democrats claimed that it was Negroes who purloined the boxes.[149]

The margin of victory of the Democrats came largely from the white counties, with Perry running exceptionally well in South Florida where it had been anticipated that a large number of settlers would vote Republican and Independent. Cleveland ran slightly behind Perry in the South Florida counties, indicating that some Republicans voted for the Democratic state ticket.[150] Earlier, the Daytona *Halifax Journal* mentioned that two businessmen who voted Republican in 1882 feared damage to their businesses and did not plan to vote in 1884.[151]

In the statewide election returns Perry had 32,087 to Pope's 27,845. Mabry defeated Greeley, and both congressional districts went Democratic. Walls experienced a humiliating defeat, polling only 215 votes. This destroyed the myth that Negroes would always prefer a Negro candidate, since Bisbee clearly received the bulk of the Negro votes. The Democrats won control of both the senate and the assembly, carrying the senate twenty to twelve and the aseembly sixty-five to twenty-three. Both parties had supported a constitutional convention, and it was approved by a vote of 31,884 to 8,473. Pope carried the Black Belt by 800 votes fewer than Conover in 1880. As in 1880, Gadsden and Jackson were the predominantly Negro counties that voted Democratic. The disappointing vote of the Independents in the Black Belt was caused partly by the ballot box stealing in Madison County, which cut Pope's vote from 1,548 in 1882 to 629, and partly by a factional fight in Leon County where Pope polled 600 fewer than Conover had polled in 1880. A fair count in Madison would have placed Pope even with Conover in the number of Black Belt votes cast. In Duval County, home of Bisbee and Cheney, Pope polled 3,267 votes, his highest county total and 750 more votes than Conover had received in 1880. Obviously, in Jacksonville Bisbee had gotten out the maximum number of voters for Pope.

Pope ran well in the cracker counties of North Florida, even carrying Hamilton on the Georgia line. He was barely nosed out in Escambia, Perry's home, and had a respectable showing in the remainder of West Florida, carrying Washington. The counties he carried in Middle and Northeast Florida were all predominantly black except Hamilton. He failed to carry a single county in South Florida.[152] A certain amount of political expediency may have been involved, since ex-Northern political leaders with liberal views, such as "Farmer" Mann, had not joined the Independent movement but had chosen to remain within the Democratic ranks. There was a decisive difference of opinion between them and the Bourbons on such issues as public lands, railroads, and Negro rights. Yet the hard line taken by Dougherty during his successful congressional race indicated that a sizable number of South Flor-

Edward A. Perry, Democrat
Frank W. Pope, Independent

Perry: 32,087
Pope: 27,845

Independent counties

Democratic counties

7. Gubernatorial Vote by County in Election of 1884. (Statistics from the Official Certificate of the Board of State Canvassers of the General Election held November 4, 1884, published in the Tallahassee *Weekly Floridian*, December 9, 1884.)

idians displayed little sympathy toward the blacks. Overall,
though, with a smaller Negro population in South Florida, the issue
of white supremacy was not as important there as in the northern
part of the state.

Both Pope and Locke, claiming fraud, refused to concede defeat. Bisbee, although much disappointed, admitted losing. He attributed his party's setback to the "silence" of the national committee and the expressed opinions of certain prominent Northern
Republicans. Pope claimed a statewide majority of 1,732 votes
and accused the Democrats of ballot box stuffing in Jackson,
Gadsden, Leon, and Jefferson counties.[153] In a statement to the
press the fiery Independent declared: "I am determined in my
fight against Bourbonism in Florida. The people have declared
by their vote against it and I shall see that their rights in the prem-
ises shall be protected. Again, I repeat, the votes shall be counted
as cast."[154] Locke reported 146 tissue ballots illegally cast at Quincy
by Democrats, making 146 more ballots in that Gadsden County
box than there were people voting. He also charged that frauds
had been committed in Jackson County. He stated that he had
hoped that the election would help him take off weight but that
the corn bread and bacon of South and West Florida had agreed
with him so well that he weighed the same as when he started.
Locke was willing to admit from the total vote that Davidson
had probably won.[155]

Unlike George F. Drew in 1876, Pope could not gain a hearing
in his attempt to take his claim of fraud to the courts and go
behind the returns in the Black Belt counties, where most of the
alleged irregularities had taken place. However, although the
Democrats won, the heavy Independent vote indicated that a large
percentage of the voters—if not a majority—desired reform in
state government and were opposed to Bourbon rule. If a large
number of white voters had not had an aversion to joining with
the Negroes, the election might have gone the other way.

As a result of its defeat, the Independent party collapsed immediately. Its heterogeneous factions were now in a state of complete disorganization. Federal patronage would go to the Democrats with Cleveland's victory, making Florida more than ever a
one-party state. Nominal Independent leader Frank W. Pope did
not have the desire, the ability, or the money to organize a movement on the order of General William H. Mahone's Virginia

Readjusters. His own gubernatorial nomination had largely been caused by a vacuum of qualified top-level leadership within the new party. Moving to Jacksonville, Pope rejoined the Democratic party, becoming affiliated with the Senator Wilk Call–anti-railroad–anti-Bourbon faction in Duval County. Pope's oratorical ability would henceforth be used mainly in the role of a criminal lawyer.[156] His right hand man during the campaign, Joseph N. Stripling, rejoined the Republicans and also specialized in criminal law.[157] Remaining out of the ranks of either party, Daniel L. McKinnon later attempted a political comeback as a Populist.[158]

The defeat fell hardest on the Negro Independent leaders. It was they who had swung the phalanx of Negro votes away from the Republican party. Now they stood discredited. Some of their constituents were beginning to feel that Negro political activity was the basic cause for the growing ill-feeling between white and Negro.[159] Chief Ring Negro lieutenant Joseph E. Lee was interviewed by a *Times-Union* reporter concerning the changed political situation. The reporter described Lee as "a well-informed, thoughtful man, ever jealous for the rights and watchful for the interests of his race." Lee credited Cleveland with being honest and the Democrats with having carried the state. He also mentioned that the Democrats had promised fair treatment, and he did not think that the legal rights and privileges of the Negroes would be abridged, since "no law under our system of government can be made that will affect one citizen and not another." Lee did not ask for social equality, because family and social matters regulate themselves.[160]

With Cleveland elected and the state firmly in Democratic hands, the members of the Jacksonville Ring and the other Republican officeholders faced the prospect of four lean patronage years. Those who remained in Florida turned to business, a number joining the Bourbons as representatives of absentee ownership.[161]

Editor J. W. Thompson of the Jacksonville *People's Journal* openly supported the Bourbons and was optimistic about the future of his race in Florida. Thompson thought that after their victory the whites would be less likely to mistreat the Negro. He foresaw an era of good feeling for the South. Bourbon editor Don McLeod of the Tallahassee *Land of Flowers* called Thompson "a sensible Negro."[162]

7

The Bourbons Triumphant

Despite political victory at the polls, the Bourbon proponents of the New South were not without passive economic opposition in Florida. Excited as the people of St. Augustine were concerning the coming of the new railroad from Jacksonville, city council members continued to graze their cattle and horses on the town square.[1] The economic awakening of predominantly agrarian Florida was gradual, despite the impatience of the dynamic trio of William D. Chipley, Henry M. Flagler, and Henry B. Plant.

It was evident from Governor Edward A. Perry's inaugural speech that his administration would follow a path well worn by his two predecessors. Words of encouragement backed by action went to industry and immigration; conciliatory platitudes were directed to the Negro.[2] The legislature, reflecting the increased interest in the Lost Cause which the election of the ex-Confederate general had stimulated, voted Florida's disabled Confederate veterans a five-dollar-a-month pension.[3] Other main items on the agenda were election of a United States senator and arrangements for the constitutional convention.[4]

Not all the anti-Bourbons within the Democratic party had deserted in 1882 and 1884 to join the Independent movement. The racial issue and reluctance to cooperate with Republicans kept many of the yeoman farmers Democratic. But the policy of Bloxham of aligning the Democratic party with railroad promoters and land developers had largely contributed to his failure to gain a

renomination. Homesteaders residing on the public domain without clear title were becoming apprehensive concerning the policy
of the Internal Improvement Fund trustees of considering almost
all the domain as swamp and overflow, thus available for railroad
land grants.[5] Alone among Florida's major officeholders, Senator
Wilk Call took up the cause of these homesteaders, declaring war
on the railroads and empire builders in the spring of 1884. Ex-
Whig Call, a former railroad lawyer, aimed his first shot at the
Florida Railroad Company, whose history was intertwined with
that of his old political foe, David L. Yulee. In May, Call introduced a bill calling for the forfeiture of its land grant.[6] Proponents
of the New South, resenting Call's interference with railroad land
granting, saw him as a dangerous demagogue who catered to the
white yeoman farmer vote.[7] The pro-railroad Bourbons vigorously
opposed Call's renomination when the Democratic legislators
caucused on the night of January 9. Feeling against Call was so
strong that when Adam C. White of Jackson introduced a resolution calling for all caucus members to be bound by its selection
in the legislature, the meeting broke up. However, seeing that the
ardently pro-Call followers from the grass roots of the white
counties not only had the votes but would force the issue, the
Bourbons were reluctant to risk a split in the newly mended ranks.
On January 13 the Democratic legislators again caucused, and Call
was nominated with little opposition.[8] Speaking for the Bourbons,
Editor Charles H. Jones of the Jacksonville *Florida Times-Union*
thought the nomination in accordance with the wishes of the majority of Floridians. At the same time, he cautioned Call that his
endorsement placed him under renewed obligations to the Democratic party.[9]

On January 20 the legislature formally approved the caucus
decision to return Call to Washington for a second term. Republicans cast their few votes for Jonathan C. Greeley. Though the
Democrats voted in a bloc for Call, one of their rural leaders
was particularly unhappy about his renomination. Speaking to his
colleagues in the senate immediately following the vote, "Farmer"
Mann of Hernando commented: "The gentleman put in nomination
it is well known to all here is not my personal choice, yet he
is seemingly the choice of my party, and the party having spoken it
is my duty to obey; I therefore cast my vote for Wilkinson Call."[10]

Interest in the forthcoming election of constitutional convention delegates continued to be lukewarm. The complete defeat of the Independents and the temporary desertion of politics by their leader, Frank W. Pope, made it almost a certainty that reform would remain in the background at the convention. Delegates to the convention, the legislature decided, were to be apportioned among the counties and senatorial districts in proportion to their representation in the legislature and were to number 108.[11] In suggesting changes to be incorporated in the new constitution, several Bourbon newspaper editors attempted to weaken the state public school system. The most reactionary of these, Don McLeod of the Tallahassee *Land of Flowers,* called for the abolition of the office of superintendent of public instruction and the placing of the free school system under the attorney general as an added duty. This would have reduced public education to a minor function of the state.[12]

In cotton-growing Marion and in urban Duval, middle-of-the-road politicians of both parties, realizing that their predominantly black counties would elect Republicans who would have no influence in framing the new constitution, proposed fusion tickets. Frank W. Harris, longtime editor of the Democratic *Ocala Banner,* and Joseph E. Lee, veteran Jacksonville Negro leader, were two who made such propositions. Lee, a Republican nominee for convention delegate from Duval County, suggested that he withdraw and be replaced by Colonel J. J. Daniel, a prominent "Gate City" attorney and a member of one of its old families. The tolerant atmosphere of noblesse oblige that existed in Jacksonville between black and white had been nurtured by such aristocrats as Daniel. That this atmosphere existed is vouched for by former Jacksonville resident James Weldon Johnson, an original organizer of the National Association for the Advancement of Colored People.[13] Negro leader J. Willis Menard, however, rebuked Lee for deserting the Republican party. Lee retorted that the blacks had been loyal to the Republicans for twenty-five years but that it was now desirable to change. Questioning Menard's loyalty to his fellow Negroes, Lee recalled that on Menard's advice the black mill laborers had struck two years before, only to have the ex-Louisiana congressman-elect abandon them. Now Negroes should concentrate on gaining education and on saving. They should befriend the whites who would aid them in accomplishing the two objectives even if those whites were Democrats.[14] Menard's view prevailed as the Duval Republican organization accepted Lee's resignation and replaced him with another Republican.[15]

Editor Harris suggested a fusion ticket for Marion consisting of two Republicans and one Democrat. This proposal received a chilly reception in most white Democratic counties where the majority had no intention of compromising with the minority.[16] In a few white counties, however, single Republican candidates received support from Democrats. After Marion's Republicans rebuffed Harris, he decided to use his newspaper as a communication device for his county's Democrats. Since under the old constitution the governor had appointed Democrats to county office, Harris warned against tampering with the governor's power of appointment.[17] A popular election of county officials at this time would have returned the Republicans to power in Marion. The large majority of Black Belt Democrats would rather have centralization of power in Tallahassee than Negroes, carpetbaggers, and scalawags in local offices.

There was a light turnout in the special election held on May 5, 1885, to select the constitutional delegates.[18] Now possessing the only party completely organized throughout the state, the Democrats coasted to an easy victory. Young Northerners, coming to Florida, were not following in the political footsteps of the carpetbaggers whose thinning ranks badly needed reinforcement. Only Duval, Leon, Marion, and Nassau, having a majority of Negroes, and Hamilton, a North Florida white county, would send anti-Democratic delegations to the convention. Even the candidacy of ex-Governor George F. Drew failed to bring victory to Duval's Democrats.[19] The Jasper *Times,* a weekly newspaper published at the county seat of Hamilton, commenting on the county's going Republican, lamented, "God help us."[20]

With Jefferson and Madison joining Alachua, Gadsden, and Jackson in the Democratic column, the Black Belt would send a sizable number of white Democratic delegates to the convention. In Madison County, which had voted Republican the previous year, that party's candidates polled fewer than two hundred votes. Jefferson County voted Democratic for the first time since the start of Radical Reconstruction.[21] The explanation was that the Rev. George Washington Witherspoon and other Negro politicians, their views apparently influenced by Democratic money, had urged its Negroes to abandon the racial issue.[22] Surprisingly, in eight white

Democratic counties in North and West Florida, single Republicans were elected. Eighty-two delegates would be Democrats, twenty-three Republicans, and three Independents.[23]

Convention delegates arriving at Tallahassee would find the town undergoing a moderate boom. Where formerly Negro fish peddlers pitched their stalls stood a new $21,000 stone and brick courthouse, "by far the prettiest in the state." Though one of the two main hotels had recently burned and was not yet rebuilt, the other, formerly the City Hotel, had undergone remodeling and renaming and was now the Morgan Hotel.[24] A new newspaper, the *Tallahassean*, edited by Don McLeod, greeted the delegates with the suggestion that now the time was ripe to end the insidious printing monopoly of the *Floridian* and Charles E. Dyke, Sr.[25] McLeod's suggestion fell upon deaf ears.

Although Negroes were not represented in proportion to their number, only seven delegates being Negroes, the convention represented a fair cross section of the state's middle-class white voters. Thirty-five delegates were lawyers, twenty-eight farmers, ten merchants, six doctors, six teachers, and two ministers. All but a small minority of delegates were born in the Deep South. The eighty-three Democratic delegates represented separate county organizations. No single railroad or other business group would dominate the convention. There were no indications, though, that the Democrats would break ranks and share decision-making with the Republicans and Independents.[26]

The unity of the Democratic party was demonstrated at the beginning of the convention when Samuel Pasco was unanimously elected president. A delegate from Jefferson, Pasco had been chairman of the Democratic state committee since 1876.[27] Like Governor Perry, the convention's presiding officer was not a native Southerner. Born in England and Harvard-educated, Pasco had come as a schoolteacher to Wakeenah Academy in Jefferson County. During the Civil War he had served with distinction in the Confederate army; after the war he returned home and entered into the practice of law. With his Black Belt county overwhelmingly Republican, Pasco assumed command of its few Democrats. Rising steadily within his party as state chairman, he had led the Democrats to five consecutive victories, the latest being the defeat of the Independents. Moderate in his views, Pasco was usually able to harmonize the various factions within the Democratic party.[28] In his acceptance speech, he showed these qualities of conciliation, praising the Negro for his progress and calling for a constitution which provided the "greatest good for the greatest number."[29]

Getting down to work, the Democratic majority quickly squelched one of its number who proposed that a stenographer record the proceedings.[30] It was decided that the format of the legislative journals would be followed, with only a bare outline of the proceedings printed. To make it more difficult for the Republicans and Independents to wield the balance of power in the event of a split between white county and Black Belt Democrats or between pro-railroad and anti-railroad groups, the dominant Democrats voted that to be adopted any proposal for a part of the constitution must receive the support of the majority of all the delegates at the convention. A majority of the quorum present at the time of the proposal would not be enough.[31]

To assist him in framing the new constitution, Pasco selected staunch party regulars to head the twenty-two standing committees. Four powerful county leaders headed the major committees. Circuit Judge A. E. Maxwell of Escambia, chairman of the committee on the executive and administrative department, had served Florida previously as an antebellum congressman and Confederate States senator. Ex–Lieutenant Governor Livingston Bethel of Monroe, Bloxham's recent adversary, received the chairmanship of the legislative committee. "Farmer" Mann, Hernando citrus grower and leader of the anti-Call faction in the South Florida rural white counties, headed the committee on suffrage and eligibility. Largely responsible for the overthrow of Wall-Dennis Republican control in Alachua, Edward C. F. Sanchez of Gainesville became presiding officer of the judicial committee.[32] These four and Pasco largely provided the leadership of the Democratic majority.

On the racial issue Democrats were sharply divided. James P. Coker, delegate from Jackson County, had once been termed "generalissimo of his section's Ku Klux," while David S. Walker, Jr., Leon County delegate and an independent Democrat, was active in encouraging Negro participation in politics. William A. Blount, attorney for the Louisville and Nashville Railroad Company, a delegate from Escambia, and William A. Hocker, a strongly pro-railroad Sumter County delegate, were there to do battle with any land reformers or advocates of a railroad commission. In dealing with the highly controversial educational issue, Pasco passed over the obviously better qualified Alachua County superintendent of schools, William N. Sheats, to name Dr. John P. Wall of Hillsborough chairman of the education committee.[33]

Although the Republicans lacked both strength and a program, the convention provided the stage for the final public appearance of the party leaders as a group. In Jonathan C. Greeley of Duval, defeated candidate for lieutenant governor, ex–Chief Justice Edwin M. Randall, also of Duval, and ex-Senator Simon B. Conover of Leon, the white Republicans had three capable representatives. Among the seven Negro members, H. W. Chandler, ex-instructor at Howard University, representing Marion, and Thomas V. Gibbs, Jacksonville lawyer and son of the late secretary of state Jonathan C. Gibbs, stood out.[34]

As the framework of the new constitution developed it soon became apparent that the convention was completely decentralizing the state government and stripping the governor of his power of appointment. Under the proposed changes, the office of cabinet member was made elective, and a governor could no longer be reelected to consecutive terms. The former proposal strengthened the power of the Democratic state convention. The latter proposal was probably meant to prevent the recurrence of a fight similar to one staged between Bloxham and Drew for a second term. The Bloxham-Drew feud had nearly split the party wide open on the eve of the campaign against the strong Independent movement. The office of lieutenant governor was abolished, its duties falling on the president of the state senate.[35] Impatient at the slow progress of the convention, Republican Charles W. Lewis, Yulee's former land agent, wrote Samuel A. Swann that although he was anxious to go home, there was little chance, since "others" had jobs to attend to.[36]

In the main, the attack against the Bourbon county leaders in the saddle was led by a few Democratic reformers; Independents and Republicans invariably gave support to these Democratic braves who were off the reservation. The railroad commission issue was brought up on June 23 by Joseph M. Tolbert of Columbia, an ex-Confederate and ex-legislator. Unfortunately, the anti-railroad forces were so weak in the convention that Tolbert did not have sufficient backing to force a vote on the issue.[37] On June

25 a second reformer came forward to battle the Bourbons, this time in the area of law and order. The Reverend Robert F. Rogers, a Missionary Baptist preacher from Suwannee County— home of the iniquitous Dutton convict-labor turpentine empire— proposed that the state operate its own prison and farm. This reform was immediately opposed on economic grounds by William A. Hocker, chairman of the committee on public institutions. Hocker reasoned that future legislatures should be free to develop a prison as the state's finances improved, as humane ideas grew, and as the needs of society demanded. Hocker's view easily prevailed, and this source of cheap labor continued to be available to Bourbons and Northern capitalists alike.[38] Within the year phosphate was discovered in Florida,[39] and phosphate mining would have the same effect on convict leasing as the invention of the cotton gin had had on slavery.

The early deliberations of the convention convinced J. Dennis Wolfe, reform-minded editor of the Pensacola *Commercial*, that the Bourbons were firmly in control.[40] But the day of the blank check for railroad interests was over. Chairman Alexander McCaskill of the committee on taxation and finance, a frugal Scottish farmer from Argyle in Walton, inserted a prohibition against state support for railroad construction. McCaskill also recommended that the constitution forbid the issuing of state bonds. Once during the Whig era and once during Reconstruction, Florida had issued bonds to aid private corporations and had then repudiated them. McCaskill was determined to divorce the credit of the state from promotion schemes.[41]

To prevent the Republicans from wielding the balance of power between differing Democratic groups, the Democrats resorted to the caucus. In the caucus on the night of July 9, the foremost proponent of the white county view of home rule and local elections, "Farmer" Mann, clashed with Pasco, who feared that these two objectives would deprive the Black Belt Democrats of the county rule which they had enjoyed since 1877. Mann then suggested a compromise which provided for minority representation.[42] The exclusion from decision-making caused some Republican tempers to flare. On July 10, H. C. Baker, a representative from Nassau County, accused Pasco of ruling arbitrarily, unjustly, and unfairly on a motion to correct the journal. Pasco, however, appears to have been uniformly severe on the time-consuming antics of delegates.[43] On July 14 Edwin C. F. Sanchez, delegate from Alachua, clearly set forth the case of the county leaders against the governor's appointive power. In advocating the election of all officers of the state, Sanchez asserted that the governor now appointed 1,638 officials, and that in every county there was a handful of men who were the appointees of the administration. For seventeen years, he recalled, the Democratic party had been assailing the constitution because it substituted gubernatorial patronage for home rule. He made no mention of the cooperation of Governors Drew, Bloxham, and Perry with the county leaders in the exercise of this appointive power, the abuse of which was a fundamental cause of Independentism.[44] Sanchez's stand allied Alachua, a Black Belt county, with the white counties.

On July 17 Judge James G. Speer of Orange, chairman of the temperance committee, successfully steered a local option law through the convention, the vote being seventy-four to twenty-three. However, local option would be voted on separately from the constitution.[45]

The major controversial issue of the convention proved to be the poll tax. Unsympathetic to the efforts of Black Belt Democrats to disfranchise Negroes, "Farmer" Mann, chairman of the suffrage and eligibility committee, supported by a majority of committee members, attempted in Article XIV (Article VI in the finished constitution) to divorce the poll tax from the constitution. The poll tax measure was not popular in the white counties, and Mann warned the convention that to inject this issue into the constitution would be hazardous. To compromise with the tax's ardent supporters from the Black Belt and the port-city county of Escambia, he suggested that it be voted on as a separate ordinance.[46] The poll tax Democrats rejected Mann's compromise, and a sizable group of reformers and white county Democrats moved to his aid as the fight began. Rumors circulated that the pro-Mann anti-poll tax Democrats had effected an alliance with the Republicans.[47] Thomas V. Gibbs rallied the Republicans to shake off their lethargy and strengthen the effort to defeat the poll tax.[48] The *Floridian* reported that a stormy session ensued on July 22, when ex–Chief Justice Edwin M. Randall gained permission to spread on the convention journal a memorial from the Workingman's Association of Jacksonville, protesting the poll tax.[49] The memorial, entitled "A Solemn Protest," was the first effort of organized laboring men to present their interests to the convention. Heretofore, only the businessman and the farmer had been heard from. The Jacksonville laborers, the majority white Democrats but with Independent leadership, objected to the poll tax because, they claimed, it would work an injury on working people. Their manifesto warned that it would lead to a diabolical traffic in the elective franchise which would convert a democracy into an aristocracy. The petition closed by threatening that if the convention did not heed the protest, the Workingman's Association would work for the defeat of the constitution.[50] Mann, supporting their aims, declared that a poll tax was unfair to the hard-working laboring class. Refuting Mann's claim to be speaking for the workers, William H. Cook of Putnam County rejoined that the memorandum did not reflect the opinion of the majority since it had been passed with only twenty-five workingmen present at the meeting.[51]

Meanwhile, the convention members complained about the water furnished from cisterns on the roof of the capitol and worried about spending all of the $35,000 which the legislature had appropriated for their use.[52]

While the Bourbons organized their forces to steamroller the poll tax through, William N. Sheats led an attack on their flank in his fight to strengthen the public school system of the state. Completely overshadowing the other members of the education committee, he wrote into Article IX of the proposed constitution (Article XII in the finished constitution) a financial bulwark for the segregated schools. The hatred of the ultra-Bourbons was now unleashed against Sheats. John Temple Graves in the Jacksonville *Daily Florida Herald* thundered that the "school crank" was trying to confiscate the property of the state in order to educate Negroes. Though the state's educational system was still in the pioneer stage, Graves did not see the need for as large a school fund as the constitution provided.[53] The Democrats were unable to resolve the education issue in caucus. When the vote was taken on the convention floor, the Republicans and a few Independents lined up solidly beside the education Democrats to pass Article IX by a vote of fifty-nine to thirty-two. The Alachua delegation stood loyally behind Sheats, along with Pasco and a number of white county Democrats. An almost solid phalanx of Black Belt Democrats were in the minority, although Section 12 of Article XII of the finished constitution provided for separate but equal schools.[54]

Despite Sheats's advocacy, the convention voted down a proposal for a state normal school for Negroes.[55] Thus in higher education, no college was the rule rather than a separate college.

On July 30 a solid bloc of Democrats passed Article XIII on census and apportionment (Article VI in the finished constitution); the Republicans opposed. The main feature of this article was the reduction of the maximum membership of a county in the house of representatives (the old assembly) to three. This provision was directed at the more heavily populated counties of the Black Belt. Jefferson, Duval, Alachua, and Leon would each lose a representative.[56]

On Saturday, August 1, Article XIV on suffrage and eligibility again came before the convention. On the previous day the Republicans as a group openly denied in a letter to the *Florida Times-Union* that they had entered into a coalition with "Farmer" Mann, as had been charged by John Temple Graves in the Jacksonville *Daily Florida Herald* on July 27.[57] Time was running short, because the allotted funds for convention expenses had already been expended. Continuing his fight for election reform, David S. Walker, Jr., attempted to insert a provision in the article forbidding anyone guilty of bribery, fraud, or violation of election law from holding office. Walker's amendment was promptly tabled. The minority report of James E. Yonge of Escambia, which inserted the poll tax into the constitution, was substituted for the majority report and passed eighty-six to twelve. Not only the Bourbons but practically all the Democrats from the white yeoman counties supported the poll tax, although it would mean disfranchisement of the poor whites as well as the bulk of the blacks. A few Republicans, including ex-Senator Conover of Leon and Hannibal Rowe of Santa Rosa and Negro William F. Thompson of Leon, oddly enough voted in favor of this measure despite its obvious adverse effect on the Republican party.[58]

From the day the convention opened with the election of Pasco as chairman, through the appointment of the committees and the framing of the constitution, the Bourbons lost only the battle on education. Compromising on education and allowing the prohibitionists to inject the local option issue was as much as they would yield. The Jacksonville *Florida Times-Union* could well report that the Black Belt was safe.[59] Obviously, "safe" meant that the Negro vote there was no longer a serious threat. Young David

S. Walker, Jr., was unwilling to accept this verdict. The strong vote of the Independents in 1884 indicated that election reform, rather than disfranchisement of the blacks, was desired by a large percentage of the state's voters. Disgusted by the refusal of the Democratic dominated convention to effect election reforms, Walker was now completely ready to break with the Democratic party. He had hopes that South Florida's Northern settlers would join him in a continuation of the Independent movement. Writing to ex-Lieutenant Governor William H. Gleason, one of the few Northern settlers who had remained Republican, Walker requested his assistance in bringing about an understanding between Independents and Republicans in order to "deliver the state from the terror of the tyrannical and arbitrary party now holding power."[60] The strongest leader of South Florida's Northern settlers, "Farmer" Mann, though remaining a loyal Democrat, was none too pleased about two decisions of his party. The first was the reelection of Wilk Call and the second the inserting of the poll tax in the new constitution. A grass roots politician, Mann was aware of the antidemocratic tendencies of the Bourbons.

As might be expected, the finished constitution pleased mainly the conservative Bourbon element. Editor George R. Fairbanks, one of this group's press spokesmen, immediately came out in the Fernandina *Florida Mirror* for its ratification. Fairbanks was enthusiastic about the provisions which called for the election of cabinet officers and supreme court judges. The appointment of county commissioners also met with his approval.[61] Carpetbagger ex-Senator Simon B. Conover, who normally leaned toward the Bourbons, also took a public stand advocating the ratification of the constitution. Conover attributed the satisfactory condition of the constitution to certain unnamed Northern Democrats.[62]

Whereas the Republican Constitution of 1868 provided for a strong governor, the Democratic Constitution of 1885 diffused the state's power to the counties. The weak governor provided for could neither run for reelection nor appoint his own cabinet. Further, financial changes in the new constitution favored county coffers over the state treasury.[63] The provision whereby the governor appointed county commissioners appeared to give him power on the grass roots level, but this provision was really a device to deprive the Republicans of those offices in the Black Belt. A gov-

ernor was expected to rubber-stamp the appointment of the nominees selected by a county's Democrats.

If the constitution were ratified, the Democratic state convention
would replace the governorship as the most important political
institution in Florida. The convention would determine the nomination—tantamount to election—of the governor, cabinet officers,
and supreme court judges. Since cabinet members would be
eligible for reelection and the governor would not, certain county
leaders were effectively blocking the possibility of the rise of a
strong political leader who would limit their freedom. The position
of the county leaders is easy to understand in view of the threat
that Frank W. Pope had posed, blazing through the state and
threatening to pull down political fences.

An immediate effect of the constitutional convention was the
elevation of Sam Pasco to a position of leadership in state politics
that rivaled the position Governor Perry held because of his
office. Perry was now in the situation that Drew had earlier faced
with Bloxham. As Pasco spoke and worked for the ratification of
the constitution in the 1886 election, only sporadic and apathetic
opposition developed. Edwin M. Cheney's optimistic prediction
in 1884 concerning the growth of the Republican party was not
being fulfilled. Young Northerners settling in Florida showed little
interest in the rejuvenation of a party which hitherto had largely
depended upon black votes. Further, the Democratic national
victory of 1884 had stripped the state Republican organization of
its federal patronage. Only in Duval, Marion, and Leon did the
Republicans maintain strong county organizations; in the rest of
the state the party was no longer effective. At the same time, the
political voice of the black was now weak. The proposed constitution provided the greatest good for those represented at the convention, the white middle class.

Pasco kept up a constant barrage of letters to newspapers. The
poll tax, he claimed, was not an anti-Negro measure but rather
a means of school revenue. Every citizen should support the government, and the tax would protect against the election of ignorant
and incompetent officeholders. At the same time, it would not
protect the Black Belt because the Negro would sell his neighbor's
last chicken to vote. Labeling the new constitution an official
Democratic party document, Pasco warned that to reject it would

condemn the state to the Republican Constitution of 1868. The new constitution, he claimed, would abolish life tenure in office.[64]

For Pasco to claim that the poll tax was not anti-Negro but a means of school revenue was an example of the subterfuge of the Democrats. Since the Negro members of the convention had not been members of the majority party caucus, they had been excluded once again from decision-making. This major issue, which had caused their dissatisfaction with both parties and their support of the Independent movement, had been ignored. Only in the area of public education, decided on the floor because of the strong advocacy of this issue by Sheats, did the blacks receive consideration in the convention. The new constitution could well be considered a white supremacy document.

Democratic state newspapers almost unanimously favored ratification of the constitution.[65] The lone press opposition to ratification came from Editor Frank Harris of the *Ocala Banner*. Harris foresaw that the new constitution would do in a surreptitious fashion that which the old constitution did openly. Terming the new document a patchwork of compromises, Harris attacked the proposed election of supreme court judges and the elimination of the lieutenant governor.[66] Weak opposition to the constitution also came from a group of Palatkans who ironically called themselves Anti-Mann Democrats and blamed him for the poll tax.[67] Governor Perry, while objecting to many features of the new constitution, on the eve of the election wrote a lukewarm letter to the Jacksonville *Florida Times-Union* favoring its ratification.[68]

In the major election contests held at the same time as the vote for ratification, Charles B. Pendleton, an independent Democrat from Key West, opposed Congressman Robert H. M. Davidson in the First District. Jonathan C. Greeley, becoming a perennial minority candidate, carried the Republican banner in a race with Charles Dougherty, the incumbent. Before winning the Democratic nomination, Davidson had to overcome the strongly supported candidacy of Stephen R. Mallory, the Younger, a Pensacola lawyer.

In the election, held November 2, 1886, the new constitution was passed by a little less than three to two, the vote being 31,803 to 21,243. Surprisingly, although Jefferson sent Pasco to the assembly, it voted against ratification by a large majority. Elsewhere in the Black Belt, Jackson and Leon joined Jefferson in voting against ratification. Nassau and Escambia, two of the three port-city counties, did likewise. It was evident that many white Democrats in counties having a large Negro population did not favor the election of local officials. Levy, Baker, and Columbia in North Florida and Volusia in South Florida were the only other counties to vote against the new constitution.

Davidson, his district now safely Democratic, defeated Pendleton by a margin of almost two to one. Greeley, receiving a large majority from Duval and polling a strong vote in East Florida, lost to Dougherty by a little over two thousand votes. The collapse of the Republican party in Madison County provided the Democrats with a large share of their margin of victory.[69] The legislature again would be strongly Democratic, only Duval and Leon going Republican. Editor Don McLeod of the *Tallahassean* complained that because of the local Republican victory, a mob of half-civilized creatures with drums, bells, tin pans, and brazen throats paraded the street howling, "Walker our leader."[70] But with the demise of the two-party system, the state government was firmly in the hands of conservative county leaders, who as long as there had been danger of opposition had not had a free hand.

8

Afterglow of the Independent Fire

Senator Call considered his reelection a mandate to continue the fight against promiscuous granting of Florida's public domain to railroad promoters. In a speech on the Senate floor late in March 1885, he attacked the actions of Wailes in serving simultaneously as railroad land agent and state lobbyist: as an employee of the Florida Railway and Navigation Company, Call charged, Wailes was claiming for the railroad land which had already been settled, and was selling orange groves and other improvements of evicted homesteaders. Because of the intense desire of Dyke, Bloxham, and the majority of county leaders to encourage out-of-state capitalists to invest in Florida, not since the antebellum era had a major officeholder dared attack the sacred railroad interests. Disregarding the proverb "Let sleeping dogs lie," Call revealed that the track of the FR & N had been built entirely from land proceeds and without any outlay of private means, and requested a Senate investigation of its business practices.[1] Wilk Call spoke from firsthand knowledge; earlier he had been the lawyer for the Florida Atlantic and Gulf Central Railroad, one of the smaller companies consolidated to form the FR & N, and his older brother, George W. Call, had been Yulee's righthand man in the building of the main line.[2]

Meanwhile, homesteaders who had entered public domain previously declared swamp and overflow, in accordance with the railroad land grant policy of the state administration were having their entries suspended. Thirty-five of these suspensions by the General Land Office occurred in November 1885 alone.[3] During the same period, only one settler voluntarily requested that his entry be canceled because the land entered was swampy and totally unfit for cultivation.[4] In December, to correct the abuse of the law by the railroad builders and their fellow Bourbon political allies, Call introduced a resolution calling for a special committee to investigate the unlawful and fraudulent appropriation of Florida public lands by railroad interests. To substantiate his charges, Call produced fourteen letters from settlers protesting harsh treatment at the hands of railroad land agents. The resolution was referred to the Committee on Public Lands.[5] Settlers gained some relief a year later when a U.S. Land Office circular gave them permission to make pre-emption filings for land claimed by the state under the swamp and overflow land grant.[6] Supporting the Florida senator's fight to keep his state's public domain open to homesteaders, the Savannah *Daily News* reported that Call was submitting bills in Congress for the forfeiture of all Florida railroad land grants which had not properly complied with the granting conditions. The Georgia newspaper praised Call for protecting the rights of homesteaders in Florida.[7]

Meanwhile, Governor Perry was involved in the utilization of railroad men in attempting to settle the Indian War claim. In this effort Perry made several trips to Washington. The Pensacola *Commercial*, resenting his leaning toward the railroads, reported that on his trip in January 1886 he was closely guarded by agents of Chipley's Pensacola and Atlantic.[8] In a speech to the Senate that same month, Call made it clear that he would not cooperate with Perry in claim proceedings if the governor persisted in retaining S. I. Wailes as state lobbyist. Call considered it "a public scandal that a vast sum of money should be paid to lawyers or pretended agents for votes to be given in Congress . . . upon which the history of the country has been fixed for years . . . on . . . reimbursing the States for expenses incurred in suppressing Indian hostilities."[9]

In early February Perry returned to Washington and conferred with Wailes and Chipley. The pro-railroad Jacksonville *Times-Union* explained to its readers that this visit had been necessitated by the muddle which Call had made of the Indian War claim.[10] The strongly anti-railroad Pensacola *Commercial* began a campaign against railroads, particularly singling out the Pensacola and Atlantic, whose promoter, Chipley, was a bitter political enemy of Editor J. Dennis Wolfe. Call's speeches calling for forfeiture of railroad land grants were faithfully published in the *Commercial*.[11] Deviating from his previous neutral course on land grants and perhaps seeing the issue growing in importance, Congressman Davidson of the First District introduced two bills from South Florida citizens asking for the forfeiture of unearned land claimed by the Florida Railway and Navigation Company.[12] The remaining two of Florida's congressional delegation, Senator Charles W. Jones and Congressman Charles Dougherty, both conservatives, maintained a discreet silence.[13]

Early in March the homesteaders were heartened by a decision of Commissioner William A. S. Sparks of the United States Land Office. Sparks held that since there had been no authoritative location of the FR & N route from Waldo to Tampa prior to the expiration of the grant in 1866, no legal location could be made subsequently and qualify under the 1856 grant. In 1860 and 1875 the railroad's map of location had been rejected by the Department of the Interior. In 1880, reversing the earlier decisions, Secretary of the Interior Carl Schurz had accepted the map now rejected by Sparks. The projected line affected by the unfavorable decision was 150 miles in length, of which one-half had been completed. About one-half million acres of public domain claimed by the railroad were involved in the controversy.[14]

On March 4 Call brought to the attention of the Senate the complaints of Dr. James Kellum of Fort Myers and F. C. M. Boggess of Fort Ogden, both residents of South Florida. Kellum had written Call that Monroe County, in common with the rest of Florida, had been victimized by land sharks. He claimed that out of one hundred tracts selected as swamp and overflow, ninety-five would not have water standing on them. Boggess reported that Fort Ogden homesteaders were becoming concerned at the selection of nearby hill country as swamp and overflow land.[15] In April, continuing his attack on Florida railroad land grants, Call gave the Senate a resumé of the history of these subsidies. Yulee's road was once again principal target as he pointed out that thirty years had elapsed since the original grant, but the railroad was yet to be completed from Fernandina to Tampa. Next he turned to Chipley's claim that his Pensacola and Atlantic Railroad should inherit the unearned portion of the old Pensacola and Georgia Railroad land grant in addition to its special grant of 20,000 acres a mile. Call included in his speech a critical letter from Chipley sharply reminding him that as senator he represented the railroads as well as other interests. The irate Pensacolian demanded that Call name one Florida railroad which had shown a profit, and he pointed out that the Florida legislature had approved the P & A land grant. Chipley scoffed at Call's claim that settlers were writing him to request that the P & G claim be forfeited rather than given to the P & A. He demanded that Call produce such letters.[16] Not only did the Pensacola *Commercial* reprint Call's speech with approving editorial comment, but the Savannah *News* stated that his constituents would approve his efforts to have the unearned land grants in the state forfeited.[17]

Opposition to railroad land grants showed indications of extending to British land speculators. An anonymous letter to the Titusville *Florida Star* in the heart of the newly settled Indian River country complained that all troubles among the working classes came from land robbery. In Florida the working classes were being robbed, according to the writer, by the sale of a million acres to English and Scottish lords. These British nobles were establishing the same system of landlordism that pauperized Ireland. Civil war and dynamite would follow, concluded the writer, if Congress did not restore the land to its rightful owners; Americans would not sit quietly while wives and children starved. Later the Ocala Demands of the Farmers' Alliance would include curbs on alien land ownership.[18]

The traditional division of Democrat vs. Republican was now forgotten as Floridians began dividing on the issue of the railroad land grant. The Knights of Labor, with some strength in Pensacola, demanded in an open letter published by the *Commercial* "that the public lands, the heritage of the people, be reserved for actual settlers; not another acre for railroads or speculators, and that all lands now held for speculative purposes to be taxed to their full value."[19]

With the obvious exception of the *Commercial,* newspapers in railroad towns generally rallied to the support of their community's leading industry. In Fernandina, where the home offices of the FR & N were located, Editor George R. Fairbanks of the *Florida Mirror* accused Call of injuring the state and its people by his opposition to railroads.[20] Fighting back at Call, three veteran railroad men, John A. Henderson, William D. Chipley, and E. N. Dickerson, journeyed to Washington to appear before the Senate Committee on Public Lands in opposition to the resolution forfeiting the FR & N land grant. The Washington correspondent of the Jacksonville *Florida Times-Union*, reporting on their visit, assured his readers that the land grant would not be forfeited.[21] Further opposition to Call's position on land grants came from the Boards of Trade of Jacksonville and Tampa. The completion of the Fernandina to Tampa line would provide a direct connection between Jacksonville and Tampa. With an inadequate transportation system a prime handicap, the merchants of the two cities petitioned Congress to grant a further extension of time to the FR & N with the expectation that such assistance would aid in the completion of the railroad.[22]

Letters from citizens to newspapers generally favored Call. James P. Perkins, a former resident of Fort Myers, in a typical letter wrote the *Tallahassean* praising Call's heroic attitude in the Senate as the champion of the poor. He also deplored the activities in South Florida of rascally, impudent, and corrupt monopolistic corporations.[23] Settlers also continued to write Call protesting further land grants. A Manatee County settler, whose petition to Call was published in the Pensacola *Commercial* on May 29, complained that by the government selection of June 13, 1885, seven-tenths of the land of Manatee County was swamp and overflow. On the basis of this selection, railroad land agents were evicting homesteaders who had invested from $75 to $5,000 in their property. Many of these settlers had paid federal surveyors twice and had duplicate homestead and pre-emption receipts.[24] A letter to the Palatka *Herald* signed "Hernando" warned that while the railroad had the most money, the homesteaders had the most votes. "Hernando" cautioned editors and politicians against getting on the wrong side of the fence and praised Call for having the courage of his convictions.[25]

Meanwhile, Receiver H. R. Duval of the FR & N continued to request an additional land grant worth $2 million to complete the remaining fifty-five miles to Tampa. This was necessary, he explained, because the owners of the railroad were unwilling to put up the $1 million required to finish the road. Suits by creditors against the FR & N had caused the owners to take this attitude.

Call demolished Duval's argument by stating that the creditors of the road were also the owners of it.[26]

Going into the summer of 1886, the campaign against the pro-railroad Bourbons appeared to be going in Call's favor. A great many newspapers were publishing favorable editorials. However, no politician with a state-wide following joined Call. Despite this, Call strongly supported the bid of fellow ex-Whig Robert H. M. Davidson for renomination to Congress from the First District, even accompanying him on his canvass. When both spoke at Pensacola on July 7, Call was presented with a petition signed by five hundred local citizens, calling for the restoration of the forfeited railroad land grants to the people. Chipley's query concerning what citizens were interested in railroad land grants was effectively answered by his fellow townsmen.[27]

Pro-railroad newspapers began to attempt to offset the bad name Call was giving the railroads. In August the Tallahassee *Weekly Floridian*, long the spokesman of the state's conservative interests, pictured the railroad builders as altruistic benefactors of Florida. Businessmen would expect five times as much from a venture as the railroad men had received. Furthermore, corporations had rights as well as the people, concluded its editor.[28] Promptly replying to the *Floridian*, the Pensacola *Commercial*'s editor, J. Dennis Wolfe, described the Tallahassee weekly as the organ of railroads and the state administration. Wolfe pointed out that contributing to the development of Florida did not give a prior claim on the property or personal and political rights of the people. If the railroads could not pay their way by normal business activities, he suggested, they should cease to operate.[29] Governor Perry, disturbed and put on the defensive by Wolfe's charge of an alliance between the state administration and the railroad faction, explained that his hands were tied by the laws of Florida in regard to railroad land grants.[30] Perry was a man of principle, but his sympathies were on the side of the railroads. His conservative philosophy, friendships, and business background made him a natural ally.

Florida's small but extremely vocal anti-railroad faction received a second, more serious setback on January 31, 1887, when the U.S. Senate Committee on Public Lands reported adversely on Call's resolution for an investigation of Florida land grants. Undismayed by this setback, Call renewed his attack, asserting that the newly opened up South Florida lands were going largely to the railroads and the Disston land companies. Out of thirty-three million arable acres in Florida, he estimated, twenty-three million had been granted for the benefit of corporations. In a brief debate, Senator John T. Morgan, an Alabama Bourbon, defended Florida's railroads.[31] In February, two adverse reports on Call-sponsored bills by the committee on Public Lands made it a certainty that this session of Congress would do nothing to aid homesteaders in their fight to obtain the better lands in the public domain at the low federal price. The committee held that the Department of the Interior was able with its normal machinery to correct the injustices brought to the attention of the Senate by Call.[32]

The winter of 1886-87 marked the entrance of California as a competitor of Florida for the tourist business. Attractive railroad rates were secured by the Far Westerners, and the country was flooded with Golden State literature. Because of a perceptible decrease in Florida's tourist industry, in the spring of 1887 the citizens of Jacksonville held a mass meeting where it was decided to establish a yearly exposition to be called the Sub-Tropical.[33]

While Jacksonville's citizens were concerning themselves with this new threat to the tourist trade, Governor Perry was becoming increasingly concerned with the prolonged absence of fellow townsman Charles W. Jones from the Senate. Senator Jones, reversing the path of the "snowbirds," absented himself from Washington during December 1885, and moved to Detroit. There the antics of the self-educated ex-carpenter as he tried to move in society and pursued an heiress made a sad spectacle.[34] Jones's sanity was very much in question. He had never been a political power in Florida; his likable and bland personality had been his chief stock in trade. But with the state's one active senator, Call, at odds with the Perry administration and the powerful railroad forces, considerable pressure was placed on the governor to replace Jones, pressure to which he finally yielded. On February 28, 1887, Perry designated ex-Congressman Jesse Johnson Finley of Jacksonville as acting senator until the legislature could fill the vacancy. Perry intimated to Finley that he desired to move from the governor's chair to the Senate. The Senate's presiding officer held that Jones was still senator. However, the Senate later adopted a resolution paying Finley's salary from March 4 to May 19.[35]

In his message to the legislature, which under the new constitution began its sessions in April instead of January, Perry emphasized the similarity between the people's interests and the railroads' interests. The legislature, however, was not in accord with the governor. White county leaders were beginning to fear railroad intrusion into their heretofore isolated spheres. To curb the railroad interests, the white counties seized upon one of the major reforms proposed by the Independents, whom they had labeled soreheads and radicals just three years earlier. John H. McKinne, a Euchee Valley Scottish farmer, introduced the commission bill, reflecting the belief of the yeomen of West Florida that their new railroad was a mixed blessing. State Senator "Farmer" Mann of Hernando, though an implacable political enemy of Wilk Call, not only took the lead to urge the state senate to pass the railroad reform bill, but also urged that an investigation be made of railroad land grants.[36] That Mann and Call could agree on objectives and yet carry on a feud would be a major obstacle to reform. Lacking the strong leadership which William A. Hocker had provided in the past, the pro-railroad legislators made no organized effort to oppose a railroad commission, the bill passing with unanimous vote in the house and only three negative votes in the senate.[37] On June 2 Perry signed the bill into law.[38]

Though Perry had been a strong party choice for governor in 1884 and his actions in office had offended few, strong opposition developed in the legislature against advancing him to the Senate. The Democratic party had been badly split in 1884 by the Bloxham-Drew feud and the desertions to the Independent movement. Perry had appealed to the county leaders then because he was a war hero without a partisan political taint. Now that he was in the middle of the political arena as governor, this appeal no longer existed. When the Democrats caucused on April 12, the anti-Perry legislators centered their support on ex-Governor Bloxham.[39] Since both men were mildly conservative, the main issue was that of personality. The caucus decided that a two-thirds majority would be necessary to nominate. Since Perry and Bloxham had almost the same number of votes, the caucus was deadlocked. Perry was accused by Editor Don McLeod of the *Tallahassean* of withholding appointments suggested by legislators who were not supporting his candidacy.[40] Bloxham had always been popular in his home town. But his entrance into this race caused the reemergence of ex-Governor George F. Drew into state politics. Considerably disturbed by the possibility that his old political adversary might become senator, Drew informed a Jacksonville *Times-Union* reporter that he would spend his last cent and his last moment of life to prevent this eventuality.[41]

The caucus now presented a trial of strength between the state administration and dissenting county leaders. While the legislature stalled, it became apparent after more than fifty ballots in the caucus that neither Perry nor Bloxham could be nominated. Now Samuel Pasco's chairmanship of the state party and his handling of the constitutional convention were to pay a major dividend. Taking advantage of the deadlock, William B. Lamar, a fellow Jefferson County representative, placed Speaker Pasco's name in nomination. Finally, on the night of May 18, after the caucus had balloted for more than a month, Bloxham and Perry withdrew and Pasco was nominated.[42] The next day the legislature made Pasco's nomination official.[43] Now both senators were from predominantly black counties.

In reapportioning the legislature in accordance with the directives set forth in the Constitution of 1885, the white county leaders at the convention demonstrated their power at the expense of the Black Belt. Santa Rosa, a West Florida white county with a population of 7,490, would elect three members of the House, the same number as Black Belt Alachua County with a population of 25,947.[44] This inequality was caused by Article Seven, section three, of the constitution, which stated that a maximum of three representatives would be allotted to a county.[45]

The bitter fight over the poll tax during the constitutional convention was not forgotten by the legislature, which killed the poll tax measure brought before it.[46] An anti-Negro measure providing separate railway cars for the races passed almost unanimously, one Negro legislator voting obsequiously in its favor.[47] The increase in population in South Florida was recognized by the formation of Pasco, Citrus, Osceola, Lake, Lee, and DeSoto counties.[48]

The actions and personnel of the 1887 legislature demonstrated that neither revolution nor even a noticeable, orderly change had been immediately brought about by the Constitution of 1885. The failure of Perry to be elected senator demonstrated that political power was in the hands of county politicians without strong leadership. These grass roots legislators could only be counted on to unite in face of a Republican or Independent threat. The slightest pressure from the state administration in behalf of Governor Perry was a contributory cause of his defeat in the senate race. Some leadership was asserted in the legislature by "Farmer" Mann as he strongly indicated that he would make a bid to take over the leadership of the anti-railroad Democrats from Senator Wilk Call.

Call, for his part, remained active in the Senate in his fight against Florida railroad land grants. In the following April he succeeded in getting a resolution through calling for the investigation of these grants. The Committee on Public Lands investigated to determine whether or not there had been illegal and fraudulent conveyance of public lands in Florida.[49] At a subcommittee hearing the chief witnesses were Call and Albert Akers, special agent for the General Land Office of the Department of the Interior. Call repeated earlier claims that the railroads had not been completed within the time limit and emphasized the fact that most of Florida was high and dry and not swamp and overflow.[50] Akers testified that numbers of settlers had complained to him that after homesteading high, rolling ground in South Florida, they were informed that they had entered public domain selected by the Disston company. When redress was sought from the Federal General Land Office, these settlers were informed that the matter was out of its jurisdiction since the state had already patented the land. The settlers, therefore, relied on Call as their court of last resort. From Akers's description, most of these homesteaders were of the poor cracker element. Handicapped by limited education and means, they were being forced off the better lands in the public domain by the railroads and the Disston land companies, which were eager to obtain these lands for resale.[51]

When the Democratic state convention met at St. Augustine, May 29, 1888, anti-Call Democrats were completely in charge. Only conservative party regulars were considered as candidates for governor. The convention shackled these candidates with the pledge that if nominated they would regard county recommendations in making the few appointments remaining to the governor. Gubernatorial hopefuls included General Robert Bullock, veteran leader of Marion's Democrats, Robert W. Davis, Palatka railroad lawyer and a clever orator known as "Our Bob" to his rapidly growing number of ardent followers, and Francis P. Fleming, junior law partner in the Jacksonville firm of Fleming and Daniel headed by his half brother, Louis Fleming. All three candidates were southern men and ex-Confederate soldiers, reflecting the composition of the convention.[52] Delegates carefully inspected the Ponce de Leon Hotel, built by Standard Oil tycoon Henry M. Flagler.[53] St. Augustine had become headquarters for Flagler's railroad, which he was soon to extend down the east coast.[54] The issue in the convention was one of personalities. Marion County, never having had a major officeholder, held out for Bullock to the bitter end. Fleming, however, had the stronger backing, winning on the fortieth ballot. Davis, an out-and-out railroad man, was never strongly in the running.[55]

Since Pasco had been elected senator it was necessary to replace him as chairman of the state Democratic executive committee. The committee's pro-railroad majority chose William D. Chipley. Upon returning to Pensacola, Chipley was serenaded by fellow townsmen in honor of his new office. Amid the strains of Dixie, Chipley announced to the serenaders that as chairman he would "utterly" disclaim personal politics and have one ambition—party unity, party harmony, and party success.[56] Commenting on his selection, editor Charles H. Jones stated in the Jacksonville *Florida Times-Union* that he was recognized as one of the boldest, shrewdest and most earnest, indefatigable workers and organizers in the state.[57] His election, however, was a definite setback to the Call faction, which had largely been kept within the ranks by the diplomatic Pasco.

Florida was now a two-party state in name only. The Republicans, badly organized and poorly led, went through the formality of waging a campaign. The once-numerous Black Belt Negro machines had disappeared one by one. In Jefferson County, Captain Jesse D. Cole, one of the few remaining white Republicans in the Black Belt, was rescued from a Democratic lynch mob by planter E. B. Bailey, who told him to pack his carpetbag and leave.[58] Without Cole, the Republican party in Jefferson collapsed completely. Only in Duval, Marion, and Leon, all predominantly Negro counties, did the Republicans continue to have strong organizations. In several Middle Florida counties, including Madison and Columbia, there was an ineffective effort to revive the Independent movement.[59] The Cuban insurrection did enable the Republicans to do a bit of flag waving. The state convention in April at Palatka, besides selecting delegates to the national convention, censured the Cleveland administration for cringing before the Spanish. One of the few young Republicans at this meeting, H. S. Chubb of Orange County, naively informed the delegates that the Republicans represented the virtue, integrity, and wealth of the state. On the other hand, those who were called anarchists in Chicago would be Democrats in Florida.[60] Meeting again in August, the Republicans found themselves in the predicament of having no one of prominence who would make the race for governor. The nomination finally went to V. J. Shipman, an ex-Union soldier who was engaged in growing strawberries at Lawtey in North Florida. Shipman was described by the Jacksonville *Florida Times-Union* as a gallant soldier and an earnest, clean, honorable man—unusual words for a Florida Democratic newspaper to use concerning a Republican candidate.[61]

While the Republican platform was decidedly pro-railroad and anti-railroad commission, an effort was made by the party to obtain the endorsement of the newly organized Florida Farmers' Alliance,[62] which was emphasizing improved agricultural methods and closer cooperation by the farmers. The Alliance had been started in June 1887, when two young organizers, Oswald Wilson and James B. Young, arrived from Texas. Wilson organized a sub-alliance in Jackson County and Young one in Citrus. The movement immediately became popular, and by the first statewide meeting in October there were sixty-five local alliances with a total membership of 2,000. Less than twenty-seven years old, Wilson became the state Alliance president. In January 1888, the local independent farmers' unions which had banded together under the leadership of the Reverend Robert F. Rogers merged with the Farmers' Alliance.[63] Wilson, continuing as president, rejected any coalition with the Republicans and personally supported Cleveland in the national election.[64] Further demonstrating the effort that the Florida Republican party was making to justify its existence, J. J. Holland, general state representative of the Knights of Labor, was actively participating as a Republican. This and the flirtation with the Farmers' Alliance indicated that the Florida Republicans were either more liberal or more desperate than the national group.[65]

Weighing three hundred pounds and possessing a good-natured disposition, candidate Shipman introduced himself at political rallies as Barnum's white elephant. Speaking from the same platform as Shipman at Tallahassee in September, ex-Congressman

Josiah T. Walls, trying valiantly to keep his race in the political ring, told the Negroes to leave all political offices to friendly whites. A little enthusiasm was injected into the Republican meeting by the singing of the following campaign song: "Oh Lord, it's all I want, it's a little more votes for Shipman . . . [Chorus:] I'll never sell out no more."[66] Disagreeing with Walls's strategy, and disgruntled at seeing the last county office, that of tax assessor, go to a white man in the Leon County Republican convention, H. S. Harmon, a Tallahassee Negro cabinet maker and former state leader of his race, asked: "If the colored man cannot have the office of Assessor, then for God's sake what can he have?"[67]

The issues in the campaign were almost nullified by the Jacksonville yellow fever epidemic. In May 1887, yellow fever had made its appearance in epidemic form at Key West, later being brought by fruit smugglers to Tampa, Manatee, and Plant City, though it was thought by some that the Plant Line transported the fever to Tampa on their fast mail service between Tampa and Havana. The disease survived a mild winter in Florida, and on July 28, 1888, a case was discovered in Jacksonville. The presence of the disease was confirmed on August 8 by the Jacksonville Board of Health and the pronouncement caused a panic; thousands of people, mostly white, crowded trains and boats to flee the city. Quarantine against Jacksonville was immediately declared by a large part of the United States. From Jacksonville the disease spread over East Florida, reaching the epidemic stage in Mac-Clenny, with cases discovered in Fernandina, Gainesville, Live Oak, and Green Cove Springs.[68] The return home of the East Florida state militia from duty at Fernandina during the Negro longshoremen's strike in September played an important part in the spread of the disease. Earlier in the year a black labor society with a membership of six hundred had been organized in the Amelia Island port by a Negro labor leader from Pensacola, stronghold of the state's black longshoremen. A strike called by the society for higher wages removed five hundred workers from the lumber wharves, leaving only twenty workers on the job. The lumber companies, banding together under ex-Governor George F. Drew, then retaliated by bringing in Negro strikebreakers from Madison. Violence ensued with the labor society defying the sheriff of Nassau County. Unable to restore order, the sheriff telegraphed Governor Perry, requesting assistance. Perry called out the East

Florida state militia. Mass arrests followed the arrival of the soldiers in Fernandina, and the strike was promptly broken. Cases
of yellow fever broke out in the home communities of the militia
shortly after their return.[69] Concerned about Florida's yellow fever
epidemic, Congress took steps to alleviate the suffering in Jacksonville and prevent the recurrence of the disease.[70]

In another matter concerning Florida, a subcommittee of the
Committee of Public Lands was hearing testimony on Florida land
grants. In a strong, notarized statement to the subcommittee on
September 7, Hamilton Disston denounced as false the testimony
by special federal land agent Albert Akers. Explaining the operation of his land companies in detail, Disston denied that they had
forcibly evicted homesteaders. The decision before the subcommittee was whether to acquiesce in the status quo, which would
connote approval of the policy of the General Land Office per-
mitting the Florida state administration to continue to patent
arable and dry land to subsidize railroad building, or to demand
a strict conformity to the swamp and overflow provision which
would mean the forfeiture of land grants and would be a serious
blow to the Florida state administration. Would the small farmer
and homesteader be favored or the railroader? The committee
decision on September 28 favored the railroaders.[71] Undismayed,
however, Call continued his fight.

Back in Florida a mild fall caused a continuation of the yellow
fever epidemic. Before federal funds had been received by Jacksonville relief workers, scores of Negroes, purportedly immune
to the fever, flocked to the city, drawn by extravagant stories of
free food and easy money.[72] Actually there were 324 white deaths
and 103 Negro deaths reported, indicating that the blacks were
more resistant to the disease but far from immune.[73] There was
some fear that the exodus of white voters caused by the epidemic
might, if the Negroes turned out in numbers, give the state to
the Republicans.[74] On election day crowds of Negro voters lolled
about the polling places, regarding with curiosity the appearance
of the few white Democrats and Republicans still in the city.[75]

Elsewhere in the state it was a Democratic landslide, Fleming
polling 40,255 votes to Shipman's 26,485. Only Duval of the predominantly Negro counties went Republican.[76] One of the defeated Democrats there, Napoleon Bonaparte Broward, a colorful
young riverboat captain and member of an old planter family,

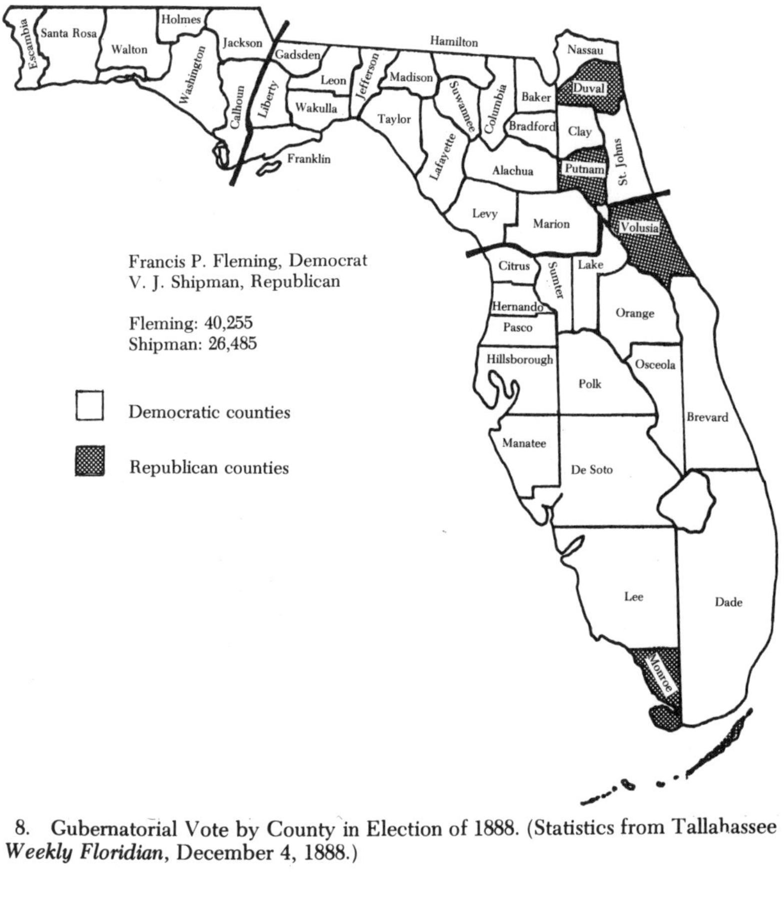
Escambia
Santa Rosa
Walton
Holmes
Washington
Jackson
Calhoun
Liberty
Gadsden
Leon
Wakulla
Franklin
Jefferson
Madison
Taylor
Hamilton
Suwannee
Lafayette
Columbia
Baker
Bradford
Nassau
Duval
Clay
Putnam
St. Johns
Alachua
Levy
Marion
Volusia
Citrus
Sumter
Lake
Hernando
Pasco
Orange
Hillsborough
Polk
Osceola
Brevard
Manatee
De Soto
Lee
Dade
Monroe
Francis P. Fleming, Democrat
V. J. Shipman, Republican
Fleming: 40,255
Shipman: 26,485
Democratic counties
Republican counties

8. Gubernatorial Vote by County in Election of 1888. (Statistics from Tallahassee *Weekly Floridian*, December 4, 1888.)

had been appointed sheriff by Governor Perry.[77] In white counties Columbia, Holmes, Walton and Putnam, single Republicans were elected to the state House of Representatives, showing that latent dissatisfaction with the Democratic party existed in these yeoman farmer areas. In South Florida the influx of Northern settlers apparently caused the election of a Republican state senator and two representatives in Volusia.[78]

U.S. Attorney General W. H. H. Miller and Judge Charles Swayne of the Northern District of Florida were unwilling to accept the election returns at face value. Miller charged that Florida election officials had refused to register seven thousand prospective Republican voters and would not permit another ten thousand Republican voters to cast their ballots. Judge Swayne, assisted by U.S. Attorney Joseph N. Stripling, took an aggressive stand against voting frauds and intimidation. Stripling was still keeping the Independent movement alive in the Black Belt and obtaining indictments against white Democrats. A black Republican, John Bird of Madison County, a witness in Stripling's investigation, was killed after returning to Madison from federal court in Jacksonville. Judge Swayne's aggressiveness would later lead to a confrontation between his court and the state government.[79]

In his inaugural address on January 8, Governor Fleming spoke of encouraging immigration and of calling a special session of the legislature to formulate state health laws to curb yellow fever. His speech, as reported in the *Floridian*, significantly omitted mention of Negro rights.[80] This was the first time since the end of the Reconstruction that an incoming Democratic governor had not specifically reassured the Negroes. Their declining political influence was most noticeable here; their failure to elect a sizable number of legislators was having its effect. In February the legislature met in special session at Fleming's request to establish a state board of health.[81] Problems brought about by yellow fever epidemics outweighed the need for governmental frugality. Dr. Joseph Y. Porter, a prominent physician of Key West, was appointed the first administrative officer of the new board.[82]

The regular session of the legislature in April quickly answered H. S. Harmon's campaign question about the Negro's political role. A caucus of Democratic legislators voted to adopt South Carolina's practice of using a separate ballot box for each office to confuse the Negro voter. William H. Milton, Jr., a grandson of Florida's wartime governor and a Bourbon representative from Jackson County, introduced the bill. Its only opposition came from Republicans and a few independent Democrats, every Black Belt Democrat voting for it in both houses. The vote in the House was forty-four to thirteen, in the Senate seventeen to seven. Further to prevent Negro voting, a poll tax was passed.[83] For all practical purposes, these actions of the legislature almost completely eliminated the Negro as an active participant in Florida politics. Only Wilk Coulter, a Democratic state senator from the piney woods of cracker Levy County, spoke out in the legislature against the passing of the eight ballot box law. Such a complicated bill, he maintained, was not in accord with true democratic principles. Election laws should be plain and simple.[84] Representative M. P. Delgado of Monroe, elected by the large Cuban cigar-making colony in Key West, naively announced that he voted for the measure because it was an educational requirement which compelled every man to vote according to the decision of his conscience and not in subjection to party bosses.[85] How a device to prevent black voting could be educational was not explained by Delgado.

The process of eliminating the black vote had been long and drawn out, starting with the violence in Jackson County in the early 1870s. The fact that the Negro was now in effect disfranchised strongly indicated grass roots sentiment in Florida. Not one of the major Democratic officeholders since the end of Reconstruction had openly advocated disfranchisement of the black man. No Florida demagogue had seized upon the Negro issue to move to a position of power within the party. It was a ground swell of Democratic opinion rising from the yeoman farmer, the small town merchant, and white lawyers in general as reflected in the legislature that eliminated the Negro, and the action of the 1889 legislature was the coup de grace. Northern settlers in South Florida, despite the myth that Northerners were more liberal on the racial issue, failed to give civil rights for the blacks substantial support. The legislature also created a board of immigration composed of the governor, secretary of state, and commissioner of agriculture.[86] Three general classifications of Northern migrants were coming into Florida: those with limited finances and bodily ailments, who expected a cure from the balmy climate; the wealthy owners of orange grove villas, who occupied them in the wintertime only; and the make-a-living toilers, whose Northern energy and common sense played an important part in the economic advancement of Florida.[87]

Simultaneously with meeting the legislature and becoming oriented to his new duties, Fleming unhappily discovered that William D. Chipley, in his capacity as Democratic state executive chairman, considered himself the party leader. In suggesting appointees to Fleming, Chipley maintained that he had a mandate from the St. Augustine Democratic convention. Fleming replied testily that he did not consider himself bound by the recommendations of the state Democratic committee and that he would not have accepted the nomination under the restrictions which Chipley now attempted to impose.[88] Although Fleming and Chipley were both pro-railroad Bourbons, their relationship was obviously strained by Chipley's aggressiveness.

Since the Indian War claim was still unsettled, Fleming retained S. I. Wailes as the state lobbyist. Wailes, who was also land agent for the state, complained that, because of the controversy raised by Call, for the past two years the United States Land Office had not been issuing patents on swamplands and had been sending investigating agents into the state.[89] The feud between Call and Chipley was now threatening to disrupt the Democratic party. On July 15 Call sent an open letter to the Jacksonville *Times-Union* asking his defamers to remove their masks for a public debate. Chipley, forgetting earlier promises of working for party harmony, on August 14 publicly accepted Call's challenge. In answer, Call taunted Chipley with being profoundly ignorant of the good sense of the people, although not lacking in boldness. Call also attacked the "vicious" railroad lobby present at the last session of Florida's legislature.[90]

Fleming felt that Chipley should remain passive as a matter of duty, because as chairman of the state Democratic executive committee he was responsible for maintaining harmony within the party. Writing Pensacola attorney Charles B. Parkhill in September, Fleming stated that although he was bitterly opposed to Call, he regretted Chipley's acceptance of Call's challenge. At the same time, the governor admitted he had never admired Chipley and would depose him as both chairman and a member of the executive committee if he had the power.[91] Chipley, however, continued as chairman until November, when he resigned from both the chairmanship and the committee, giving his controversy with

Call as the reason for his withdrawal.[92] Possibly the governor had played a role in this decision.

To spur the settlement of the Seminole War claim of Florida, Comptroller W. D. Barnes conferred with Treasury officials in Washington in the summer. He then reported back to Fleming that the outlook for settlement was favorable. Fleming in turn solicited the assistance of Senators Call and Pasco, inviting the two to Tallahassee for a conference before Congress met.[93] With the money accruing from the long-standing claim Fleming planned to construct a state prison.[94] This would have ended the highly objectionable convict-lease system and would have been the first major reform of the Bourbons since taking over the state in 1877. Though Pasco joined forces with Fleming and Wailes to pressure Congress into settling Florida's long-standing Indian War claim, Call obstinately continued to oppose their efforts.[95] In an effort to obtain Northern Republican votes for the claim bill passage, Fleming enlisted the support of Hamilton Disston, imploring the wealthy Philadelphian to "please use your influence with Congress." The need for immediate funds was urgent, Fleming informed Disston, because the new constitution had shifted expenses from the counties to the state without an accompanying shift in revenue, and local option in dry counties had cut state liquor receipts.[96] Suwannee County, for example, had just voted dry by a majority exceeding three hundred.[97] Fleming neglected to add that the faction of the Democratic party to which he belonged had largely written the constitution. In a letter in which he agreed to work for the passage of the Indian War claim, Disston also displayed enthusiasm concerning his investments in Florida and mentioned that he was receiving good reports from his sugar plantation at St. Cloud.[98] The exchange of letters was indicative of the tie-in between Florida Bourbonism and Northern industry.

Strange Bedfellows

From 1880 to 1890 the population of Florida increased from 269,493 to 391,422.[1] Along with this increase Florida added 10,790 farms, with the average farm undergoing a marked decrease in size, indicative of the influx of yeoman farmers who would swell the ranks of the Florida Farmers' Alliance.[2] Membership in the state alliance was estimated at twenty thousand in July 1889, with a total of 372 local alliances. By December the membership had risen to twenty-five thousand. In April of the following year, local alliances flourished in all but four counties, none of which were important agriculturally.[3]

Although the Florida Farmers' Alliance had started out as a nonpartisan grass roots organization, it soon attracted the politically ambitious.[4] As interest in politics increased, two factions emerged: the conservative group, led by the Reverend Robert F. Rogers of Suwannee County; and the agrarian reform group, headed by A. P. Baskin of Marion County. A compromise between the two factions was achieved in January 1889, whereby Rogers became president of the Alliance and Baskin the secretary. The *Florida Farmers' Alliance* made its appearance as the official paper, only to merge in January 1889 with the Jacksonville *Florida Dispatch*. During 1890 and 1891, at least seven other pro-Alliance papers were published.[5]

The rise of the Farmers' Alliance did not immediately affect Democratic party machinery. In January 1890, Stephen M. Sparkman, Tampa political leader and attorney for railroader Henry

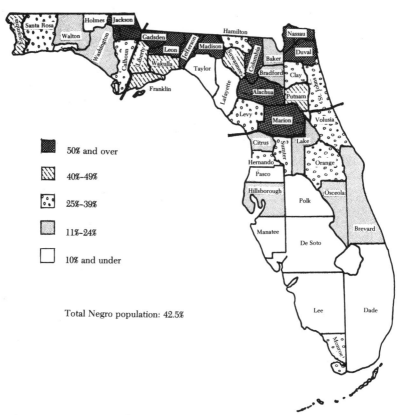

Santa Rosa
Holmes **Jackson**
Escambia
Walton
Washington
Calhoun
Gadsden
Liberty
Leon **Jefferson** **Madison** **Hamilton**
Wakulla **Suwannee**
Franklin **Taylor** **Lafayette** **Columbia** **Baker** **Nassau**
Bradford **Duval**
Alachua **Clay**
Levy **Putnam** **St. Johns**
Marion **Volusia**
Citrus **Sumter** **Lake**
Hernando **Orange**
Pasco
Hillsborough **Osceola**
Polk **Brevard**
Manatee
De Soto
Lee **Dade**
Monroe

50% and over

40%–49%

25%–39%

11%–24%

10% and under

Total Negro population: 42.5%

9. Ratio of Negro Distribution by County, 1890. (Statistics from the U.S. Census Office, Eleventh Census, 1890.)

B. Plant's enterprises, became chairman of the Democratic State Executive Committee.[6] But the anxiety of the farmers to inject agrarian reform into politics was beginning to attract the attention of the conservative element in the state. The *Pensacola Daily News*, acting as spokesman for the ever aggressive leader of this faction, William D. Chipley, warned the farmers in its editorial columns not to bring the Alliance into the Democratic party but to continue to participate in that party as individuals, because it had always been the farmer's friend. There were other interests deserving of representation besides those of the farmer, the editorial significantly added; those who would use the Alliance for political purposes were enemies of the farmer.[7]

Meanwhile, without joining the Alliance, Senator Call continued his fight for homesteads and against railroad land grants. Feeling that Call was misrepresenting these issues, in late January 1890, Governor Fleming wrote him defending the policy of the Democratic party of encouraging railroad construction by offering land grants. There was plenty of free land, according to Fleming, and any citizen of the state could buy eighty acres at twenty-five cents an acre.[8]

One of the few issues in which Call and Fleming were in agreement involved the efforts of federal Judge Charles Swayne to make it possible for black voters in Middle Florida to cast their ballots without fraud and intimidation. Veteran South-watcher Senator William E. Chandler of New Hampshire brought the matter of intimidation, murder, and election frauds in Middle Florida to the floor of the Senate in February 1891. "Murder," he charged, "is an old weapon of the Democrats of Florida." Chandler was a longtime adversary of Southern Democrats, having been a national Republican investigator in Florida as early as 1876 and later the cabinet official charged with Southern affairs in the Arthur administration. Now he accused Governor Fleming and Senators Pasco and Call of being more interested in hunting down Judge Swayne, U.S. Attorney Stripling, and U.S. Marshal John R. Mizell than in bringing murderers to trial. Pasco blamed the decline in votes between 1884 and 1888 on the yellow fever epidemic but failed to explain why, if the Negroes were immune, their vote had fallen off drastically. It fell to Call to defend law enforcement in Florida, and his defence was virulent. Call accused Judge Swayne of sending desperate, reckless, and lawless men to stir up peaceful communities and cause a war of the races, giving vent to the "wild lust and passions" of the blacks. Interspersed amid racist remarks were affirmations of the "protection, friendship, and sympathy" of Southern people toward Negroes. To answer complaints about the absence of convictions insofar as law and order in Florida were concerned, he pointed out that there were unsolved Western murders. Two wrongs, apparently, made a right. Though an ex-Whig and a member of an old aristocratic Florida family, Call was now identifying himself with the cracker and white yeoman farmer who desired that the Negro be kept in his place.[9] He also advocated at this time that the United States purchase Cuba from Spain for use as a dumping ground for discontented blacks.[10]

Despite Call's attack Judge Swayne proceeded with his plans to try several white Democrats from Madison County for election frauds. The trials were to be held in Jacksonville, where Democrats feared that the juries would be packed with Republican partisans. Emotions were running so high in Middle Florida that U.S. Marshal Edmund C. Weeks, an old-time carpetbagger, was refused horse-hire and hotel accommodations while in the execution of ordinary civil cases. Feeling that Democrats could not have a fair trial under Swayne, Governor Fleming personally appealed to President Harrison. It was Harrison's decision to follow Hayes's reconciliation policy of 1876 and not force the issue of civil rights on southern states such as Florida, regardless of the evidence. Another judge was sent into Florida to replace Swayne in the vote fraud cases.[11] The refusal of the federal government to protect black civil rights in Middle Florida would eliminate what fertile ground was there for the Populist party.

With Florida now for all intents and purposes a one-party state, the Bourbon Democrats decided to purge Senator Wilk Call. Veteran railroader William D. Chipley led the fight, publishing and distributing widely throughout the state a booklet entitled *Review of Senator Call's Record*. Paradoxically ignoring the obvious fact that it was Call's anti-Bourbon activism that had caused the feud, Chipley labeled him a do-nothing senator who had ridden into office on the coattails of his uncle and brother. The Chipley booklet was essentially an effort to eliminate grass roots support for Florida's crusty senior senator. Chipley accused Call of being a lobbyist, of cheating a poor Negro out of his homestead, of being involved in a bank scandal, and of acting in bad faith in opposing settlement of the Indian War claim. He also charged that Call had been involved in the Swepson-Littlefield railroad frauds in Reconstruction and had been disloyal to the Democratic party by encouraging the Independent movement in 1884. Further, Call had wrongfully stated that homesteaders opposed land grants. The Louisville and Nashville Railroad (owner of the Pensacola and Atlantic), Chipley stated, had had no litigation with Florida settlers for the last six years.[12]

Call answered Chipley's charges in the Senate on June 2, 1890. The senior Florida senator was then on such important committees as Appropriations, Fisheries, Immigration, and Mines and Mining. To the criticism concerning inactivity, Call replied that 238 bills he had introduced had eventually become law. The Indian War claim if settled would give state lobbyist Wailes a large fee at the expense of the just claims of soldiers and widows. His part in the Swepson-Littlefield frauds was an attempt to keep Swepson and Littlefield from obtaining control of a railroad. Turning to the offensive, Call termed Chipley a legislative lobbyist and convention manipulator whose chief political work as chairman of the Democratic State Executive Committee consisted of sending out quantities of documents, chiefly concerning himself. Call thought that Chipley was an embarrassment and obstacle to Florida's Democratic party. In answer to the assertion that the Louisville and Nashville had not had litigation for the past six years, Call read to his fellow senators a letter from a settler who claimed that the railroad had sold his homestead from under him.[13]

Call and Chipley agreed to debate their differences July 1, in the heart of the South Florida land grant country at Arcadia. Speaking first, Chipley faced a slightly hostile pro-Call audience. A Call lieutenant, Frank Clark, a young Bartow lawyer, interrupted several times. But a show of fair play was made by the gathering and Chipley was able to complete his speech, consisting mainly of repetition of his pamphlet accusations. Belittling Call's claim that some of the swamp and overflow lands were as high and dry as the United States capitol, he asserted that only two hills in Florida were as high as that.

In answering Chipley, Call had the audience with him all the way as he pictured his rival as a stranger who represented a corporation and corporate powers. Call disparaged the Chipley pamphlet, asserting that "A piney woods boy could do better."

Taking full advantage of his hold on the South Florida farmers, Call invited his "cracker" friends to stay with him when they visited Washington. When the meeting closed neither speaker had touched conclusively on the main issue: priority for public lands— homestead or railroad land grant.[14]

Newspaper reports conflicted, some giving the verdict to Call and some to Chipley, but neither gained stature by the debate. The Palatka *Times* dubbed Call the "swamp angel" who would rather make personal attacks like a schoolboy than refute charges. The result was a Call victory, according to the pro-Call Jacksonville *Florida Times-Union*. The *Tampa Tribune*, however, came nearest to the truth in its statement that the Call people were sure that their man won, while the Chipley crowd was just as certain of victory.[15]

A second major clash between Call and Chipley occurred at the Democratic State Convention at Ocala. Here Chipley had the support of the state administration, the Democratic State Executive Committee, and the majority of county leaders. Just prior to the meeting, Governor Fleming informed Chipley with obvious pleasure that Leon County was sending an anti-Call delegation to Ocala.[16] Despite a pro-Call delegation from Duval, James P. Talliaferro, a conservative anti-Call man from the same county, was reelected chairman of the Democratic State Executive Committee, a strong indication that the Bourbons did not plan to offer a compromise to the Call forces.[17]

In strange contrast to the cold reception which the Call faction met, the representatives of the Farmers' Alliance were enthusiastically received. Robert W. "Our Bob" Davis, silver-tongued orator of the railroad interests, officially welcomed the Florida Farmers' Alliance into the Democratic party and nominated its president, the Reverend Robert F. Rogers, to be vice-president of the convention. Accepting this purely honorary post, Rogers affirmed his belief in the Democratic party.[18] An Alliance newspaper, the *Florida Farmers Advocate*, revealed the part which the Rogers faction expected the Alliance to play when it praised Chipley as a loyal Democrat and announced that the combined forces of honest Democrats and loyal Alliancemen would defeat Call.[19] Although the coalition of Alliancemen and Bourbons to defeat Call seemed on the surface a strange union of opposites, underneath there were several factors that made the fusion possible. First, "Farmer"

Mann and several agrarian leaders considered Call a demagogue, lacking sincerity in his support of the small farmer.[20] Second, those of the conservative wing of the Alliance held views similar to those of the railroad and business interests. Members of this wing of the Alliance would not leave the Democratic party for Populism. Their philosophy was basically conservative, not radical. Significantly, when Call spoke in September at the Semi-Tropical Alliance day meeting, he paid tribute to A. P. Baskin, leader of the radical wing of the Florida Alliance. Baskin was not a Call man.[21] He and Call would debate in early October.[22]

Considering the conservatism of the major wing of the Florida Alliance, it was not surprising that in late September C. B. Collins, a strong Allianceman, advocated the nomination for senator of former state Senator John F. Dunn of Ocala. Collins asserted that he spoke for thousands of Alliancemen.[23] A man of limited education and of charitable disposition, Dunn had achieved wealth in the central Florida phosphate boom. Known as "Phosphate King" Dunn, he regularly supplied gifts at county fairs, a habit which had made him quite popular with rural people.[24] Dunn had also extracted the Florida Alliance from an embarrassing situation at the December 1889 St. Louis meeting when a delegation led by President Rogers had invited the National Farmers' Alliance to hold its 1890 convention in Florida. Up to this time no national convention of any sort had ever been held in the state. In extending the invitation Rogers had in mind the Alliance's utilizing Jacksonville's thriving tourist facilities. Large hotels were available to house the delegates and the Sub-Tropical Exposition building had sufficient space for the meetings. Excellent rail and water connections made the port city most accessible to travelers. Unfortunately, Rogers had done no prior planning. Both the Sub-Tropical Exposition officials and the Jacksonville Board of Trade, representing the business community, reacted coldly to the idea of playing hosts to the agrarian reform movement. No substantial concessions were forthcoming. Realizing that he had a convention and no city, Rogers appealed for help to the Florida Alliance's wealthy friend, John F. Dunn.

Although Ocala had a population of slightly less than three thousand, Dunn responded with an immediate invitation, pledging $5,000 of his own money and promising that Ocala would provide an equal amount. Dunn's invitation extended free use of the Ocala

Semi-Tropical Building and grounds, which for the duration of
the meeting would be under Alliance management. All gate receipts were to go to the Alliance. Convention delegates were to
be entertained at half price, and the National Alliance officers were
to be housed, fed, and entertained free of charge. Dunn promised
to make an effort to get the railroads to reduce their rates. Later
Ocala increased its appropriation to $7,000 to aid the Florida
Alliance in setting up its exhibits. In all, Ocala's offer was worth
about $15,000. Ironically, the one large hotel in Ocala was the
Ocala House, owned by railroader Henry B. Plant. Thus, the sons
of agrarian reform were coming to Florida at the invitation of
a national banker to be housed by a railroad man. To supplement
the hotel in handling the expected overflow crowd, seventy-five
cottages were built.[25]

In the off-year political contests in the fall of 1890, the Republicans succeeded in nominating a full slate of candidates for the
statewide offices. When Stephen R. Mallory, the Younger, replaced
Robert H. M. Davidson as Democratic nominee in the First Congressional District, the Republicans countered by nominating the
incumbent's scalawag brother. When he declined, ex-Governor
Harrison Reed became the Republican nominee. Always a vigorous and fearless campaigner, Reed denounced the Democrats
for not allowing equal civil rights, maintaining that they had won
in 1876 through fraud and in fourteen years of rule had raised
taxes, cheated the ignorant, and squandered the public domain.
At the same time, he proclaimed that the Republican cornerstone
was that all men are born free and endowed with the inalienable
rights of life, liberty, and the pursuit of happiness.[26]

In the fall, openly breaking with the Bourbon-dominated Democratic State Executive Committee, Call conducted an independent
canvass of the state.[27] More like a lieutenant of Chipley than the
leader of the radical wing of the Alliance, A. P. Baskin debated
the anti-Bourbon senator at Ocala in early October. Baskin asserted
that Call had not answered Chipley's charges and had voted for
a national bank charter bill in 1882. Instead of going on the defensive and answering Baskin, Call attacked monopoly, autocracy,
and plutocracy. He called on the Democratic party to deprive
the railroad owners of their great power, and he declared that
Chipley was spending $30,000 to defeat him. He also read a letter
from Baskin, written the previous April, in which Baskin called

Governor Fleming too much a railroad man and urged Call to "spit back on them on every occasion." Call was clearly the winner of the debate, his speech constantly interrupted by applause.[28] Later in the month, Baskin suffered defeat in seeking renomination for the legislature from Marion County. The *Ocala Banner* looked on the result of this contest as an Alliance defeat and a victory for the railroads.[29] Without political office, Baskin's leadership position was weakened. Thus when the state Alliance met at Monticello in the closing days of the month, "Farmer" Mann, instead of Baskin, was placed in nomination by the radical wing to unseat Rogers as president of the Alliance. Rogers won reelection easily.[30]

Also in October ex-Independent leader Frank W. Pope spoke at an Ocala Democratic rally. Pope's topic was American history and the constitution. Through with third party reform movements, Pope told his listeners that the Democratic party was the party of the people. The *Ocala Banner* described his speech as broad, commanding, and patriotic.[31]

The state election came off quietly in early November despite an abortive attempt by Pensacola Republicans to trade four hundred Negro votes to certain Democratic legislative candidates in return for local offices.[32] Throughout the state, black voters were completely befuddled by the eight ballot box system of surreptitious disfranchisement.[33] The Republican party was completely defeated. Its sole representative in the state legislature, Senator O. B. Smith, would come from St. Johns, a white county.[34] The Black Belt was solidly Democratic for the first time since the end of the Civil War. A large majority of the members of the legislature claimed membership in the Alliance.[35]

Attention within Florida turned immediately from the election to the National Farmers' Alliance Convention which opened on December 2 at Ocala with all the fanfare Florida could generate. After Southern Alliance President Leonidas L. Polk had called the meeting to order, the assembly sang "Pull for the Farmer," the official Kansas campaign song. Governor Fleming welcomed the delegates with bland words describing the beauties of Florida and Florida women.[36] While the Alliance's national leaders planned agrarian reform, John F. Dunn, continuing to act as chief benefactor of the Florida Alliance, offered several premiums ranging from $100 to $150 for the best general exhibits of local alliances.

A half-page national bank advertisement in the program, however, reminded Alliance members of Dunn's presidency of an institution opposed by the National Alliance.[37] Unabashed by the fact that their Florida hospitality was being provided by the hated corporations, the National Alliancemen continued along the radical path towards a third party. Even President Rogers of the Florida Alliance exclaimed in his speech of welcome: "The Alliance has revolutionized American politics and filled the bloody chasm. Let the solid West lead the way, and the solid South will join it in chaining and taming the lion of the East."[38]

The St. Louis Demands, announced by the Southern Alliance and Knights of Labor in December 1889, provided the keynote for President Polk. The Ocala Demands, adopted on the last day of the meeting, were passed by a vote of seventy-nine to ten, Florida's delegates voting solidly in the affirmative. The Ocala Demands called for the abolition of national banks and the substitution of sub-treasuries which would make loans on farm products for a low rate of interest, for increasing the circulating medium to not less than $50 per capita, and for the free and unlimited coinage of silver. The Demands also contained provisions for an income tax and were against high protective tariffs, for government control of transportation, and against dealings in commodity futures.[39]

Third party advocates, led by the Kansas delegates, were anxious to formulate plans along national lines. Successes scored by the Alliance in 1890 elections greatly stimulated this agitation. The Southern Alliance, however, was not interested in splitting the white vote and was primarily concerned with securing control of the Democratic party. To avert a split between the Western and Southern wings of the Alliance, a compromise offered by W. C. McCune, chairman of the National Executive Committee of the Alliance, was adopted. This postponed the decision on a third party until February 1892, the time of the next national convention. Advocates of a third party, dissatisfied with the McCune compromise, issued a call for a third-party organizing convention to meet in Cincinnati in February 1891. A minority of Southern Alliance delegates signed the third party call; the Florida Alliance officially remained aloof.[40]

While the Florida Alliance had had advertising Florida in mind in inviting the national group, and tours planned by "Farmer"

Mann had accomplished this objective, there were other results. The conservative wing, particularly in South Florida, was considerably disheartened by the radical flavor of the Ocala Demands. Within two months of meeting, the Sarasota Alliance dissolved because of the sub-treasury plan. Other local alliances were torn by internal strife.[41] Instead of attempting to reconcile the differences within the Alliance, President Rogers now became engrossed in politics. In a determined effort to make John F. Dunn the next United States senator, Rogers, Dunn, Chipley, and E. J. Triay traveled the state, conducting secret meetings which were obviously used for planning anti-Call strategy.[42] It was plain that the conservative leadership of the Florida Alliance had entered into a coalition with the railroad politicians. Agrarian reform was abandoned for practical politics.

The legislative meeting to convene in April would provide the test of strength for the Alliance. Alone among the major office-holders, Wilk Call had fought the battle for the white yeoman farmers and crackers of the piney woods. Would he be abandoned for new friends who talked agrarian reform and yet consorted with national bankers and railroad men? There were, according to different estimates, from fifty-five to sixty-two Alliance legislators, giving the Alliance control if it operated as a solid bloc.[43] Of this number, however, only twenty-nine were primarily farmers.[44]

At the start of the legislative session, the venerable Tallahassee *Floridian* appeared as a daily, its editorials and news columns devoted to defeating Call. The once mighty spokesman of the state Democratic party was reduced to the menial role of smear sheet.[45] Now a member of the legislature and still pro-Call, Frank Clark later asserted that the *Daily Floridian* was subsidized by John F. Dunn, William D. Chipley, and other anti-Call politicians.[46]

On the night of April 6 the Democratic legislators caucused to elect the president of the Senate and Speaker of the House. The election of Call men in both positions showed that the Alliancemen were not voting a bloc. Jefferson B. Browne, a Key West lawyer, defeated Joseph F. Baya of Columbia for president; Dr. J. L. Gaskins, relatively unknown politically, was the choice of the House over ex-Congressman Charles Dougherty. Neither Browne nor Gaskins was a farmer. The defeat of Dougherty was a major setback to the railroad interests. The solitary Republican legislator was described by a witty reporter as being perpetually in caucus.[47] Present in the legislature as a state senator from Suwannee County, President Rogers of the Alliance led the attack on Call, requesting Alliancemen not to endorse a gold Democrat. At the same time, Rogers reluctantly announced that the Alliance would not support Dunn because he was a national banker.[48] Dunn was at this time counting on a nucleus of forty Alliance votes.[49] It was evident that this last-minute desertion was caused by pressure from the radical wing of the Alliance. Commenting on the withdrawal of Alliance support from Dunn, A. P. Baskin, the radical faction leader, stated in the *Ocala Banner*: "Were Mr. Dunn the director of the plow and not a national till box we should rejoice to support him."[50] Abandoned by his fair-weather Alliance friends, Dunn withdrew from the contest.[51]

The legislative session showed promise of being the stormiest since the end of Reconstruction. It had hardly begun when Frank Clark introduced a measure to eliminate the railroad commission.[52] The commission had met with moderate success; its freight schedules, except for phosphate, had been complied with; and in 1891, only the Florida Southern Railroad, in the hands of a receiver, was not complying with its passenger rates. The commission's only serious defeat had been at the hands of William D. Chipley, who carried an adverse ruling against the Pensacola and Atlantic rates to the state supreme court, where it was reversed.[53] Several years later Clark gave as his reason for the bill the expected nomination of E. J. Triay, an extreme pro-railroad man, by Governor Fleming, indicating that the anti-railroad group preferred no railroad commission to one dominated by the railroads.[54]

The Alliance was now without a candidate. Combining with a few lukewarm Call supporters, the anti-Call legislators had managed to have the two-thirds rule adopted by the Democratic caucus by a vote of fifty-six to forty.[55] To prevent Call from being nominated on the first ballot, the Alliance entered ex-Governor Bloxham in the race. Ironically, the man responsible for the Disston Sale had his name seconded by President Rogers. Though he had endorsed none of the Ocala Demands, the Alliance's political future temporarily depended on Bloxham. On the first ballot Call had sixty votes to Bloxham's thirty-five, needing only a change of three votes for election. A large number of the Alliance members were now supporting Call.[56] To bring these legislators back

into the Alliance ranks and defeat Call, Rogers withdrew Bloxham's name and nominated an Allianceman. Judge James G.
Speer, like Rogers, came from the conservative faction of the Alliance and had been a member of the Constitutional Convention
of 1885. "Farmer" Mann seconded Speer's nomination.[57] Mann was
bitterly opposed to a third term for Call, and his harsh laugh could
be heard over the clamor of politics as he sought to reunite the
Alliance.[58]

Bribery attempts and a shooting scrape further disrupted the
session of the legislature, which was accomplishing little as its
Democratic members caucused. The shooting involved S. S. Har-
vey, a prominent Pensacola Allianceman, and James Alexander,
Call's secretary. Neither participant was injured but both were
fined by the town authorities for creating a disturbance.[59] Bribery
accusations were leveled by both factions. State Representative
Walton Whitehurst of Hillsborough was the first to report a bribe,
claiming that he had been offered $500 by ex-State Senator J. H.
McClellan to vote for Call. This attempt was promptly condemned
by Call, and Whitehurst amended his original charge by stating
McClellan told him that it was worth $500 to vote for Call.[60] A
second, more serious, bribery attempt involved a letter from J.
R. Newlen, an anti-Call lobbyist, to John L. Bryant of Polk County.
Newlen promised Bryant $100 to vote against Call. The letter was
made public in the house of representatives by Dannite H. Mays,
a rising young Jefferson County planter-lawyer.[61] Both episodes
were allowed to die by the legislature; neither investigation nor
punitive action followed.

As the balloting continued daily in caucus, it became evident
that Speer was not attracting the Alliancemen who were supporting Call. To explain the weakness of the Alliance in politics, C.
B. Collins, the "Sandspur philosopher," and state lecturer of the
Alliance, rationalized in a letter to the Tallahassee *Daily Floridian*
that "our Alliance people have been farming and not in public
life."[62] Unperturbed by the deadlock, Call continued to conduct
his campaign with quiet dignity. His manner, according to the
Ocala Banner, if gaining him no friends, did not make enemies.[63]
The legislature continued to split its vote, awaiting the decision
of the Democratic caucus.[64]

On May 5 the Alliance withdrew Speer's name and placed
Dannite H. Mays in the race. Allianceman State Senator Thomas

F. Swearingen of Wakulla protested against the arbitrary actions of the Alliance leaders and announced that he would continue to vote for Call.[65] Because both Mays and Senator Samuel Pasco resided in Monticello, the election of Mays would have been a serious blow to Pasco's chances for a second term; therefore, Pasco opposed his candidacy. As senator, Pasco was steering a middle course between the railroad and anti-railroad factions. The nomination of Mays by the Alliance-railroad group caused him to make a temporary alliance with the anti-railroaders.[66] Alliance members were split evenly in caucus, twenty-eight voting for Call and twenty-eight supporting Mays. After the eighty-sixth caucus ballot on May 25, seeing that a compromise was impossible, state Senator D. H. Yancey of Lake moved that the caucus be dissolved *sine die*. Frank Clark seconded this Call maneuver which was carried by the narrow margin of forty-nine to forty-eight.[67]

The following day, seventeen of the thirty-two senators absented themselves to prevent any balloting. However, since the legislature balloted in joint session and a majority was present, President Jefferson B. Browne ruled that a quorum existed. In the balloting Call received fifty-one votes, Mays one.[68] The *Ocala Banner*, which originally supported Dunn, remarked that nearly every newspaper in the state had been against Call, and that every prominent member of the Alliance, the allied railroads, and the most intelligent and progressive members of the legislature had been against his renomination. His victory, the *Banner* concluded, demonstrated the strong hold he had on the people.[69] The Titusville *Florida Star* attributed Call's reelection to Chipley, because it was his opposition to Call that solidified the anti-railroad elements in the state.[70]

Unaware that Call was being renominated, sixteen of the missing senators picnicked with a few representatives in the woods north of Tallahassee. Prominent among them were President Rogers, "Farmer" Mann, and Charles Dougherty. Upon their return to Tallahassee, they were serenaded by the Tallahassee Silver Cornet Band in front of the Leon Hotel. The *Daily Floridian* called them "Fugitives from Injustice."[71] The Jacksonville *Daily Florida Times-Union* ridiculed them as "babes in the woods," a name by which the incident became known.[72] The *Times-Union* was owned by John N. C. Stockton, a national banker and strong Call supporter. The senator's enemies claimed that by accepting such support,

Call showed he was not sincere in his fight against the corporation interests.[73] Stockton, however, was an independent-minded individual and not tied in with the Bourbons.

The second major issue before the legislature, repeal of the railroad commission, caused a new lineup. Call supporters joined President Rogers of the Alliance in destroying the commission, an action which cost the Florida farmers thousands of dollars.[74] This move amazed even the strongly pro-railroad *Daily Floridian*, which editorially asked why the Alliancemen destroyed the railroad commission, opposed Call, took a critical attitude toward the Florida Agricultural College and Experiment Station, and did away with the Bureau of Immigration.[75] The answer to this question had already been supplied by the DeLand *Florida Agriculturist*. This combination newspaper and farmer's magazine, which strongly opposed the Alliance participation in politics, stated that many legislators were Alliancemen for revenue only.[76] In the 1891 legislature, President Rogers and the conservative wing used the Alliance to aid Chipley against Call, the nomination of Alliancemen for senator being for that alone, not for agrarian reform. The repeal of the railroad commission, the lack of interest in higher education, and the elimination of the Bureau of Immigration were indicative of a return to the policy of the Bourbons of the previous decade, the policy of encouraging railroads, practicing economy in government, and opposing higher education. Instead of the reform legislature which many farmers hoped for, except for the election of Call, conservatism dominated. More than ever before, radical members of the Alliance wanted to abandon the Democratic party. Writing to the DeLand *Volusia County Record*, one of the discontented, who signed himself "Farmer," stated that the old parties had nothing to offer except old dead issues of the past. "Let the bloody shirt be buried, and the animosities of race relegated to the archives of ancient history," was his advice.[77]

Governor Fleming refused to recognize Call's reelection as valid and in September appointed ex-Congressman Robert H. M. Davidson to be United States senator. In an interview with a reporter from the *Weekly Floridian*, Davidson announced that he did not believe Call had been legally elected; therefore, he was going to make a fight for the seat.[78] Dr. John L. Crawford, the Florida secretary of state and a strong Call man, refused to sign Davidson's commission. Upon its return unsigned, Fleming without comment sent it a second time to the secretary of state. Crawford went storming into the governor's office, slammed the commission down on his desk, and angrily affirmed: "I'll be damned if I do."[79] Since the attorney general, William B. Lamar, was also a Call man, Fleming employed private counsel and brought legal proceedings against Crawford, forcing him to sign Davidson's appointment. Fleming next published a pamphlet, entitled *Did the Florida Legislature of 1891 Elect a Senator?*[80] A copy of this pamphlet was sent to each United States senator. On December 8, Call was seated by the United States Senate, and the contested election was referred to the Senate Committee on Privileges and Elections.[81] Senator James Z. George of Mississippi, speaking on the contest, criticized Governor Fleming for usurping power belonging to the Senate.[82] The report by the Committee on Privileges and Elections favored Call, and its adoption by the Senate ended the contest.[83] The conservative Bourbons had suffered their first serious defeat since Reconstruction. How much Call's stand for white supremacy helped him in his senatorial fight is open to conjecture.

10

The Populist Fiasco

Though their first venture into politics had ended in disaster, the Alliancemen did not return to a non-political basis. But following the legislative session there were definite signs that the Alliance was on the downgrade. By August, seven of the 676 local Alliances had turned in their charters. The annual meeting in October revealed that the number of dues-paying Alliancemen had been reduced from the 7,688 of the previous year to 5,460. It was announced at the meeting, sessions of which were held behind closed doors, that the decline was caused by increased dues and salaries.[1] Important as these factors might have been, they were minor compared to the failure of the Alliance's political activity. In the main address at the annual meeting, President Robert F. Rogers recommended that the Alliance elect a new state president. Speaking of the rising third party sentiment within the Florida Alliance, Rogers reaffirmed his strong belief in the Democratic party. There was no need for a third party, he asserted, and this position was strengthened by the presence at the meeting of Senator Pasco, who assured the Alliancemen that their interests would best be served within the Democratic fold. Led by Rogers, however, the convention adopted the Ocala Demands by a vote of seventy-one to five, only Orange County and Senator Pasco opposing.[2] Renominated, Rogers was given deafening and continuous applause by the convention, which then proceeded to reelect A. P. Baskin as secretary by a vote of forty-one to thirty.[3]

More than ever before the Farmers' Alliance was now politically active. Ex-Confederate brigadier Robert Bullock was reported in

May 1892 to be worried over a clash with the Alliance concerning the state's Seminole War claim.[4] The Alliance, however, went into the Democratic state convention in Tampa without endorsing a single candidate. The Bourbons—the Fleming administration, the railroads, and conservative county leaders—had as their candidate state circuit Judge Henry L. Mitchell of Tampa. But hard as ex-Congressman Charles Dougherty was working, prior to the convention the Bourbons did not have a majority of delegates pledged to Mitchell.[5] Mitchell was not "to the manner born." As a youth he had migrated to Florida with his father driving an ox-team. During the Civil War he had held the rank of captain in the Fourth Florida Infantry. In addition to being a circuit judge, he had served on the state supreme court and in the legislature. He also had a reputation for "scrupulous and exact official honesty."[6] His narrow concept that a frugal government was the best government no doubt pleased the Bourbons.

Delegates arriving in Tampa on May 30 were greeted by a full-page advertisement in the *Tampa Daily Tribune* which proclaimed: "Tampa is the coming Metropolis of Florida."[7] The wigwam in which the convention was held was a remarkable open structure on the old Fort Brooke reservation. The roof of the wigwam was built to permit moss-clad liveoaks to pass through. Pillars supporting the roof were covered with palmetto and entwined with streamers and flags.[8] While the Mitchell Club met to make final arrangements, an anti-Mitchell group attempted to center its strength on a second conservative, "Our Bob" Davis. Surprisingly quiet for the past six months, the Alliancemen came boldly to the front in the opening days of the meeting, threatening that if the convention did not endorse the Ocala Demands, the Alliance as a body would join the third party.[9]

Contested delegations arrived from Sumter, Polk, and Duval counties. Stephen M. Sparkman, the temporary chairman, seated the conservative factions after vigorous questioning by Alexander St. Clair Abrams, spokesman for the Call anti-Bourbon supporters. The convention vote of 237 to 178 sustaining Sparkman indicated that conservatives controlled the meeting. A delegation from Duval led by Senator Wilk Call was among those not seated.[10] The committee on credentials later endorsed Sparkman's decisions.

On the night of June 1, the Farmers' Alliance delegates caucused and again combined with the railroad faction, agreeing to Mitchell in return for a pro-Alliance platform. The following day, Mitchell was nominated without opposition; "Our Bob" Davis saved face by seconding his nomination. The Alliance was represented on the committee on platform by A. W. Weeks, its state lecturer. While not completely accepting the Ocala Demands, the majority report attempted to include enough agrarian reform planks in the platform to hold the farmer to the Democratic party. The platform called for redress for the farmer, financial reform, abolition of national banks, government control of railroads, free silver, and fifty dollars per capita of currency in circulation. Weeks dissented, holding out for complete adoption of the Ocala Demands. During the debate that ensued, St. Clair Abrams asked Weeks, who he assumed was an official spokesman of the Alliance, whether he would support the Democratic nominees if the vote were adverse to him. Weeks answered, "I yield to the majority."[11] This can only be interpreted to mean that the Alliance accepted the decision of the convention to approve the majority report. The Democrats did, however, make more concessions to the Alliance. Two of its most prominent members were nominated for cabinet posts: C. B. Collins of Marion County for state treasurer, and W. M. Sheats of Alachua County for superintendent of public instruction.[12] Highly pleased with the concessions gained at the Tampa convention, conservative Alliancemen asserted that the threat of a third-party movement had been averted.[13]

Toward the end of June, however, rumor was rampant that the Alliance would bolt the Democratic party in the coming election,[14] and the rumors were confirmed on June 23, when the Titusville *Florida Star* carried the announcement that a third-party convention would be held in Jacksonville on July 14. Not a pro-Alliance newspaper, the *Star* took A. P. Baskin and A. W. Weeks to task for participating in the Tampa Democratic convention and then refusing to support the party because their demands were not met. It described their followers as a "heterogeneous squad of disaffects, restless agitators, disbanded Republicans, and tabooed scalawags."[15]

The new third party would go into the campaign with every daily and most weeklies in the state supporting the Democrats. The *Tampa Daily Tribune*, on receiving news of the emergence of a third-party movement, attacked Weeks, Baskin, and "Farmer" Mann. The *Pensacola Daily News*, which only a year before had been a staunch defender of the Alliance in the fight against Call, ridiculed the new party.[16] The Populists resorted to the tactics of the Independents in answering their critics. The Alliance page in the *Ocala Banner* declared: "Our own Baskin has heard the wild eagle's shriek from the mountain and has now loosed his feet from the rotten rigging of the old ship to rise above the rocky crags of prejudice and party, divorce the State Alliance from her bonds of matrimony to Democracy, and with the orange blossoms from this unholy wedlock soar away. . . . The thunder in November will shake the Solid South to pieces."[17]

The strange coalition between Allianceman and Bourbon, engendered by hatred of Senator Call, was now at an end. After years of working within the Democratic party, even playing a major role in preventing the spread of Independentism in South Florida in 1884, "Farmer" Mann had bolted, claiming that the Alliance had been sold out at Tampa. Farmers' Alliance meetings such as one held at Fellowship in Marion County were fast becoming third-party affairs. Although he permitted the Alliance to use a page in the *Ocala Banner,* Editor Frank E. Harris remained a Democrat and used his influence at the Fellowship gathering to attempt to persuade the eight hundred to one thousand people there to do likewise.[18]

With the Alliance endorsing the third party movement, a considerable number of its conservative members withdrew, accusing the radicals of being rabid for a third party. A former Marion County Alliance official, H. W. Long, berated the Populist leadership for not standing behind the Tampa convention agreement.[19] "Farmer" Mann answered Long in a *Times-Union* interview on July 11. Easily the strongest political leader in Florida Populism, Mann revealed that a large part of his own dissatisfaction had been caused by the refusal of the Democratic party to support election reforms. A campaigner against voting frauds ever since his chairmanship of the suffrage committee in the Constitutional Convention of 1885, the veteran South Florida political leader idealistically asked if his wish for the repeal of present election laws and the substitution of the Australian ballot system was unreasonable.[20]

Supporting the Democratic ticket but anti-Bourbon, the *Times-Union* accused the bolting Alliancemen of insincerity. For proof it reminded its readers that just two years before, President Rogers with Baskin's consent had effected a coalition with the railroad-corporation faction of the Democratic party.[21] The *Times-Union's* stand indicated that the Call people, despite their opposition to the Bourbons and their support of reform, would not bolt. Further, there was bitter enmity between "Farmer" Mann and Call. Mann considered Call to be a "windbag" not truly interested in reform but only in his own political advancement.[22]

Attempting to take advantage of the Democratic split, state Republican chairman Dennis Eagan issued a circular letter urging support for the Populists. In fusing with the Populists, Eagan gave as his reasons that they were fighting the old enemy and would repeal the "infamous election laws in this state."[23] His views had obviously changed since 1884 when he had sabotaged the Independent movement. The Jacksonville *Florida Republican* accused Duval's county commissioners of being irresponsible party bosses,[24] and veteran Republican J. D. Goss of Ocala attempted a political comeback as a Populist party organizer.[25] Otherwise, Republicans were generally inactive, particularly in Middle Florida. The DeLand *Florida Agriculturist*, thoroughly soured on the political situation and the Democratic party, announced that the voice of the candidates, "loud with love of the dear people will be silent after October." The new legislature would forget its constituents and as usual forget to amend the fertilizer law—the major issue to the *Florida Agriculturist*—and take fifty or sixty days to elect a new senator.[29]

On July 20, the People's Party (the official name of the Populists) held its convention in the Sub-Tropical Building at Jacksonville. For the second time since the end of Reconstruction, disgruntled Democratic reformers effected a coalition with Negroes. On the executive committee was J. L. Mooree, president of the state Colored Farmers' Alliance. Ex-Congressman Josiah T. Walls also appeared at the convention. A motion to thank the railroads for transportation was promptly voted down with a show of antagonism. Because the Jacksonville *Florida Dispatch*, official Alliance newspaper, was remaining aloof from politics, the Populists lacked a party organ. To overcome this handicap, Mann announced that plans were being formulated for publishing a Populist newspaper in Jacksonville. With only slight opposition, Mann was nominated for Congress and Baskin for governor. An almost complete slate of nominees included the old ex-Independent David L. McKinnon for the supreme court.[27] J. D. Goss, on the nomination of Baskin, rashly stated that he would get every black Republican vote.[28] The Democratic press immediately made the wooing of the Negro vote by the Populists a major issue in an effort to keep disaffected Democrats from bolting. The Starke *Bradford County Telegraph* quoted the views of Judge Mitchell, the Democratic candidate: "The democratic party is amply able to correct all the mistakes it may have made; . . . it is the white man's party and . . . white men will rule Florida."[29] The issue of white supremacy was once more a major weapon of the Democrats. The *Pensacola Daily News*, expressing the views of the railroad faction of the Democratic party, termed the Populist convention a gathering of Republicans, cranks, and recreant Democrats. The success of the third-party movement, it thought, depended on Republican support.[30]

In an effort to get out the Negro vote, Baskin, Mann, and Walls conferred at Ocala in August. The Starke *Bradford County Telegraph* accused Mann of having said at the conference that the Negroes should enforce their voting privileges on the day of the election even "at the muzzle of their guns."[31] By late August it was evident that the campaign was going badly for the Populists. Even the official Alliance spokesman, the Jacksonville *Florida Dispatch*, abandoned earlier neutrality and came out for the Democratic candidates, stating: "We prefer to cleave to old names and old parties. The place for reform is in the primaries."[32] Earlier the *Dispatch* had attacked Negro education as hopeless and mentioned that the Farmers' Alliance of Manatee County would not join the Populists.[33] Now that the Farmers' Alliance was of no further use to William D. Chipley, the *Pensacola Daily News* attacked both it and the Populist party. A letter supposedly from an East Bay farmer published in the *Daily News* accused Farmers' Alliance leaders of taking the money of the farmers and then trying to lead them into third partyism. "Lay off that old Third party coat, put on a new Democratic robe," advised "East Bay Farmer."[34] The only newspaper support for the Populists came from a few rural weeklies.

The state Republican party, ineffectually fused with the Populists, was so demoralized that only a feeble effort was made for an electoral ticket favorable to Harrison. The defeatism of Republicans was expressed by the October 1 issue of the Jacksonville *Florida Republican,* which was completely devoid of politics, although the paper was originally established as the state party organ.[35]

Under the revised election laws, two elections were held. The first, for state offices, was scheduled in October, and the second, for presidential electors and congressmen, in November. Weather conditions were ideal for the state offices election, yet voting was light. The *Weekly Floridian* attributed the light vote to the poll tax and the eight ballot box law.[36] The Populists carried Walton and Calhoun in West Florida, and tied in Washington. In the peninsula, only Baker and Taylor, with a sizable number of crackers in North Florida, went Populist. The final vote was Mitchell 32,064, Baskin 8,309. Baskin had suffered the worst defeat of any major gubernatorial candidate thus far in the history of the state.[37]

There were two major reasons for the overwhelming defeat of Florida's Populists. First and foremost was the issue of white supremacy. Because of the poll tax and the eight ballot box law—in addition to intimidation from whites and apathy on the part of blacks—Negroes were now not an effective pressure group in Florida politics. The few who voted in the Black Belt voted mostly Democratic. Without presidential backing, the campaign for Negro civil rights by Judge Swayne and U.S. Attorney Stripling had completely collapsed; in Leon and Jefferson counties, both of which had gone Independent in 1884, not a single Populist vote was cast.[38] The second reason involved the failure of Farmers' Alliance members in South Florida to become Populists. Here, despite opposition to high railroad rates and Bourbon land policy, the citrus and truck farmers stuck to the Democratic party just as they had voted against Independentism in 1884, and for the same reasons. Although the large number of ex-Northern settlers in this region were not as strong on white supremacy as Southerners, the belief that they were tolerant in the area of race relations is an unsubstantiated myth. The general overall conservatism of Florida Democrats was the main issue here. The strength of Populism was in West Florida and the white counties of North Florida where distrust of railroads, of large real estate interests, and of other

Henry L. Mitchell, Democrat
A. P. Baskin, Populist

Mitchell: 32,064
Baskin: 8,309

☐ Democratic counties

▨ Populist counties

10. Gubernatorial Vote by County in Election of 1892. (Statistics from Tallahassee *Weekly Floridian*, October 22, 1892, and Allen Morris, comp., *Florida Handbook*, 1949-50.)

corporations outweighed for the crackers and the farmers the white supremacy issue.[39]

In November the Populist-Republican electoral ticket failed to carry a single county. "Farmer" Mann trailed in his race for Congress in every county in South Florida where for a decade he had been a strong and extremely popular political leader of the settlers. This showed conclusively that even with good leadership, South Florida's settlers would not bolt the Democratic party. Mann carried only cracker Baker County in North Florida, running against a relatively weak Democratic opponent.[40]

After the election, an extremely feeble state Populist party continued to exist with the Farmers' Alliance as an adjunct. But the day had passed when the Farmers' Alliance could boast of a majority in the legislature and attempt to fasten the Ocala Demands on a Democratic state convention.[41] The Bourbon-conservative-railroad interests were now firmly in control of the single major party. Only Senator Wilk Call and his anti-Bourbon faction opposed them. Since Call's followers carried the local offices in Duval County, the victory of the Bourbons was not yet complete. Governor Fleming commented to Chipley, "The success of the State ticket is all that the most sanguine democrat could have desired. I wish I could say the same as to Duval. The end is not yet."[42]

Though nominated at the Tampa Convention by a coalition of Farmers' Alliance men and conservatives, Henry L. Mitchell in his inaugural speech quickly served notice that no measures of agrarian reform would be sponsored by his administration. Economy in government was the keynote of his speech. Significantly, William D. Chipley and his Pensacola Tammany organization occupied prominent places in the inaugural proceedings.[43] The concessions to the Ocala Demands made earlier in the platform of the state Democrats were ignored by Governor Mitchell in his message to the legislature in April. A doctrinaire conservative rather than an opportunist, Mitchell naively placed his administration squarely behind the state's railroad and corporation interests with the frank statement that "there should be no contest between the corporations and the people, because capital so invested benefits both the people and the corporations." Furthermore, Florida's resources and prosperity were attracting out-of-state capital, and this capital would continue to come in provided that there was no unfriendly legislation.[44] That the homesteader needed protection from those who benefited from extensive land grants, and that the small farmer who shipped to Northern markets for a profit could not absorb exorbitant rates, does not seem to have occurred to Mitchell. But, like Fleming, he was concerned about abuses involved in convict leasing. He particularly singled out the phosphate mine operators for their ruthless exploitation of prisoners. To alleviate this deplorable situation, he called for an overhauling of the system.[45] As before, Negroes made up a large percentage of the convicts. That the exploitation was part and parcel of the larger problem of racial discrimination possibly did not occur to Mitchell. Mitchell, like Fleming before him, was to ignore the racial issue completely. Apparently to the Boubons the disfranchisement of the Negro eliminated him from any consideration in Florida politics except when votes could be garnered by using the white supremacy issue.

The do-nothingness of the 1893 legislature contrasted sharply with the aggressiveness of the predominantly Farmers' Alliance body of 1891. Little was accomplished aside from the reelection of Senator Pasco and the passing of routine bills. Efforts to revive the railroad commission were frustrated. Backers of the Australian ballot found little enthusiasm for long overdue election reforms. The chief opposition to the conservatives came from the Jacksonville Call group, known as the Straightouts. The extreme bitterness between the two factions was evidenced when the aristocratic leader of the state administration's forces in Duval County, James P. Taliaferro, received a severe beating from Straightout J. M. Barrs, the fight taking place just outside the House chamber.[46]

Disappointed by Mitchell's conservative pro-Bourbon position, the Jacksonville Times-Union's owners, the Stockton brothers, who had supported the Tampan in his contest against Baskin, now bitterly opposed him. One editorial accused Mitchell of representing only corporation interests.[47] Hurt by the Jacksonville newspaper's attacks, Mitchell wrote South Florida cattle baron Francis A. Hendry that the Times-Union was bound to rule or ruin. To counterbalance its anti-administration policies a "first class opposition paper" would be started in Jacksonville shortly.[48] Opposition to the Duval Straightouts and the Call faction was now being supported by railroad and oil magnate Henry M. Flagler. Like Sanford in 1884, Flagler planned to start a newspaper, to control federal patronage, and to be a political power. John N. C. Stockton castigated Flagler in a letter to Call, claiming that the Standard Oil Company through Flagler and his paid attorneys were hovering over the Stocktons "like buzzards do over dead animals in the woods." Stockton attacked high railroad rates, the granting of large bodies of public land, and a "thousand other insidious schemes to defraud the public in the name of the law." He also claimed to be the only Jacksonville banker who stood with the people and was opposed by every corporation in the state. He did not think that his opposition could start another newspaper if the Cleveland people stood behind him.[49]

Writing President Cleveland in the fall and again in late December, Flagler opposed the appointment of either John N. C. or T. T. Stockton to the office of collector of internal revenue at Jacksonville. While Call was busy supporting the nomination of T. T. Stockton, Flagler accused John N. C. of backing a "miserable set of demagogues who were not only discouraging capital from coming into the State but would be glad to drive out much of the capital already there." Flagler informed Cleveland that he planned to start a new daily that would support the national administration. He asserted to the President that he was speaking also for railroader Henry B. Plant.[50] William Chipley, James P. Taliaferro, and Stephen Sparkman, Tampa lieutenant of Plant, journeyed to Washington to aid in the fight to strip Senator Wilk Call of federal patronage.[51] Cleveland favored the Bourbon-conservative-railroad forces, a major defeat for the Call faction.[52]

In Florida the shadows of Henry B. Plant, William D. Chipley, and Henry M. Flagler now stretched as far as their respective railroad lines. In 1897 Chipley would come within one vote in the legislature of being elected senator as Call would finally be defeated. Yet despite the success of the Bourbons in defeating Call, Florida politics would continue to be factional. Both the Independent and Populist revolts had failed to displace the Bourbons, and by coming to their assistance when they were the dominant element in the state, Cleveland could claim some credit in the forthcoming defeat and disintegration of the Call faction. Yet no single interest would now be able to control Florida politics. The first two governors in the twentieth century would be progressives William S. Jennings, son-in-law of "Farmer" Mann, and Napoleon Bonaparte Broward, ex-sheriff of Duval County and a Straightout.

11

Conclusion

The period from 1877 to 1893, the era of independent Democratic county leaders, saw the moulding of the pattern of present-day Florida politics. In 1877, despite the antiquity of St. Augustine, Florida was the southern frontier of the United States. A poor state and sparsely settled (3.4 inhabitants per square mile in 1870), it had many attributes of the western frontier, including cowboys and Indians. For having followed the leadership of the other Southern states it underwent Reconstruction. In North Florida, the older section, there were few large plantations, many yeoman farms, and virtually no manufacturing. The wealth of the port cities was in trade, not industry. In South Florida, where millions of acres of virgin land awaited the settler, a few Seminoles roamed in the vicinity of the Everglades and Big Cypress Swamp. To open South Florida and the panhandle, railroads were needed, and public land was offered by Republicans and Democrats alike as an inducement for railroad building.

Because the Negroes were a sizable minority in Florida, black votes constituted a serious threat to white Democratic rule as late as 1884. The majority of counties were rural white; the Black Belt counties and the port-city counties, Duval and Nassau, had Negro majorities. When the Democratic party returned to power in 1877, its legislative leadership was largely based upon white county leaders—small town merchants, lawyers, successful farmers—who, because of the relative isolation of much of Florida, were not answerable to a statewide political machine or political

leaders with large statewide followings. The last powerful antebellum chieftain, ex-Senator David L. Yulee, remained out of
politics after the Civil War except as it concerned his railroad.
Closest to a state machine was the gathering of ex-Confederate,
so-called Bourbon county leaders in the office of the Tallahassee
Weekly Floridian seeking the advice of Editor Charles E. Dyke,
Sr.

When Governor George F. Drew (chosen in 1876 because of
his wealth, Northern birth, and Whig-Unionist background) realized he had been a successful governor and desired a second term,
a crisis arose. Drew had not been a member of the small group
of diehard Democrats who fought the Republicans throughout Reconstruction. In 1876 he had been a newcomer to statewide politics. Furthermore, though Drew was a Bourbon economically, politically and ideologically he was not. His moderate views on race
were suspect, and Dyke in particular did not trust him. The veteran
editor's loyalty was with Secretary of State William D. Bloxham,
planter and ex-Confederate veteran. No doubt Dyke's influence
with a number of Democratic county leaders played a major role
in depriving Drew of renomination.

Whereas Drew had been a cautious governor with respect to
railroad promoters and land grants, Bloxham opened the flood
gates by effecting the Disston Sale. The purchase of four million
acres of Florida public domain by the wealthy Philadelphia in-
dustrialist for twenty-five cents an acre heralded a new Northern
invasion, much more acceptable than the one which ended at
Olustee and Natural Bridge. Because the influx of fresh investment
capital meant settlers, railroads, and a business boom, the more
conservative—or Bourbon—Democratic politicians eagerly endorsed the Bloxham administration. This enthusiasm was not, however, shared by a triumvirate of young, idealistic, white, Black
Belt lawyers: Frank W. Pope of Madison, Daniel L. McKinnon
of Jackson, and David S. Walker, Jr., of Leon. All three were
to the "manner born" and disillusioned by the election frauds and
lawlessness condoned by the Bourbons. They were also impatient
with the monopolizing of major offices by ex-Confederate veterans.
The failure of the Bloxham administration to take positive action
to protect the civil and political rights of Negroes was another
prime cause of the Independent movement. In addition, there was
the emphasis which the Florida Republican party placed on patron-

age and the increasing disillusionment of black leaders, particularly ex-Congressman Josiah T. Walls, with the leadership of Congressman Horatio Bisbee, Jr., and the Jacksonville Ring. Substantial financial support for the Independent movement was expected to come from Henry S. Sanford, a wealthy and influential national Republican with extensive citrus groves on Lake Monroe in South Florida. Unable to get the support of the Arthur administration for the Independents, Sanford reneged on his promised assistance. However, Negroes from the Black Belt and port cities led by Walls deserted the carpetbag-dominated Republican party and together with reform Republicans joined the Independents in a determined effort to defeat the Democrats in 1884.

As the gubernatorial candidate of the Independents, Pope conducted a vigorous campaign throughout the state, calling for a railroad commission, local option, fair treatment of Negroes, and homesteads. The Bourbons, their ranks and coffers reinforced by the railroad builders, countered Pope's idealism by recalling the incident in which Pope as a youth fatally shot his schoolteacher and by invoking memories of the Lost Cause. The gallant commander of the Florida Brigade, General Edward A. Perry, became their nominee. Thus, an ex-Yankee hero possessing conservative political views opposed a young Southern idealist who denounced lynching and the Disston Sale. The tight grip of the Democrats on election machinery and the solid support of South Florida, home of the Disston land empire and the Northern settlers, were the deciding factors in the Democratic victory. The Independents failed to carry a single county in the Northern settler country south of Marion, and even the reform-minded ex-Yankee "Farmer" A. S. Mann refused to bolt.

The Independent revolt marked the last major attempt to involve the Negroes in Florida politics until the New Deal. It was a joint effort of capable black leaders, young Southern moderates, and reform Republicans. Discrimination, which has been inherent in American society since the institutionalizing of slavery in the seventeenth century, was the prime cause of the gradual exclusion of the Negroes. Other causes included the failure of a substantial number of blacks to become independent yeoman farmers, professional men, and businessmen. Persistent efforts by a few Democrats holding the concept of noblesse oblige to build a Negro wing of their party met with little success.

It was the Democratic white county leaders who dominated the Constitutional Convention of 1885. Legislative seats granted them by the new constitution were far out of proportion to the number of their constituents. The home rule provisions went further than the Black Belt Democrats desired. The provision against state borrowing put an end to the use of the state's credit by railroad builders. The convention marked the high-water point of influence of the white county leaders.

At the time the new constitution was framed, however, representatives of the railroads and new capital were already making their power felt within the Democratic party. Led by William D. Chipley, representing the Louisville and Nashville Railroad interests in Florida, they were gradually carrying the integration of capital and the Democratic party far beyond the original concessions of Bloxham. Only Senator Wilk Call, a veteran ex-Whig, stood in the way, as Chipley aggressively threatened to dominate and upset the balance maintained by the county leaders. In the middle 1880s, Call, never before an advocate of reform, began a long fight against railroad land grants and the administration policy of favoring newly arrived businessmen and promoters over yeoman farmers. A controversial figure and clever stump speaker, Call was opposed not only by the Bourbons but by "Farmer" Mann and other agrarian reformers who looked upon him as a self-seeking demagogue.

Taking a leading part in launching the Florida Farmers' Alliance in politics, Mann and other Alliance leaders effected a coalition with Chipley against Call in order to obtain Call's senatorial seat for an Alliance candidate. President Robert F. Rogers, leader of the conservative wing of the Florida Alliance, while uttering platitudes of agrarian reform, carefully groomed John F. Dunn, a national banker, for the post. Dunn in return largely underwrote the expenses of the Ocala meeting of the National Farmers' Alliance in 1890. The election earlier in that year of an Alliance-dominated legislature seemingly guaranteed his nomination. Before the legislature met in April 1891, however, the radical wing of the Alliance, led by A. P. Baskin, forced the withdrawal of support from Dunn because of his being a national banker. Without a strong candidate against Call, the Alliance failed to rally its members.

In the state Democratic convention at Tampa in 1892, the Alliance again effected a coalition with the railroad faction. It agreed to support the railroad faction's nominee for governor, Henry L. Mitchell, in return for a major portion of the platform and two cabinet positions. Dissatisfied despite these concessions, the radicals in the Alliance led by Mann and Baskin withdrew it from the Democratic party. The newly organized Populist party attracted a few farmers and a small number of Negroes and Republicans. Its failure to gain substantial support and its resulting defeat left the Democratic party without a major rival in the state.

In 1877 the Republicans and Democrats were of about equal strength. The scattered population of South Florida and the white counties of North and West Florida were strongly Democratic. The Black Belt and port-city regions were Republican. As South Florida's population grew it continued to be almost solidly Democratic. Northern settlers would not join the Republican party largely because of its patronage policies and its Negro rank and file. On the other hand, the Negro vote was drastically decreased by fraud and intimidation and all but eliminated by the poll tax and other legislation in the late 1880s. Without a substantial Negro vote and with only a few Democrats bolting, the Populists followed the Independents and Republicans into defeat and political oblivion.

From the typical white rural Florida county came a frontier spirit of every man for himself and his community. This sometimes caused the Democrats to enter their state conventions badly split, with no one faction in control. However, strong opposition from the Republicans, Independents, and Farmers' Alliance caused the regular Democrats to bury their differences, to compromise and present a united front in canvass and election. Democratic gubernatorial candidates, except for Bloxham, were politically inexperienced and largely dependent on county organizations for their victories. Two who were governors, Perry and Bloxham, desired to become senators. Neither made it. The power of the Democratic party came from the grass roots. This was the situation from the end of Reconstruction until the defeat of the Populists.

Notes

1

1. Plant interview, *Success*, Nov. 1898, p. 6; Stowe, *Palmetto Leaves*, pp. 116-18.

2. *King, Southern States*, 2:382.

3. Webb and Fenlon, "Florida's Early Industrial Development: 1850-1890," p. 1.

4. Florida *Senate Journal*, 1865, p. 37; Brevard, *History of Florida*, 2:83; Hanna and Hanna. *Florida's Golden Sands*, pp. 137-38; Davis, *Civil War and Reconstruction in Florida*, pp. 250-51, 297-313, 324, 331-32.

5. *Florida Union* (Jacksonville), 8 Apr., 1865; Gammon, "Governor Milton," pp. 256-60.

6. *Florida Union*, 29 July, 1865.

7. *Floridian* (Tallahassee), 26 Sept., 1865; Davis, *Civil War and Reconstruction in Florida*, p. 359.

8. Davis, *Civil War and Reconstruction in Florida*, pp. 361-65; Ackerman, "Florida Reconstruction," pp. 40-49; *Floridian*, 27 Oct., 3, 7, 10 Nov., 1 Dec., 1865; Florida *Convention Journal*, 1865, passim.

9. Wallace, *Carpetbag Rule in Florida*, p. 17; Davis, *Civil War and Reconstruction in Florida*, pp. 365-66, 368, 429; Ackerman, "Florida Reconstruction," p. 50.

10. Florida *Senate Journal*, 1865, pp. 84-87; 1866, pp. 144-47; Wallace, *Carpetbag Rule in Florida*, pp. 27-36; *Floridian*, 5 Jan., 1866.

11. Robertson, *Soldiers of Florida*, pp. 55, 156.

12. Doherty, "Florida Whigs," p. 227.

13. *Tallahassee Sentinel*, 9 Apr., 15 Aug., 22 Nov., 1867; Davis, *Civil War and Reconstruction in Florida*, pp. 438-39, 446-48, 454-463, 466-67, 470; Ackerman, "Florida Reconstruction," pp. 85-88.

14. Simkins, "Why the Ku Klux," pp. 737-38; Bentley, "Florida Freedmen's Bureau," pp. 28-37; Davis, *Civil War and Reconstruction in Florida*, pp. 377-407; Ackerman, "Florida Reconstruction," pp. 69-76; Bush, "Florida Education Outlook," p. 318.

15. Thrift, *Florida Circuit Rider*, pp. 95-96, 105-10; Pennington, "Florida Episcopal Church," pp. 48-50, 58-59.

16. Wallace, *Carpetbag Rule in Florida*, pp. 42-47; Davis, *Civil War and Re-

construction in Florida, pp. 375-76, 401; Ackerman, "Florida Reconstruction," pp. 76-79; *Florida Industrial Record,* pp. 5-6; Webber, *Eden of the South,* pp. 33-36.

17. Overy, *Wisconsin Carpetbaggers in Dixie,* pp. 11-12.

18. J. C. Greeley to M. Williams, 7 May, 1867, Yulee Papers.

19. H. Reed to D. L. Yulee, 25 May, 1877, Yulee Papers.

20. D. L. Yulee directed the rebuilding of the railroad from the Fort Pulaski prison. D. L. Yulee to T. Baltzell, 30 Oct., 1865; Meader to D. L. Yulee, 13 Nov., 1865; D. L. Yulee to Meader, 23 Mar., 1866, Yulee Papers; C. Wickliffe Yulee, "Senator Yulee," pp. 15-16; Hanna and Hanna, *Florida's Golden Sands,* pp. 128-36. Yulee made a number of switches in his career, including changing his name from Levy to Yulee. His deft hand was revealed in 1855 when the Florida legislature passed an internal improvement act extremely favorable to his railroad construction plans. He and his supporters hoped that the Florida Railroad would become part of a rail-water route from the east coast to California. His chief financial support came from E. N. Dickerson, with offices on Wall Street.

21. C. W. Yulee to D. L. Yulee, 27 July, 1878, Yulee Papers.

22. Lanier, *Florida,* pp. 39-66.

23. *Floridian,* 11 Oct., 1867; Davis, *Civil War and Reconstruction in Florida,* pp. 492-93; Ackerman, "Florida Reconstruction," p. 107; Dovell, *Florida,* 2:552-53.

24. *Florida Convention Journal,* 1868, passim; *Sentinel,* 30 Jan., 1868; *Florida Union,* 28 Feb., 4, 11 Apr., 1868; *Floridian,* 11 Oct., 1867, 21 Jan., 11 Feb., 1868; Davis, *Civil War and Reconstruction in Florida,* pp. 494-515; Ackerman, "Florida Reconstruction," pp. 108-25; Wallace, *Carpetbag Rule in Florida,* pp. 49-65.

25. Ackerman, "Florida Reconstruction," pp. 128-51, 154-57, 160-63, 185-90.

26. "Comptroller's Report," Florida *Assembly Journal,* 1873, Appendix, p. 2; *Holland v. Florida;* Brown, "Florida Investments of Swepson," pp. 281-83; Davis, *Civil War and Reconstruction in Florida,* p. 662; Dovell, *Florida,* 2:571-72.

27. *Vose v. Reed;* Rerick, *Memoirs of Florida,* 2:180-86; Florida *Assembly Journal,* 1873, Appendix, pp. 51-109.

28. *Floridian,* 15 Nov., 1870; Ackerman, "Florida Reconstruction," pp. 195-201.

29. Ackerman, "Florida Reconstruction," pp. 218-21.

30. Davis, *Civil War and Reconstruction in Florida,* pp. 558-59, 565-79; Stanley, *History of Jackson County,* pp. 205-21; Congressional *Joint Select Committee Testimony* (1872), pp. 78, 221, 289-91.

31. Florida *Assembly Journal,* 1873, p. 132; Rerick, *Memoirs of Florida,* 1:327.

32. Florida *Assembly Journal,* 1875, p. 240; *Floridian,* 2, 9, 16 Feb., 1875; 30 Dec., 1886.

33. *Commercial* (Pensacola), 20 Jan., 11 Apr., 1886.

34. Davis, *Civil War and Reconstruction in Florida,* pp. 494-95; Rerick, *Memoirs of Florida,* 1:333; Wallace, *Carpetbag Rule in Florida,* p. 55. Gibbs, a Dartmouth graduate, came to Florida as a missionary, branching out into politics. Early recognized as a capable leader of his race, he held cabinet positions under all three of Florida's Republican governors. His most notable contribution came in the field of free school education. In 1874 he died suddenly in his prime, depriving the Negroes of much needed leadership at a critical time.

35. *Congressional Biographical Directory 1774-1927,* p. 1662; interview by author with Benmont Tench, 31 Oct., 1950.

36. *Makers of America,* Fla. Ed., 1: 395-97; *Floridian,* 2 Jan., 5 June, 1877; Carson, "Bloxham," pp. 91-92, 134; Shofner, "A Note on Governor Drew," pp. 412-14.

37. Going, *Bourbon Democracy in Alabama 1874-1890*, pp. 12-13, 18.

38. Davis, *Civil War and Reconstruction in Florida*, pp. 689-91.

39. Sen. Report 611, 44th Cong., 2d sess., pp. 388-401; H. R. Misc. Doc. 31, Pt. 2, 45th Cong., 3d sess., pp. 3-171; Davis, *Civil War and Reconstruction in Florida*, pp. 693-710; "Florida 1876 Election."

40. Capt. E. M. L'Engle to Mrs. E. M. L'Engle, 29 Oct., 1876.

41. *Drew v. State Canvassing Board;* Davis, *Civil War and Reconstruction in Florida*, pp. 732, 736-37; Shofner, "Electoral Count of 1876," pp. 122-50.

42. *Congressional Biographical Directory 1774-1927*, p. 703.

43. *Floridian*, 17 Oct., 1876.

44. Wallace, *Carpetbag Rule in Florida*, p. 336.

45. W. H. Gleason to G. W. Holmes, 30 Oct., 1890; Brevard County Records, Deed Book A, p. 187, Deed Book F, p. 226; Ackerman, "Florida Reconstruction," pp. 237-38; Pratt, "Florida Prison System," p. 32.

46. Brown, "Swepson's Florida Investments," pp. 275-88.

47. "Report of the Comptroller," Florida *Senate Journal*, 1877, p. 4; *Principles of Florida Republican Party*, 1875, pp. 13-15; Florida *Assembly Journal*, 1868. pp. 223-25; Ackerman, "Florida Reconstruction," pp. 237-38.

2

1. *Floridian*, 5 June, 1877; Barbour, *Florida for Tourists*, pp. 79-80; *Florida Handbook, 1949-1950*, p. 150.

2. Wallace, *Carpetbag Rule in Florida*, p. 343; *Floridian*, 2 Jan., 1877.

3. M. L. Stearns to T. W. Osborn, 21 Feb., 1877, Hayes Papers.

4. *Floridian*, 2 Jan., 1877; *Daily Florida Union*, 3 Jan., 1877; Wallace, *Carpetbag Rule in Florida*, pp. 343-44. Eppes (*Through Some Eventful Years*, pp. 375-77) mentions the presence of armed white men guarding Drew's inauguration. Both Wallace and Eppes show a tendency to exaggerate.

5. *Daily Florida Union*, 3 Jan., 1877.

6. Carson, "Bloxham," p. 128; *Floridian*, 27 Mar., 1883.

7. Rerick, *Memoirs*, 1:339; *Makers of America*, Fla. ed., 3:38-39; *Florida Sun* (Jacksonville), 16 Jan., 1877; C. E. Dyke, Jr., to W. T. Bacon, 9 Jan., 1877, Drew Letter Book; Dickison, *Dickison and His Men*, p. 56.

8. Governor Milton died in office. *Florida Union*, 8 April, 1865.

9. Barbour, *Florida for Tourists*, pp. 80-81; Knauss, *Territorial Florida*, p. 75; Carson, "Bloxham," pp. 146-47.

10. *Floridian*, 1846-77, passim.

11. *Daily Florida Union*, 4 Jan., 1877.

12. Ibid., 5 Jan., 1877.

13. Florida *Senate Journal*, 1877, pp. 7-9; Florida *Assembly Journal*, 1877. pp. 4-5.

14. Florida *Senate Journal*, 1877, pp. 4-5.

15. Ibid., pp. 3-4; Florida *Assembly Journal*, 1877, pp. 3-4, 11-12.

16. Florida *Assembly Journal*, 1877, pp. 9-10; Florida *Senate Journal*, 1877, p. 6.

17. Florida *Senate Journal*, 1877, p. 29.

18. Ibid., pp. 37-39. It finally turned out that the $39,087 was not missing. The scare was the result of a careless error by a clerk in the comptroller's office. *Floridian*, 20 Mar., 1877.

19. *Floridian*, 16 Jan., 1877.

20. *Daily Florida Union*, 13 Jan., 1877.

21. Florida *Senate Journal*, 1877, pp. 138-43; Florida *Assembly Journal*, 1877, pp. 70-72.

22. Florida *Assembly Journal*, 1877, pp. 94-95.

23. *Daily Florida Union*, 16 Jan., 1877.

24. Florida *Assembly Journal*, 1877, pp. 23-25, 35-39, 117, 227; Florida *Senate Journal*, 1877, pp. 136-43.

25. *Daily Florida Union*, 20 Jan., 1877.

26. *Nation* 24, no. 614 (5 April 1877): 202.

27. E. G. Hill Diary, 19 Jan., 1877.

28. Florida *Senate Journal*, 1877, pp. 124-25.

29. U.S. Electoral Commission, *Proceedings*, 1876, pp. 195-99; *Florida Election, 1876*, Sen. Report 611, 44th Cong., 2d sess., p. 3.

30. *Congressional Record*, 44th Cong., 2d sess., p. 2068.

31. Bush, *Florida Statute Law*, pp. 7-14; Shofner, "Constitution of 1868," pp. 368-69.

32. C. E. Dyke, Jr., to G. G. McWhorter, 7 Apr., 1877; C. E. Dyke, Jr., to H. T. Lykes, 1 June, 1877, Drew Letter Book.

33. *Daily Florida Union*, 6, 8 Jan., 1877.

34. C. E. Dyke, Jr., to G. G. McWhorter, 7 Apr., 1877; C. E. Dyke, Jr., to H. T. Lykes, 1 Jun., 1877, Drew Letter Book.

35. C. E. Dyke, Jr., to T. F. King, 30 Jan., 1877 (two letters); G. F. Drew to N. A. Hull, 30 Jan., 1877, Drew Letter Book.

36. Florida *Senate Journal*, 1877, p. 26.

37. C. E. Dyke, Jr., to R. B. Ballard, 12 Feb., 1877, Drew Letter Book.

38. *Daily Florida Union*, 23 Jan., 1877; *Florida Sun*, 16 Jan., 1877.

39. Florida *Senate Journal*, 1877, pp. 152-53.

40. *Floridian*, 23 Jan., 1877.

41. Florida *Assembly Journal*, 1877, pp. 255-56; "Report of Superintendent of Public Instruction," 1875-76, Florida *Senate Journal*, 1877, Appendix, p. 80.

42. Florida *Senate Journal*, 1877, p. 168; Florida *Assembly Journal*, 1877, p. 41.

43. Florida *Assembly Journal*, 1877, pp. 406-8.

44. Florida *Senate Journal*, 1877, pp. 287-301; *Florida Laws, 1877*, chap. 3021.

45. Pratt, "Florida Prison System," p. 32; "Warden's Report, State Prison," Florida *Assembly Journal*, 1873, Appendix, pp. 135-37; "Report of Surgeon of Prisoners," ibid., p. 143; "Warden's Report, State Prison," ibid., 1874, Appendix, pp. 207-9; "Report of Physician of State Prison," ibid., Appendix, p. 224; "Adjutant-General's Report," ibid., 1877, Appendix, pp. 122-23; "Warden's Report, State Prison," ibid., Appendix, pp. 129-32, 159; "Surgeon's Report," ibid., Appendix, pp. 161-62. Democrats in later years maintained that the state abandoned its prison because Warden Martin was operating it as a medieval torture chamber and wasting the state's money. Cash, *The Story of Florida*, 2:494, states that the death rate at the prison during Reconstruction was very high and conditions were so disgusting as to be almost unbelievable. Cash relied on Powell, *American Siberia*, pp. 8-14, for most of his information. Powell, a convict captain for many years, attempted to justify the convict lease system by relating stories supposedly told him by prisoners concerning the state prison. It is strange that none of these stories came to light when the Democrats decided to close the state prison.

46. Florida *Assembly Journal*, 1877, pp. 563-66.

47. "Adjutant-General's Report," ibid, Appendix, pp. 122-23; "Adjutant-General's Report," ibid., 1879, Appendix, pp. 231-32, 252: Powell, *American Siberia*, pp. 11-15.

48. Florida *Assembly Journal*, 1877, p. 606; Florida *Senate Journal*, 1877, p. 443.

49. "Report of the Comptroller," Florida *Assembly Journal*, 1877, Appendix, p. 10; ibid., p. 606; *Florida Laws, 1877*, chaps. 3033–35.

50. "Biennial Report of the State Prison, Mar. 4, 1877–Dec. 1, 1878," Florida *Assembly Journal*, 1879, Appendix, p. 231; Powell, *American Siberia*, pp. 14, 16.

51. *Floridian*, 4 Mar., 1879.

52. *Florida Laws, 1877*, chaps. 2089, 3052.

53. Florida *Assembly Journal*, 1877, pp. 322–23; "Commissioner of Lands and Immigration Report, 1875–1876," ibid., Appendix, pp. 47–48. The sale of Internal Improvement Fund land for these two years came to $87,182.97.

54. Florida *Assembly Journal*, 1877, pp. 323–24.

55. Ibid., p. 509; Florida *Senate Journal*, 1877, p. 381.

56. Florida *Assembly Journal*, 1877, p. 616.

57. *Daily Florida Union*, 8 Jan., 1877.

3

1. Florida *Assembly Journal*, 1877, pp. 576, 578.

2. C. E. Dyke, Jr., to H. T. Lykes, 16 Apr., 1877, Drew Letter Book.

3. *Floridian*, 24 Apr., 1877.

4. Brown, "Florida Investments of Swepson," passim; *Daily Florida Union*, 8 Apr., 1877; J. B. Stewart to E. M. L'Engle, 12 Jan., 1877, L'Engle Papers.

5. *Daily Florida Union*, 10, 11, 12, 16 Apr., 1877; E. W. Thompson to E. M. L'Engle, 4 Apr., 1877, J. B. Stewart to E. M. L'Engle, 10 Apr., 1877, L'Engle Papers.

6. C. W. Yulee to D. L. Yulee, 10 July, 1877, Yulee Papers; C. E. Dyke, Jr., to C. W. Jones, 10 Oct., 1877, Drew Letter Book; *The Florida Atlantic and Gulf Ship-Canal Company Summary Report*, pp. 4–6.

7. D. L. Yulee to [G. F. Drew], 12 July, 1877, Yulee Papers.

8. C. E. Dyke, Jr., to C. W. Jones, 10 Oct., 1877; C. E. Dyke, Jr., to Col. P. C. Raiford, 8 Sept., 1877; L. B. Wombwell to J. Shepard, 7 Nov., 1877, Drew Letter Book.

9. Powell, *American Siberia*, pp. 11–15; "Biennial Report of the State Prison, Mar. 4, 1877–Dec. 1, 1878," Florida *Senate Journal*, 1879, Appendix, pp. 232, 240–41.

10. Florida *Senate Journal*, 1879, p. 232; Powell, *American Siberia*, pp. 7, 14–15, 22–23; Pratt, "Florida Prison System," pp. 37–38; Florida *Assembly Journal* 1879, p. 492; *Floridian*, 4 Mar., 1879.

11. L. B. Wombwell to P. Cone, 7 Nov., 1877, Drew Letter Book.

12. Powell, *American Siberia*, pp. 16–17, 27.

13. Ibid., p. 27; "Report of Adjutant-General, Dec. 31, 1880," Florida *Assembly Journal*, 1881, Appendix, p. 266.

14. Florida *Assembly Journal*, 1881, p. 255.

15. *Evening Chronicle* (Jacksonville), 14 Nov., 1877.

16. "Biennial Report of Superintendent of Public Instruction, Dec. 31, 1878," Florida *Senate Journal*, 1881, Appendix, p. 216.

17. Statement of W. Lansing Gleason, personal interview, 16 Oct., 1952; Brevard County Records, Deed Book A, p. 187, Deed Book F.

18. G. F. Drew (by L. B. Wombwell) to C. Dougherty, 1 Jan., 1878, Drew Letter Book.

19. M. L. [Stearns] to [T. W.] Osborn, 21 Feb., 1877, Hayes Papers.

20. *Floridian*, 3 Apr., 1877.

21. Ibid., 6, 20 Mar., 1877.

22. *New York Times*, 16 July, 1877.

23. Ibid., 29 July, 1877.
24. N. R. Gruelle to R. B. Hayes, 19 Apr., 1877, Hayes Papers.
25. W. Call to R. B. Hayes, 1 Aug., 1877, W. Call to Judge [S.] Matthews, 1 Aug., 1877, Hayes Papers.
26. S. B. McLin to Governor [name not legible], 4 May, 1877, Sherman Papers.
27. S. N. Williams to J. Sherman, 18 Feb., 1878, Sherman Papers.
28. N. R. Gruelle to Pres. R. B. Hayes, 15 May, 1878, Hayes Papers.
29. *The New York Times,* 11 May, 1878.
30. W. E. Chandler to Judge T. Settle, 11 Feb., 1878, Chandler Papers; *Floridian,* 2 Apr., 1878.
31. *Floridian,* 30 July, 1878.
32. Ibid., 5 Mar., 1878.
33. *New York Times,* 17 May, 1878.
34. *Floridian,* 23 July, 1878.
35. Ibid., 6 Aug., 1878.
36. A. Marvin to E. M. L'Engle, 14 July, 1878, L'Engle Papers.
37. *Floridian,* 16 July, 1878.
38. Ibid., 30 July, 1878; C. W. Yulee to D. L. Yulee, 27 July, 1878, Yulee Papers.
39. *Floridian,* 30 July, 1878.
40. Ibid., 5 Nov., 1878.
41. *Bisbee v. Hull,* H. Misc. Doc. 26, 46th Cong., 1st sess., pp. 435-37.
42. Ibid., p. 346.
43. C. W. Yulee to D. L. Yulee, 9 Aug., 1878, Yulee Papers.
44. *Bisbee v. Hull,* pp. 372-73.
45. *Floridian,* 26 Nov., 1878.
46. *Bisbee v. Hull,* pp. 32-33, 428, 517-18.
47. Ibid., pp. 13, 16-17, 25.
48. Ibid., pp. 11, 573-74; *Floridian,* 19 Nov., 1878.
49. *Bisbee v. Hull,* pp. 98-101, 163, 555-56.
50. Ibid., pp. 179-85; 188-91, 196, 569-71; W. T. Cash, "The Lower East Coast, 1870-1890," p. 65.
51. *Floridian,* 24 Dec., 1878; *Bisbee v Hull,* p. 397.
52. *Bisbee v. Hull,* pp. 1-2; *Floridian,* 28 Jan., 1879; G. F. Drew to H. Bisbee, 14 Jan., 11 Aug., 1879, Drew Letter Book.
53. *Bisbee v. Hull,* pp. 1-9, 572.
54. *Biographical Directory of the American Congress,* 1774-1927, p. 353.
55. *Bisbee v. Hull,* pp. 569,571.
56. Ibid., pp. 204-05; G. F. Drew to R. B. Hay[e]s, 27 Jan., 1879, Drew Letter Book.
57. *Floridian,* 12 Nov., 10 Dec., 1878.
58. Ibid., 17 Dec., 1878.
59. *Bisbee v. Hull,* p. 394.

4

1. J. Tyler, Jr., to J. Sherman, 26 Dec., 1878, Sherman Papers.
2. Florida *Assembly Journal,* 1879, pp. 2-3; *Floridian,* 7 Jan., 1879.
3. S. L. Niblack to D. L. Yulee, 27 June, 1878; D. L. Yulee to S. L. Niblack, 30 June, 1878; D. L. Yulee to Editors of the *Mirror* (Fernandina), 11 Jan., 1879; D. L. Yulee to W. N. Thompson, 11 Jan., 1879, Yulee Papers.
4. D. L. Yulee to W. N. Thompson, 11 Jan., 1879, Yulee Papers.

5. W. N. Thompson to D. L. Yulee, 14, 15 Jan., 1879; C. W. Yulee to D. L. Yulee, 12 Dec., 1878, Yulee Papers.

6. W. N. Thompson to D. L. Yulee, 15 Jan., 1879, Yulee Papers.

7. *Floridian*, 22 Jan., 1879.

8. Florida *Senate Journal*, 1879, pp. 75-76.

9. Rerick, *Memoirs of Florida*, 1:340.

10. "Governor's Message," Florida *Assembly Journal*, 1879, pp. 27-28; "Biennial Report of the Superintendent of Public Instruction," Florida *Senate Journal*, 1879, Appendix, p. 183.

11. *Florida Laws*, 1879, chap. 3100.

12. "Biennial Report of the Superintendent of Public Instruction," Florida *Senate Journal*, 1881, Appendix, pp. 192-215.

13. *Florida Laws*, 1877, Joint Resolution opposing passage of the Texas and Pacific Railroad Bill approved 8 Mar., 1877. *Florida Laws*, 1879, chaps. 3148, 3162, 3186, Joint Resolution favoring the Texas and Pacific Railroad approved 26 Feb., 1879. Concurrent resolution providing for voting on a new constitution approved 8 Mar., 1879.

14. Florida *Senate Journal*, 1879, pp. 355-62.

15. *Makers of America*, 3:41; *Florida Laws*, 1879, chap. 3167.

16. Florida *Senate Journal*, 1879, Senate Bill 129, p. 365.

17. D. L. Yulee to President of Florida Senate, 18 Feb., 1879, Yulee Papers.

18. Florida *Senate Journal*, 1879, p. 365.

19. Florida *Assembly Journal*, 1879, p. 442.

20. Florida *Senate Journal*, 1879, p. 369; Florida *Assembly Journal*, 1879, p. 405.

21. Florida *Senate Journal*, 1879, pp. 517-20; *Floridian*, 18 Mar., 1879.

22. *Sunland Tribune* (Tampa), 5 Apr., 1879.

23. D. S. Walker to D. L. Yulee, 2 Aug., 1879, Yulee Papers.

24. D. L. Yulee to Dr. J. P. Wall, 29 Aug., 1879, Yulee Papers.

25. Florida Board of Commissioners of Public Institutions, *Minute Book*, 26 Oct., 1869 to 13 Feb., 1892; Wyse bid accepted at Jan. 2, 1879 meeting.

26. Florida *Senate Journal*, 1879, p. 91; *Florida Laws*, 1879, chap. 3137.

27. Florida Public Institutions, *Minute Book*, 1 Mar., 1879; *Floridian*, 4 Mar., 1879.

28. C. A. Cowgill to W. E. Chandler, 11 Feb., 1879, Chandler Papers.

29. W. G. Stewart to W. E. Chandler, 10 Mar., 1879, Chandler Papers.

30. G. F. Drew to C. W. Jones, 21 Apr., 1879, Drew Letter Book.

31. G. F. Drew to J. H. Durkee, 15 July, 1879, Drew Letter Book.

32. H. Bisbee, Jr., to W. E. Chandler, 17 May, 1879, L. G. Dennis to W. E. Chandler, 18 May, 1879, Chandler Papers.

33. S. B. Conover to J. Sherman, 8 June, 1879, Sherman Papers.

34. Ibid., 13 June, 1879.

35. L. G. Dennis to W. E. Chandler, 1 Oct., 1879, Chandler Papers.

36. *Florida Industrial Record*, Sept. 1901, pp. 5-6.

37. G. F. Drew to W. N. Thompson, J. T. Lesley, J. E. Yonge, W. Judge, E. C. Love, S. Pasco, P. P. Bishop and others, 7 July, 1879; G. F. Drew to S. French, 4 Aug., 1879, Drew Letter Book.

38. C. W. Yulee to D. L. Yulee, 13 July, 1879, Yulee Papers.

39. G. F. Drew to W. B. Taylor, 8 Aug., 1879, Drew Letter Book.

40. Grismer, *Tampa*, pp. 155-56; statement of D. B. McKay, personal interview, 20 May, 1949.

41. J. T. Magbee to J. Sherman, 10 Jan., 1880, Sherman Papers.

42. Ibid., — Jan., 1880, Sherman Papers.

43. *Guardian* (Tampa), 24 Apr., 1880.

44. Ibid., 17 Apr., 1880.

45. S. C. Cobb to G. C. Tichnor, 17 Jan., 1880, Sherman Papers.

46. R. W. Ruter to F. C. Humphries [Humphreys], 21 Jan., 2 Feb., 1880, Sherman Papers.

47. S. H. Welch to G. C. Tichnor, 23 Jan., 1880, Sherman Papers.

48. F. C. Humphreys to G. C. Tichnor, 24 Jan., 1880, Sherman Papers.

49. G. E. Wentworth to J. Sherman, 5 Feb., 1880, Sherman Papers.

50. G. E. Wentworth to G. C. Tichnor, 30 Jan., 1880, Sherman Papers.

51. M. Martin to W. E. Chandler, 4 Feb., 1880, Chandler Papers.

52. T. M. Davey to J. Sherman, 25 Feb., 1880, Sherman Papers.

53. J. Fogarty to F. Weller, 9 Mar., 1880, Sherman Papers; Browne, *Key West*, p. 19.

54. A. A. Knight to S. B. Conover, 6 Mar., 1880, Sherman Papers.

55. J. B. Chaffee to W. E. Chandler, 7 Mar., 1880, Chandler Papers.

56. L. G. Dennis to W. E. Chandler, 10 Mar., 8 Apr., 1880, Chandler Papers.

57. F. C. Humphreys to W. M. Bateman, 10 Mar., 1880, Sherman Papers.

58. M. Martin to W. E. Chandler, 12 Mar., 1880, Chandler Papers.

59. Ibid., 21 Mar., 1880.

60. Ibid., 4 Apr., 1880.

61. *Guardian* (Tampa), 13 Mar., 10 Apr., 1880.

62. F. C. Humphreys to Gen. B. D. Fearing, 10 Apr., 1880, Sherman Papers.

63. S. C. Cobb to J. Sherman, 16 Apr., 1880, Sherman Papers.

64. *Floridian*, 4 May, 1880.

65. Ibid.

66. R. S. Smith to B. D. Fearing, 16 Apr., 1880, Sherman Papers.

67. Stanley, *Jackson County*, pp. 218-21.

68. *Floridian*, 11 May, 1880; *Sunland Tribune* (Tampa), 10 June, 1880.

69. Rerick, *Memoirs of Florida*, 1:347.

70. A. E. Bateman to J. Sherman, 14 May, 1880, Sherman Papers.

71. R. W. Ruter to L. Crandall, 18 May, 1880, Chandler Papers; *Floridian*, 18 May, 1880.

72. *Floridian*, 18 May, 1880.

73. Ibid.

74. Ibid.; A. E. Bateman to J. Sherman, 14 May, 1880; F. C. Humphreys and F. N. Wicker to J. Sherman, 14 May, 1880, Sherman Papers.

75. *Guardian* (Tampa), 9 Oct., 1880.

76. *Floridian*, 18 May, 1880.

77. *Sunland Tribune* (Tampa), 10 June, 1880.

78. Carson, "Bloxham," pp. 132-53; *Floridian*, 15 June, 1880.

79. Cash, *Democratic Party*, p. 72.

80. *Floridian*, 29 June, 1880.

81. Ibid., 12 Oct., 1880.

82. R. W. Ruter to L. Crandall, 18 May, 1880, Chandler Papers.

83. *Guardian* (Tampa), 9 Oct., 1880.

84. J. T. Magbee to J. Sherman, 13 June, 1880, Sherman Papers.

85. Ibid.; *Guardian* (Tampa), 10 July, 1880; G. F. Drew to W. A. Turner, 14 July, 1880, Drew Letter Book.

86. *Floridian*, 12 Oct., 1880.

87. H. S. Sanford to Mr. Astor, 27 Oct., 1880, Sanford Papers.

88. *Sunland Tribune* (Tampa), 2 Sept. 1880.

89. *Bisbee v. Finley*, H. Misc. Doc. 11, 47th Cong., 1st sess., pp. 176-83.

90. *Guardian* (Tampa), 21 Aug., 1880.

91. *Floridian,* 17 Sept., 1880.
92. *Daily Florida Union* (Jacksonville), 12 June, 1880.
93. *Floridian,* 23 July, 1880.
94. Ibid., 15 Oct., 1880.
95. *New York Times,* 4, 30 Oct., 1880.
96. Ibid., 24, 30 Oct., 1880.
97. *Floridian,* 9 Nov., 1880; *Bisbee v. Finley,* pp. 172-243; Edward Hart Diary, 2 Nov., 1880.
98. *Floridian,* 28 Dec., 1880, 4 Jan., 1881.
99. Florida *Senate Journal,* 1881, p.28.
100. T. W. Osborn to W. E. Chandler, 12 Nov., 1880, Chandler Papers; *Bisbee v. Finley,* pp. 163-71; Rowell, *Contested Election Cases,* pp. 368-71.
101. M. Martin to W. E. Chandler, 8 Nov., 1880, Chandler Papers.

5

1. *Floridian,* 4 Jan., 1881.
2. Ibid., 7 Dec., 1880.
3. C. Dougherty to A. Carter, 14 Jan., 1881, Dougherty Papers.
4. Florida *Senate Journal,* 1881, pp. 12-29; Rerick, *Memoirs of Florida,* 1:340.
5. "Report of Board of Trustees Internal Improvement Fund, 1877-78," Florida *Senate Journal,* 1879, Appendix, pp. 93-94.
6. Rerick, *Memoirs of Florida,* 1:349; D. L. Yulee to W. N. Thompson, 20 Jan., 1881, Yulee Papers.
7. Florida *Senate Journal,* 1881, pp. 80-81, 89-90; *Floridian,* 18 Jan., 1881.
8. Florida *Senate Journal,* 1881, pp. 122, 131-32.
9. Ibid., pp. 165-309; Florida *Assembly Journal,* 1881, p. 252.
10. Rerick, *Memoirs of Florida,* 1:349.
11. *Floridian,* 5 Apr., 1881.
12. Davis, "The Disston Land Purchase," p. 204; Carson, "Bloxham," pp. 198-200.
13. *Minutes of Board of Florida Internal Improvement Fund,* 2:483; H. A. Corley to S. A. Swann, 10 Mar., 1879, Internal Improvement Fund Papers.
14. Roberts interviews, 26 Sept., 2 Oct., 1947; J. Disston, Jr., interview, 26 Sept., 1947; clipping from *Sunday Times* (Philadelphia), n.d. 1876; *Public Ledger* (Philadelphia), 1 May, 1896, p. 2.
15. Roberts interview, 26 Sept., 1947; *Press* (Philadelphia), 13 May, 1881; Carson, "Bloxham," p. 200; Rose, *Swamp and Overflowed Lands of Florida,* pp. 3-4; Douglas, *Everglades,* pp. 282-83; *I. I. Fund Minutes,* 2:463-69.
16. *I. I. Fund Minutes,* 2: 500-501; "Report of Board of Trustees I. I. Fund, 1881-1882," Florida *Senate Journal,* 1883, Appendix, pp. 77-80.
17. Sharp, "Swann," pp. 190-93; S. A. Swann to Trustees I. I. Fund, 16 June, 1881; *I. I. Fund Minutes,* 2: passim.
18. *Press* (Philadelphia), 17 June, 1881.
19. *Disston Lands Catalogue,* p. 23.
20. *Florida Mirror* (Fernandina), 18 June, 1881.
21. *Floridian,* 21 June, 1881.
22. Ibid., 28 June, 1881.
23. *Florida Agriculturist* (DeLand), 22 June, 1881; *Florida Star* (Titusville), 29 June, 1881.
24. *Floridian,* 12 July, 1881.
25. Carson, "Bloxham," p. 204; Hanna and Hanna, *Lake Okeechobee,* pp. 100-

101; Dovell, "Everglades," pp. 116, 126-27.

26. E. Swann to S. A. Swann, 2 July, 1881, Swann Papers.

27. Sharp, "Swann," p. 192.

28. Carson, "Bloxham," p. 203.

29. *Disston Lands Catalogue*, p. 29.

30. "Report of Board of Trustees I. I. Fund, 1881-1882," Florida *Senate Journal*, 1883, Appendix, pp. 83-84; Hanna and Hanna, *Lake Okeechobee*, pp. 97-98; Davis, "The Disston Land Purchase," pp. 207-8.

31. H. Disston to Sen. J. P. Dolph, 7 Sept., 1888, *Public Lands in Florida*, Sen. Rpt. 2288, 50th Cong., 1st sess., p. 59.

32. Poor, *Railroads for 1882*, p. 448.

33. Davis, "The Disston Land Purchase," p. 208; *I. I. Fund Minutes*, 3:196-97.

34. Rerick, *Memoirs of Florida*, 1:351; "Report of Board of Trustees I. I. Fund, 1881-1882," Florida *Senate Journal*, 1883, Appendix, p. 83.

35. Webb and Fenlon, "Florida's Early Industrial Development: 1850-1890," passim.

36. H. Disston to W. D. Bloxham, 28 July, 1881, in *Floridian*, 9 Aug., 1881; "Report of Board of Trustees I. I. Fund, 1881-1882," Florida *Senate Journal*, 1883, Appendix, p. 81.

37. *Florida Times-Union* (Jacksonville), 1 Jan., 1891; Hanna and Hanna, *Lake Okeechobee*, pp. 102-3.

38. Plant Interview, *Success*, Nov. 1898, p. 6; Dovell, *Florida*, 2:615-16.

39. Pettengill, *Florida Railroads*, pp. 42-43; Poor, *Railroads for 1882*, p. 451.

40. "Statement of swamp lands owned by Florida and of lands sold and granted to corporations up to January 1, 1883, revised and corrected by Hugh A. Corley."

41. J. B. Hill to author, 19 Dec., 1945; Rerick, *Memoirs of Florida*, 2:482-83; Dovell, *Florida*, 2:614-15; Smith, "The Construction of the P & A," passim; McKinnon, *Walton County*, pp. 350-51.

42. W. D. Chipley to W. D. Bloxham, 14 Apr., 1884, Executive Letters.

43. Smith, "The Construction of the P & A," passim; "Major General Meade's Report on the Ashburn Murder," pp. 1-130; *News Supplement* (Pensacola), 29 Sept., 1896; Williamson, "William D. Chipley," pp. 333-36.

44. *Bisbee v. Finley*, pp. 886-87, 895, 905, 908-9; M. Martin to W. E. Chandler, 14 Feb., 1881, Chandler Papers.

45. *Bisbee v. Finley*, pp. 854, 1195-96.

46. *Savage and James v. the State*, 18 Florida Reports 909.

47. *Bisbee v. Finley*, pp. 862-64, 868; *Ex-parte Eagan*, 18 Florida Report 194.

48. *Ex-parte Eagan; Bisbee v. Finley*, pp. 868, 1195-96; M. Martin to W. E. Chandler, 14 Feb., 1881, Chandler Papers; *Savage and James v. the State*.

49. *Ex-parte Eagan; Bisbee v. Finley*, pp. 1195-96.

50. *Bisbee v. Finley*, pp. 1032-33, 1196-97; *Ex-parte Eagan*; M. Martin to W. E. Chandler, 14 Feb., 1881, Chandler Papers.

51. *Florida Industrial Record*, Sept. 1901, pp. 5-6.

52. *Motion Docket*, 1873-1905, Circuit Court of Hamilton County, pp. 60-65; Transcript, *Savage and James, Plaintiffs in Error v. the State of Florida, Defendant in Error*.

53. *Floridian*, 26 July, 1881; D. Eagan to H. S. Sanford, 11 Apr., 1881, Sanford Papers.

54. W. Call to W. E. Chandler, 10 Feb., 1881, Chandler Papers.

55. Rowell, *Contested Election Cases*, pp. 368-71; *Congressional Record*, 47th Cong., 1st sess., pp. 4444-45.

56. *Savage and James v. the State*.

57. B. B. Van Vaukenbaugh to A. A. Knight, 20 Aug., 1881, Florida Supreme Court Library, Savage and James Transcript.
58. *Daily Florida Union,* 28 Apr., 1882.
59. H. S. Sanford to President Arthur, 19 Nov., 1881, Florida Historical Society Library; *Florida Sun* (Jacksonville), 16 Jan., 1877.
60. *Floridian,* 11 Oct., 1881.
61. *Florida Daily Times* (Jacksonville), 19 Mar., 1882.
62. *Commercial* (Pensacola), 28 Apr., 1882; *Floridian,* 9 May, 1882.
63. *Floridian,* 9 May, 1882.
64. *Commercial,* 5 May, 1882.
65. Ibid., 26 May, 1882.
66. Ibid., 18 May, 1882.
67. D. L. Yulee to W. N. Thompson, 21 Jan., 1881, Yulee Papers.
68. *Daily Florida Union,* 28 May, 1882.
69. *Floridian,* 20 June, 1882.
70. *Daily Florida Union,* 16 Aug., 1882.
71. *Florida Mirror,* 26 Aug., 1882.
72. *Floridian,* 29 Aug., 1882; *Daily Florida Union,* 26 Aug., 1882.
73. W. D. Bloxham to Sheriff Hankins, 2[?] Aug., 1882, Bloxham Letter Book.
74. *Daily Florida Union,* 27 Aug., 1882.
75. *Floridian,* 29 Aug., 1882.
76. *Daily Florida Union,* 26 Aug., 1882.
77. *Florida Mirror,* 9 Sept., 1882.
78. *New York Times,* 31 Aug., 1882.
79. *Florida Mirror,* 9 Sept., 1882.
80. *Floridian,* 29 Aug., 1882.
81. *Florida Mirror,* 2 Sept., 1882; *Daily Florida Union,* 7 Sept., 1882.
82. M. Martin to D. B. Henderson, 23 Sept., 1882, Chandler Papers.
83. W. D. Bloxham to B. B. Blackwell, 16 Sept., 1882; G. P. Raney to B. B. Blackwell, 12 Oct., 1882, Bloxham Letter Book.
84. *Floridian,* 30 Aug., 1881.
85. *Florida Mirror,* 23 Sept., 1882; W. D. Bloxham to Gen J. J. Dickison, 27 Sept., 1881, Bloxham Letter Book.
86. W. D. Bloxham to Gen. J. J. Dickison, 27 Sept., 1881, Bloxham Letter Book.
87. *Florida Mirror,* 23 Sept., 1882.
88. *Bisbee v. Finley,* p. 896.
89. Bloxham to J. W. Turner, 8 Jan., 1883; Bloxham to L. W. Bethel, 25 Jan., 1 Feb., 1883, Bloxham Letter Book.
90. Richardson, *William E. Chandler,* pp. 345–46.
91. Woodward, *Origins of the New South,* p. 101.
92. Skinner, *Reminiscences,* p. 155.
93. Ibid., pp. 158–61; *Floridian,* 12 Sept., 1882.
94. *Floridian,* 12 Sept., 1882.
95. Ibid., 24 Oct., 1882.
96. Skinner, *Reminiscences,* p. 263.
97. *Floridian,* 29 Aug., 1882.
98. Ibid., 25 July, 1882.
99. Skinner, *Reminiscences,* pp. 163–69.
100. De Santis, "President Arthur and the Independent Movements," pp. 358–59; Woodward, *Origins of the New South,* p. 101.
101. *Floridian,* 8, 29 Aug., 1882.
102. *Recorder* (Madison), 4 Nov., 1882.

103. *Floridian,* 19 Dec., 1882.
104. Ibid.
105. Florida *Senate Journal,* 1883, pp. 15-36; *Floridian,* 9 Jan., 1883.
106. Florida *Senate Journal,* 1883, pp. 379-85.
107. Ibid., p. 449.
108. Ibid., p. 133.
109. *Florida Laws,* 1883, Joint Resolution [2].
110. *Floridian,* 13 Feb., 1883.
111. Ibid., 3 Apr., 1883.
112. Ibid., 28 Nov., 1882.

6

1. *Floridian,* 12 Feb., 1884; James Dean to W. E. Chandler, 22 Jan., 1884, Chandler Papers.
2. *Floridian,* 12 Feb., 1884.
3. R. W. Ruter to L. Crandall, 27 Feb., 1884, Sanford Papers.
4. Reed to H. S. Sanford, 7 Mar., 1884, Sanford Papers.
5. *Floridian,* 12 Feb., 1884.
6. *Florida Weekly Times* (Jacksonville), 31 Jan., 1884.
7. W. D. Bloxham to C. W. Jones, 11 Apr., 1884, Bloxham Letter Book.
8. W. D. Bloxham to T. J. Ashe, 15 Apr., 1884, Bloxham Letter Book.
9. W. D. Bloxham to General J. B. Gordon, 9 May, 1884, Bloxham Letter Book.
10. Carson, "Bloxham," pp. 128-29.
11. *Florida Times-Union,* 5 Sept., 1884.
12. *Bisbee v. Finley,* pp. 992-94.
13. H. Reed to H. S. Sanford, 8 Jan., 21 Dec., 1883; 7, 25, 30 Mar., 16 Apr., 5 May, 1884, Sanford Papers.
14. J. R. Hawley to H. S. Sanford, 15 Mar., 1884, Sanford Papers.
15. H. Reed to H. S. Sanford, 8 Jan., 21 Dec., 1883; 30 Jan., 7 Mar., 1884, Sanford Papers.
16. Elsie M. Lewis, "The Political Mind of the Negro 1865-1900," p. 201.
17. H. Reed to H. S. Sanford, 8 Jan., 21 Dec., 1883; 6 Mar., 1884; H. S. Sanford to W. Astor, 25 Apr., 1884 (unsigned draft), Sanford Papers.
18. Current, *Three Carpetbag Governors,* pp. 22-35.
19. *Florida Journal* (Jacksonville), 26 May, 1884.
20. S. C. Cobb to H. Reed, 5 Apr., 1884, Sanford Papers.
21. Harrison Reed to H. S. Sanford, 6, 25 Mar., 2, 16 Apr., 6, 9, 12 May, 1884; S. A. Adams to Harrison Reed, 17 Mar., 1884; S. A. Adams to H. S. Sanford, 14, 22, 23 Apr., 1, 3, 7, 8, 10 May, 1884, Sanford Papers.
22. S. C. Cobb to H. Reed, 5 Apr., 1884, Sanford Papers.
23. R. W. Ruter to L. Crandall, 5 Mar., 1884, Chandler Papers.
24. H. Reed to H. S. Sanford, 22 Apr., 1884, Sanford Papers.
25. Ibid., 5, 6, 9 May, 1884.
26. Ibid., 9 May, 1884.
27. J. E. Lee to W. E. Chandler, 9 May, 1884, Chandler Papers.
28. H. Reed to H. S. Sanford, 5 May, 1884, Sanford Papers.
29. Ibid.
30. *Florida Journal* (Jacksonville), 26 May, 1884.
31. Ibid., 29 May, 1884.
32. H. Reed to H. S. Sanford, 14 June, 1884, Sanford Papers.

33. *Florida Journal,* 29 May, 1884.
34. Ibid., 5 June, 1884.
35. H. Disston to H. S. Sanford, 19 May, 1884, Sanford Papers.
36. *The Florida Journal,* 2 June, 1884.
37. S. A. Adams to H. S. Sanford, 13 June, 1884, Sanford Papers.
38. *Florida Journal,* 16 June, 1884.
39. Ibid.
40. Ibid., 19 June, 1884.
41. *Florida Times-Union* (Jacksonville), 19 June, 1884; *Floridian,* 24 June, 1884; *Land of Flowers* (Tallahassee), 21 June, 1884; *Florida Mirror,* 5 July, 1884; *Palatka Daily News,* 10 Aug., 1884; Cash, *Democratic Party,* p. 77.
42. S. A. Adams to H. S. Sanford, 20 June, 1884, Sanford Papers.
43. *Floridian,* 24 June, 1884; *Florida Times-Union,* 19 June, 1884; *Florida Journal,* 19 June, 1884.
44. *Independent Platform and Record of the Candidates* (1884).
45. *Florida Times-Union,* 19 June, 1884; *Independent Platform and Record of the Candidates.*
46. H. Reed to H. S. Sanford, 5 May, 1884, Sanford Papers; *Florida Journal,* 19 June, 1884.
47. *Independent Platform and Record of the Candidates.*
48. Statement of Columbus Smith, 16 Oct., 1948; *Florida Times-Union,* 16 July, 1884.
49. *Florida Annual, 1884,* pp. 155-57.
50. *Land of Flowers* (Tallahassee), 21 June, 1884.
51. *Floridian,* 24 June, 1884.
52. *Florida Journal,* 19 June, 1884.
53. Ibid., 17 July, 1884.
54. Ibid., 21 July, 1884.
55. *Florida Times-Union,* 12, 15, 17, 18 June, 1884; Carson, "Bloxham," pp. 137-46.
56. *Florida Times-Union,* 15 June, 1884; Tebeau, *History of Florida,* p. 288.
57. *Florida Journal,* 26 June, 1884.
58. Ibid., 3 July, 1884.
59. *Land of Flowers,* 28 June, 1884; *Florida Mirror,* 28 June, 1884; *Floridian,* 1 July, 1884; Samuel Pasco, Jr., "Samuel Pasco (1834-1917)," p. 137.
60. *Floridian,* 1 July, 1884; *Florida Journal,* 3 July, 1884.
61. *Floridian,* 1 July, 1884.
62. W. D. Bloxham to C. B. Carlton, 7 July, 1884, Bloxham Letter Book.
63. *Floridian,* 1 July, 1884; *New Era* (Madison), 7 Aug., 1884.
64. *Pensacolian* (Pensacola), 12 July, 1884.
65. *Florida Journal,* 30 June, 1884.
66. *Florida Times-Union,* 3 July, 1884.
67. *Florida Mirror,* 12, 19 July, 1884; *Florida Journal,* 10 July, 1884.
68. *Florida Journal,* 10 July, 1884.
69. Solon A. Adams to H. S. Sanford, 19 June, 1884, Sanford Papers.
70. Hamilton Disston to H. S. Sanford, 19 May, 1884, Sanford Papers.
71. *Floridian,* 1 July, 1884; *Florida Journal,* 3 July, 1884; *Florida Times-Union,* 1, 2 July, 1884.
72. *Florida Mirror,* 19 July, 1884.
73. *Florida Journal,* 3 July, 1884.
74. Ibid., 17 July, 1884.
75. *Weekly Bee* (Gainesville), 23 Aug., 1884; *Florida Mirror,* 19 July, 1884.
76. *Florida Mirror,* 5 July, 1884.

77. Ibid., 12 July, 1884.
78. *New York Times*, 8 July, 1884.
79. *Weekly Telegraph and Messenger* (Macon), 4, 11 July, 1884.
80. *Florida Journal*, 23 June, 1884.
81. *Florida Mirror*, 19 July, 1884.
82. *Florida Times-Union*, 16 July, 1884; *Florida Mirror*, 19 July, 1884.
83. *Florida Journal*, 21 July, 1884.
84. *Florida Times-Union*, 16 Oct., 1884.
85. Ibid., 16 July, 1884.
86. *Florida Journal*, 14, 24 July, 1884.
87. H. Reed to H. S. Sanford, 5, 25 May, 1884, Sanford Papers.
88. *Florida Journal*, 31 July, 1884.
89. *Florida Times-Union*, 25, 26 July, 1884; *Land of Flowers*, 29 July, 1884.
90. *Florida Mirror*, 26 July, 1884.
91. *Florida Times-Union*, 19 July, 1884.
92. *Floridian*, 5 Aug., 1884.
93. Ibid., 29 July, 1884.
94. *Florida Journal*, 28 July, 1884.
95. *Land of Flowers*, 21 June, 1884; *Floridian*, 24 June, 1 July, 1884; *Florida Mirror*, 28 June, 1884; *Florida Times-Union*, 22 June, 1884.
96. Date of birth of Frank W. Pope taken from his tombstone in the Madison Cemetery.
97. *Floridian*, 29 July, 1884.
98. *Florida Journal*, 31 July, 1884.
99. *New Era* (Madison), 7 Aug., 1884.
100. L. D. Huston to Maria Huston, 6 Aug., 1884, Huston Papers.
101. *Halifax Journal* (Daytona), 16 Oct., 1884.
102. *Florida Star* (Titusville), 14 Aug., 1884.
103. *New York Times*, 18 Aug., 1884.
104. Ibid., 19 Aug., 1884.
105. *Florida Times-Union*, 1 Aug., 1884; *Floridian*, 12 Aug., 1884.
106. *Florida Journal*, 4 Aug., 1884.
107. *Florida Times-Union*, 1 Aug., 1884; *Florida Journal*, 31 July, 1884.
108. *Florida Journal*, 28 July, 1884.
109. H. Reed to H. S. Sanford, 5 May, 1884, Sanford Papers.
110. *Florida Mirror*, 16 Aug., 1884.
111. *Daily News* (Palatka), 22 Aug., 1884.
112. *Florida Times-Union*, 31 Aug., 1884.
113. *Floridian*, 19 Aug., 2 Sept., 1884; *Florida Mirror*, 16 Aug., 1884.
114. *Journal* (Sanford), 4 Sept., 1884.
115. *Florida Times-Union*, 2 Sept., 1884.
116. Solon A. Adams to H. S. Sanford, 2, 11, 16 Sept., 1884, Sanford Papers.
117. *Daily News* (Palatka), 24 Aug., 1884.
118. *Journal* (Sanford), 28 Aug., 1884.
119. *Floridian*, 16 Sept., 1884.
120. Ibid., 2 Sept., 1884.
121. Ibid., 26 Aug., 1884.
122. *Florida Times-Union*, 26 Aug., 1884.
123. Ibid., 10 Sept., 1884.
124. Ibid., 30 Aug., 1884.
125. *Daily News* (Palatka), 24 Aug., 1884.
126. Ashley D. Hurt to Mary Bruce Johns Hurt, 27 July, 1884, Univ. of Florida Archives.

127. W. D. Bloxham, *The Disston Sale and the State Finances; Floridian*, 2 Sept., 1884.
128. *Florida Mirror*, 6 Sept., 1884.
129. *Daily News* (Palatka), 26 Aug., 1884.
130. *Land of Flowers*, 13 Sept., 1884.
131. *Floridian*, 16, 23 Sept., 1884.
132. *Land of Flowers*, 27 Sept., 1884.
133. *Florida Times-Union*, 19, 20 Sept., 1884.
134. *Land of Flowers*, 20 Sept., 1884.
135. *Florida Mirror*, 20 Sept., 1884.
136. W. D. Barnes to S. A. Swann, 31 Aug., 1884, Swann Papers.
137. *Floridian*, 23 Sept., 1884.
138. Ibid.
139. Ibid., 21 Oct., 1884.
140. Edw. Barnott to W. H. Gleason, 20 Oct., 1884, William H. Gleason Papers; F. W. Munson Diary, 3 Oct., 1884; *Florida Star* (Titusville), 9 Oct., 1884.
141. *Florida Mirror*, 25 Oct., 1884.
142. *Florida Times-Union*, 25 Oct., 1884.
143. Ibid., 1 Nov., 1884.
144. *Floridian*, 26 Aug., 1884.
145. E. O. Locke to W. E. Chandler, 14 Oct., 1884, Chandler Papers.
146. *Florida Mirror*, 18 Oct., 1884.
147. *Florida Star* (Titusville), 6 Nov., 1884.
148. *Land of Flowers*, 15 Nov., 1884; *Florida Times-Union*, 9 Nov., 1884; *Floridian*, 11 Nov., 1884.
149. *Florida Times-Union*, 19 Nov., 1884.
150. Ibid., 27 Nov., 1884.
151. *Halifax Journal* (Daytona), 16 Oct., 1884.
152. *Floridian*, 9 Dec., 1884.
153. *Florida Times-Union*, 7, 8 Nov., 1884; *Floridian*, 11 Nov., 1884.
154. *Florida Times-Union*, 7 Nov., 1884.
155. Ibid., 8 Nov., 1884.
156. Interview with Mrs. Frank W. Pope, Jr., Daytona Beach, Florida, 16 Mar., 1952.
157. *Weekly Tallahassean*, 5 Mar., 1896; interview with Carlton Smith, Madison, Fla., 10 Mar., 1952.
158. *Bradford County Telegraph* (Starke), 29 July, 1892.
159. Statement of Thomas Moreno, 96-year-old Creole Negro, Federal Writers' Project, Pensacola, Fla., 1 June, 1937; *Florida Times-Union*, 14 Nov., 1884.
160. *Florida Times-Union*, 27 Nov., 1884.
161. E. M. Cheney to W. H. Gleason, 12 Aug., 1885, Gleason Papers; *Southern Sun* (Jacksonville), 7 May, 1885.
162. *Land of Flowers*, 6 Dec., 1884.

7

1. Enquirer to the citizens of St. Augustine [1885], City of St. Augustine Papers.
2. *Floridian*, 6 Jan., 1885.
3. *Florida Laws*, 1885, chap. 3570.
4. Florida *Senate Journal*, 1885, pp. 36, 143.

5. J. G. Willis to Atty. Gen. State Florida, 15 June, 1885, Attorney General's Papers.

6. *Commercial* (Pensacola), 24 May, 1884.

7. Interview with Mrs. W. S. Jennings, 1 Apr., 1952. Letter to author from D. B. McKay, 17 Nov., 1945.

8. *Commercial* (Pensacola), 14 Jan., 1885.

9. *Florida Times-Union*, 14 Jan., 1885.

10. Florida *Senate Journal*, 1885, p. 143.

11. *Florida Laws*, 1885, chap. 3577.

12. *Land of Flowers*, 29 Nov., 1884.

13. *Ocala Banner*, 15 Apr., 1885; *Florida Times-Union*, 18, 21 Apr., 1885; *Floridian*, 23 Aug., 1885; Johnson, *Along This Way*, p. 45.

14. *Florida Times-Union*, 1 May, 1885.

15. Ibid., 3, 5 May, 1885.

16. Collins, "Florida Constitution of 1885," p. 31.

17. *Ocala Banner*, 16 May, 1885.

18. *Florida Times-Union*, 5 May, 1885.

19. *Floridian*, 7, 14 May, 4 June, 1885.

20. Ibid., 14 May, 1885.

21. Ibid., 4 June, 1885.

22. Ibid., 7 May, 1885.

23. Ibid., 4 June, 1885.

24. *Tallahassean*, 6 June, 1885.

25. Ibid.

26. J. B. Whitfield, "Constitutional Conventions of Florida," p. 81; Collins, "Florida Constitution of 1885," p. 40.

27. *Constitutional Convention Journal*, 1885, p. 8.

28. Pasco, "Samuel Pasco," pp. 135–38.

29. *Constitutional Convention Journal*, 1885, p. 9.

30. Ibid., p. 15.

31. Ibid., pp. 41–42.

32. Ibid., p. 53; *Florida State Government, 1885 Directory*, pp. 9, 13, 17.

33. *Florida State Government, 1885 Directory*, pp. 8–18; *Constitutional Convention Journal, 1885*, p. 54; Davis, *Civil War and Reconstruction in Florida*, p. 572.

34. *Florida State Government, 1885 Directory*, pp. 8–18.

35. *Constitutional Convention Journal, 1885*, pp. 82–85.

36. C. W. Lewis to S. A. Swann, 20 June, 1885, Swann Papers.

37. *Constitutional Convention Journal, 1885*, p. 106.

38. Ibid., p. 131.

39. Dovell, *Florida: Historic*, 2:624.

40. *Commercial* (Pensacola), 27 June, 1885.

41. *Constitutional Convention Journal, 1885*, pp. 208–81.

42. *Florida Times-Union*, 10 July, 1885.

43. *Constitutional Convention Journal, 1885*, p. 282.

44. E. C. F. Sanchez, Speech of Sanchez in the Convention, 14 July, 1885.

45. *Constitutional Convention Journal, 1885*, pp. 280–81.

46. Ibid., p. 346.

47. *Florida Times-Union*, 18 July, 1885.

48. *Constitutional Convention Journal, 1885*, pp. 361–62.

49. *Floridian*, 23 July, 1885.

50. *Florida Times-Union*, 16 Apr., 23 July, 1885; *Constitutional Convention Journal, 1885*, pp. 402–4.

51. *Florida Times-Union,* 30 July, 1885.
52. *Constitutional Convention Journal, 1885,* pp. 481, 503-4.
53. Parker, "Sheats," pp. 72-80.
54. *Constitutional Convention Journal, 1885,* p. 382.
55. Ibid., p. 216.
56. Ibid., p. 526.
57. *Florida Times-Union,* 31 July, 1885.
58. *Constitutional Convention Journal, 1885,* pp. 562, 568-69.
59. *Florida Times-Union,* 5 Aug., 1885.
60. D. S. Walker, Jr., to Gov. W. H. Gleason, 27 July, 1885, Gleason Papers.
61. *Florida Mirror,* 15 Aug., 1885.
62. *Floridian,* 22 Oct., 1885.
63. F. P. Fleming to H. Disston, 1 Nov., 1889, Fleming Letter Book.
64. Collins, "Florida Constitution of 1885," pp. 125-37; *Ocala Banner,* 11 Sept., 1885.
65. *Florida Times-Union,* 14 Aug., 1885.
66. *Ocala Banner,* 29 Oct., 1886; Collins, "Florida Constitution of 1885," pp. 120-22.
67. *Palatka Daily News,* 20 Aug., 1886.
68. Collins, "Florida Constitution of 1885," pp. 137-38.
69. *Floridian,* 16 Dec., 1886.
70. *Tallahassean,* 3 Nov., 1886.

8

1. *Commercial* (Pensacola), 25 Mar., 1885.
2. Yulee Papers, passim.; *I. I. Fund Minutes,* 1:306.
3. S. M. Stocksluger to Register and Receiver, 3, 4, 5, 12 (two letters), 14 Nov., 1885; W. A. J. Sparks to Register and Receiver, 17, 19, 21, 28 Nov., 1885, Gainesville U.S. District Land Office Papers.
4. S. M. Stocksluger to Register and Receiver, 14 Nov., 1885.
5. *Congressional Record,* 49th Cong., 1st sess., p. 358.
6. S. M. Stocksluger to Register and Receiver, 11 May, 1888.
7. *Commercial,* 13 Jan., 1886.
8. Ibid., 23 Jan., 1886.
9. *Congressional Record,* 49th Cong., 1st sess., p. 966.
10. *Commercial,* 3, 6 Feb., 1886.
11. Ibid., 6 Jan., 6 Feb., 20 Apr., 1886.
12. *Congressional Record,* 49th Cong., 1st sess., pp. 1460, 1552.
13. Ibid., pp. 165, 183, 337.
14. *Commercial,* 3 Mar., 1886.
15. *Congressional Record,* 49th Cong., 1st sess., p. 2081.
16. Ibid., Appendix 87.
17. *Commercial,* 11, 20 Apr., 1886.
18. *Florida Star* (Titusville), 14 Apr., 1886; Saloutos, *Southern Farmer Movements,* p. 119.
19. *Commercial,* 19 May, 1886.
20. Ibid., 28 Apr., 1886.
21. *Tallahassean,* 5 May, 1886.
22. *Congressional Record,* 49th Cong., 1st sess., pp. 4074, 4658.
23. *Tallahassean,* 26 May, 1886.
24. *Commercial,* 29 May, 1886.

25. Ibid., 9 June, 1886.
26. Ibid., 26 May, 1886.
27. Ibid., 30 June, 10 July, 8, 18 Sept., 1886.
28. *Floridian*, 26 Aug., 1886.
29. *Commercial;* 1 Sept., 1886.
30. Ibid., 13 Oct., 1886.
31. *Congressional Record*, 49th Cong., 2d sess., pp. 1178-80.
32. Ibid., pp. 1428, 1706-7.
33. Davis, *History of Jacksonville*, pp. 176-78.
34. *Commercial*, 20 Jan., 11 Apr., 1886.
35. Mrs. M. F. Wynner to A. J. Hanna, 13 Jan., 1934, J. J. Finley biographical file; *Biographical Directory of the American Congress, 1774-1927*, pp. 393, 967, 1160.
36. Florida *Senate Journal*, 1887, pp. 72-76.
37. Ibid., p. 859; Florida *House Journal*, 1887, pp. 857-58.
38. *Florida Laws*, 1887, chap. 3746.
39. *Floridian*, 14 Apr., 1887.
40. *Tallahassean*, 20 Apr., 18 May, 1887.
41. Ibid., 27 Apr., 1887.
42. *Floridian*, 19 May, 1887.
43. Florida *Senate Journal*, 1887, pp. 509-11.
44. Ibid., p. 912.
45. *Constitutional Convention Journal, 1885*, p. 610.
46. Florida *House Journal*, 1887, p. 459.
47. Ibid., p. 447; *Florida Laws*, 1887, chap. 3743.
48. *Florida Laws*, 1887, chaps. 3768-72.
49. *Congressional Record*, 50th Cong., 1st sess., pp. 3074-76.
50. U.S. Congress, Senate, *Public Lands in Florida*, Sen. Report 2288, 50th Cong., 1st sess., p. 7.
51. Ibid., pp. 29-31.
52. *Floridian*, 7 June, 1888.
53. Ibid., 21 June, 1888.
54. Martin, *Florida's Flagler*, pp. 130-39.
55. *Floridian*, 7 June, 5 July, 1888.
56. Ibid., 21 June, 1888.
57. *Florida Times-Union*, 15 June, 1888.
58. Bailey, *Pasco Finale and Pasco's Pedigree*, p. 22; *Florida Times-Union*, 1 Aug., 1888.
59. *Congressional Record*, 51st Cong., 1st sess., p. 1474.
60. *Florida Times-Union*, 25 Apr., 1888.
61. Ibid., 3, 6 Aug., 1888.
62. Ibid., 7 Aug., 1888.
63. Knauss, "The Farmers' Alliance in Florida," pp. 301-3.
64. *Florida Times-Union*, 26 June, 1888.
65. Ibid.
66. *Floridian*, 18 Sept., 1888.
67. Ibid.
68. Fleming, *Message to Legislature*, 5 Feb., 1889, pp. 2-3; Rerick, *Memoirs of Florida*, 1:365; *Ocala Banner*, 12 Oct., 1888; Merritt, *A Century of Medicine in Jacksonville*, pp. 146-61; Adams, *Report of Jacksonville Sanitary Association*, passim; Fairlie, "Yellow Fever Epidemic of 1888 in Jacksonville," pp. 95-106.
69. *Ocala Banner*, 14 Sept., 1888; Rerick, *Memoirs of Florida*, 1:366.

70. *Congressional Record*, 50th Cong., 1st sess., pp. 8719, 8826, 8973, 9123, 9134.

71. Disston to Senator [J. N.] Dolph, 7 Sept., 1888, in *Public Lands in Florida*, Sen. Report 2288, 50th Cong., 1st sess., pp. 59-64.

72. Proctor, *Broward*, p. 44.

73. Davis, *History of Jacksonville*, p. 185.

74. *Fort Myers Press*, 27 Sept., 1888.

75. Proctor, *Broward*, p. 44.

76. *Floridian*, 20 Nov., 1888.

77. Proctor, *Broward*, pp. 40, 46.

78. *Floridian*, 20 Nov., 1888.

79. *Congressional Record*, 51st Cong., 1st sess., pp. 1473-74, 1528-36.

80. *Floridian*, 15 Jan., 1889.

81. Fleming, *Message to Legislature*, 5 Feb., 1889, pp. 1-7.

82. *Florida Laws*, 1889, chap. 3839; Rerick, *Memoirs of Florida*, 1:371.

83. Florida *Senate Journal*, 1889, pp. 766-67; Florida *House Journal*, 1889, pp. 591, 995-1000; *Florida Laws*, 1889, chaps. 3850, 3879.

84. Florida *Senate Journal*, 1889, pp. 766-67.

85. Florida *House Journal*, 1889, p. 996.

86. *Florida Laws*, 1889, chap. 3852.

87. Davidson, *Florida of To-Day*, p. 111.

88. E. J. Triay [Fleming's private secretary] to W. D. Chipley, 22 Mar., 1889, F. P. Fleming to W. D. Chipley, 25 Mar., 1889, Fleming Letter Book.

89. S. I. Wailes to F. P. Fleming, 25 Mar., 1889, incoming executive correspondence.

90. *Pensacola Daily News*, 7 Sept., 1889.

91. E. J. Triay to C. B. Parkhill, 13 Sept., 1889, Fleming Letter Book.

92. E. J. Triay to W. D. Chipley, 20 Nov., 1889, Fleming Letter Book; Pensacola *Daily News*, 19 Nov., 1889.

93. F. P. Fleming to S. Pasco, 7 Sept., 1889, F. P. Fleming to W. Call, 7 Sept., 1889, Fleming Letter Book.

94. Rerick, *Memoirs of Florida*, 1:372.

95. S. Pasco to F. P. Fleming, 9 Dec., 1889, incoming executive correspondence.

96. F. P. Fleming to H. Disston, 1 Nov., 1889, Fleming Letter Book.

97. *Times* (Orange City), 7 Sept., 1889.

98. H. Disston to F. P. Fleming, 20 Dec., 1889, incoming executive correspondence.

9

1. Florida Dept. of Agriculture, *Seventh Census of the State of Florida 1945*, p. 10.

2. U.S. Census Office, *Eleventh Census of the United States: 1890, Agriculture*, 3:2.

3. Knauss, "Farmers' Alliance in Florida," pp. 303, 307.

4. *Lake City Reporter*, 7 Oct., 1887; *News-Herald* (Jacksonville), 14 Apr., 1888.

5. Knauss, "Farmers' Alliance in Florida," p. 304.

6. E. J. Triay to W. D. Chipley, 14 Jan., 1890, Fleming Letter Book.

7. *Pensacola Daily News*, 30 Apr., 1890.

8. F. P. Fleming to W. Call, 24 Jan., 1890, Fleming Letter Book.

9. *Congressional Record*, 51st Cong., 1st sess., pp. 1473-74, 1527-35, 1640.

10. Hirshon, *Farewell to the Bloody Shirt*, p. 190.
11. Statement of A. Cockrell, 29 Dec., 1945; *Floridian*, 18, 26 Feb., 1890.
12. Chipley, *Review of Senator Call's Record*, pp. 10-60.
13. *Congressional Record*, 51st Cong., 1st sess., Appendix, pp. 549-62; Roberts, "Wilkinson Call," 2:186-87.
14. *Pensacola Daily News*, 2, 5 July, 1890.
15. Ibid., 6 July, 1890.
16. E. J. Triay to W. D. Chipley, 24 July, 1890, Fleming Letter Book.
17. *Pensacola Daily News*, 19 Aug., 1890.
18. Ibid.
19. Ibid., 21 Aug., 1890.
20. Statement of Mrs. W. S. Jennings, 1 Apr., 1952; letter to author from D. B. McKay, 17 Nov., 1945.
21. *Ocala Banner*, 26 Sept., 1890.
22. Ibid., 10 Oct., 1890.
23. Ibid., 26 Sept., 1890.
24. Ibid., 10 Oct., 1890.
25. Proctor, "Farmers' Alliance Convention of 1890," pp. 161-63.
26. *Pensacola Daily News*, 4 Oct., 1890.
27. Ibid., 3 Oct., 1890.
28. *Ocala Banner*, 10 Oct., 1890.
29. Ibid., 17 Oct., 1890.
30. *Bradford County Telegraph* (Starke), 31 Oct., 1890.
31. *Ocala Banner*, 31 Oct., 1890.
32. *Pensacola Daily News*, 1 Nov., 1890.
33. *Ocala Banner*, 7 Nov., 1890.
34. *Pensacola Daily News*, 20 Nov., 1890.
35. Ibid., 2 Apr., 1891.
36. *Ocala Banner*, 5 Dec., 1890; Proctor, "Farmers' Alliance Convention of 1890," pp. 165-69.
37. *1890-91, Annual, Farmers' Alliance Exposition at Ocala, Florida*, pp. 9, 14.
38. Chamberlain, *The Farmers' Alliance*, p. 34.
39. Proctor, "Farmers' Alliance Convention of 1890," pp. 174-178-80; Knauss, "Farmers' Alliance in Florida," p. 313.
40. Proctor, "Alliance Convention of 1890," pp. 175-76.
41. Knauss, "Farmers' Alliance in Florida," pp. 310, 313.
42. *Pensacola Daily News*, 20 Feb., 1891.
43. Ibid., 2 Apr., 1891; *Daily Floridian*, 22 Apr., 1891.
44. *Florida Agriculturist* (DeLand), 15 Apr., 1891.
45. *Daily Floridian*, 6 Apr.-7 June, 1891.
46. *Pensacola Daily News*, 12 Apr., 1894.
47. *Evening Telegram* (Jacksonville), 6, 7 Apr., 1891.
48. *Daily Floridian*, 9 Apr., 1891.
49. Ibid., 18 Apr., 1891; *New York Times*, 7 Apr., 1891.
50. *Ocala Banner*, 10 Apr., 1891.
51. Ibid., 17 Apr., 1891.
52. Florida *House Journal*, 1891, p. 11.
53. Rerick, *Memoirs of Florida*, 2:208.
54. *Pensacola Daily News*, 12 Apr., 1894.
55. *Daily Floridian*, 14 Apr., 1891; *Ocala Banner*, 17 Apr., 1891.
56. *Evening Telegram*, 15 Apr., 1891.
57. *Daily Floridian*, 16 Apr., 1891.
58. Ibid., 23 Apr., 1891.

59. *Ocala Banner,* 17 Apr., 1891.
60. *Daily Floridian,* 18 Apr., 1891.
61. *Evening Telegram* (Jacksonville), 24 Apr., 1891.
62. *Daily Floridian,* 18 Apr., 1891.
63. *Ocala Banner,* 17 Apr., 1891.
64. Florida *Senate Journal,* 1891, pp. 167–299; Roberts, "Wilkinson Call," 2:187.
65. *Daily Floridian,* 6 May, 1891.
66. Ibid., 12, 20 May, 1891.
67. Ibid., 26 May, 1891.
68. Florida *House Journal,* 1891, pp. 816–18; *Daily Floridian,* 27 May, 1891.
69. *Ocala Banner,* 29 May, 1891.
70. *Florida Star,* 28 May, 1891.
71. *Daily Floridian,* 29, 30 May, 3 June, 1891.
72. *Daily Florida Times-Union,* 30 May, 1891.
73. *Spring* (Green Cove Springs), 9 May, 1891.
74. Abbey, "Florida Versus the Principles of Populism 1896–1911," p. 463; Florida *Senate Journal,* 1891, pp. 837–38; Florida *House Journal,* 1891, pp. 672–73.
75. *Daily Floridian,* 6 June, 1891.
76. *Florida Agriculturist,* 13 May, 1891.
77. *Volusia County Record* (DeLand), 5 Aug., 1891.
78. *Weekly Floridian,* 19 Sept., 1891.
79. Statement of Alston Cockrell, 29 Dec., 1945. Mr. Cockrell, as a youth, heard Dr. Crawford relate the story.
80. Fleming, *Did the Florida Legislature of 1891 Elect a Senator?,* passim.
81. *Congressional Record, 52d Cong., 1st sess., p. 7.*
82. Ibid., p. 3.
83. Ibid., p. 846.

10

1. *Florida Times-Union,* 22 Oct., 1891; Knauss, "Farmers' Alliance in Florida," p. 304; *Florida Dispatch* (Jacksonville), 29 Oct., 1891.
2. *Florida Times-Union,* 23 Oct., 1891.
3. *Florida Dispatch* (Jacksonville), 29 Oct., 1891.
4. S. I. Wailes to F. P. Fleming, 11 May, 1892, incoming executive correspondence.
5. *Florida Times-Union,* 19 May, 1892.
6. Cash, *Democratic Party,* pp. 88–89.
7. *Tampa Daily Tribune,* 30 May, 1892.
8. *Florida Times-Union,* 2 June, 1892.
9. Ibid.
10. Ibid., 2, 3 June, 1892.
11. Ibid., 4 June, 1892.
12. *Bradford County Telegraph* (Starke), 17 June, 1892.
13. *Florida Times-Union,* 4 June, 1892.
14. *Pensacola Daily News,* 21 June, 1892.
15. *Florida Star* (Titusville), 23 June, 1892.
16. *Pensacola Daily News,* 25, 28 June, 1892.
17. *Ocala Banner,* 1 July, 1892.
18. Ibid.
19. Ibid.
20. *Florida Times-Union,* 11 July, 1892.

21. Ibid., 10 July, 1892.

22. Interview with Mrs. William S. Jennings, Jacksonville, Florida, 1 Apr., 1952.

23. De Santis, *Republicans Face the Southern Question*, pp. 238-39.

24. *Florida Republican* (Jacksonville), 16 July, 1892.

25. *Ocala Banner*, 1 July, 1892.

26. *Florida Agriculturist* (DeLand), 20 July, 1892.

27. *Florida Times-Union*, 21, 22 July, 1892.

28. Ibid., 21 July, 1892.

29. *Bradford County Telegraph*, 22 July, 1892.

30. *Pensacola Daily News*, 23 July, 1892.

31. *Bradford County Telegraph*, 12 Aug., 1892.

32. *Florida Dispatch*, 25 Aug., 1892.

33. Ibid., 11 Aug., 1892.

34. *Pensacola Daily News*, 3 Sept., 1892.

35. *Florida Republican* (Jacksonville), 1 Oct., 1892.

36. *Floridian*, 8 Oct., 1892.

37. Ibid., 22 Oct., 1892. Knauss, "Farmers' Alliance in Florida," p. 314.

38. *Floridian*, 15 Oct., 1892.

39. McKinnon, *Walton County*, p. 350.

40. *Floridian*, 3 Dec., 1893.

41. *Florida Dispatch*, 27 Oct., 10 Nov., 1892; Knauss, "Farmers' Alliance in Florida," p. 314.

42. F. Fleming to W. Chipley, 7 Oct., 1892, Fleming Letter Book.

43. *Florida Times-Union*, 4 Jan., 1893.

44. Mitchell, *Message to Legislature*, p. 3.

45. Ibid., pp. 3, 18-19.

46. *Florida Times-Union*, 2 June, 1893.

47. Ibid., 4 June, 1893.

48. H. Mitchell to F. Hendry, 15 June, 1893, Mitchell Letter Book.

49. J. N. C. Stockton to W. Call, 17 June, 1893, Cleveland Papers.

50. H. M. Flagler to Lamont, 9 Nov., 1893, Cleveland Papers; H. M. Flagler to H. T. Thurber, 29 Dec., 1893, Collector of Internal Revenue Applications; T. T. Stockton to W. Call, telegram, 4 Jan., 1894, Collector of Internal Revenue Applications.

51. H. M. Flagler to H. T. Thurber, 9 Jan., 1894, Collector of Internal Revenue Applications.

52. Collector of Internal Revenue Applications, 1893-94.

Bibliography

CONTEMPORARY SOURCES

Manuscripts

Bloxham, William D. Letter Books. 1881–84. Florida State Library. Official gubernatorial correspondence of Bloxham. Correspondence covers railroad building, land grants, lynching, and routine matters.
Call, Richard Keith. Papers. 1819–90. Florida Historical Society Library. Extensive
collection contains scattered letters by Ellen Call Long relating to politics,
personalities, and social life.
Chandler, William E. Papers. 1862–1901. Manuscripts Division, Library of Con-
gress. Because of his part in the Hayes-Tilden election aftermath in Florida,
Chandler was looked upon by many Florida Republicans as their firmest
national supporter, and they wrote him for advice and leadership.
Cleveland, Grover. Papers. 1859–1910. Manuscripts Division, Library of Congress.
Extensive collection contains letters relative to Florida politics from William
Chipley, Henry M. Flagler, Wilk Call, and others.
Collector of Internal Revenue Applications. 1893–94. National Archives. Evidence
is clear from these Treasury Department records that President Cleveland
stripped Senator Wilk Call of federal patronage to reward Henry M. Flagler.
Dougherty, Charles. Papers. 1878–88. P. K. Yonge Library of Florida History, University of Florida. A small collection of letters of a Florida congressman
describing politics and life in the Halifax River region.
Drew, George F. Letter Books. 1877–80. Florida State Library. Official correspondence of Florida's first Democratic governor following Reconstruction.
Fleming, Francis P. Letter Books. 1889–92. Florida State Library. Official gubernatorial correspondence of Fleming. Contains copies of important political
letters, but the copies of several letters to William D. Chipley are missing
from the books.
Florida Attorney General. Papers. 1885. Florida State Library. A small collection,
mostly routine matters.
Gainesville U.S. District Land Office. Papers. 1826–1931. University of Florida

217

Library. A most extensive and valuable collection of land records, starting
   when the land office was at Tallahassee.
Gleason, William H. Papers. 1866-93. P. K. Yonge Library of Florida History,
   University of Florida. An extensive collection consisting of personal, business,
   and political correspondence of a Republican Reconstruction leader who also
   was a large-scale real estate developer on Florida's East Coast.
Hart, Edward. Diary, 1879-80. P. K. Yonge Library of Florida History, University
   of Florida. Concerns the everyday existence of a Northern settler in the St.
   Johns River valley.
Hayes, Rutherford B. Papers. 1834-92. Hayes Memorial Library. Included in this
   extensive collection are a number of letters from Florida Republicans vitally
   concerned with Hayes's policy of conciliation.
Hill, Erastus G. Diary. 1877. In possession of Mrs. L. H. Hill, Lawtey, Florida.
   Hill was a Northern settler who quickly developed a Southern frame of refer-
   ence. His diary contains an excellent description of towns along the route
   of the Florida Railroad.
Hurt, Ashley D., to Mary Bruce Johns Hurt, July 27, 1884. University of Florida
   Archives. Describes Tallahassee and Florida in 1884. Hurt came to Florida
   as the new president of the Florida Agricultural College.
Huston, L. D. Papers. 1874-84. In the Possession of Mrs. Frank W. Pope, Jr.,
   Daytona Beach, Fla. Collection contains description of a large political rally
   in 1884 and details of the settlement of the Halifax River region.
Incoming Executive Correspondence. Miscellaneous gubernatorial letters, unar-
   ranged. Florida State Library. The letter from W. D. Chipley to W. D. Bloxham, 14 Apr., 1884, is of particular importance because it clearly expresses
   the viewpoint of the railroad political leader in the land grant controversy.
   Unfortunately, no collection of Chipley's papers has been preserved.
L'Engle, Edward M. Papers. 1834-97. Southern Historical Collection, University
   of North Carolina. Personal correspondence and business and legal papers
   of L'Engle, particularly valuable in respect to Florida Central Railroad of
   which he was president.
L'Engle, Capt. E[dward] M., to Mrs. E. M. L'Engle, 29 Oct., 1876. In possession
   of Miss Gertrude L'Engle, Jacksonville, Fla. A detailed letter concerning
   Democratic plans for victory in Florida in the 1876 election; also evaluates
   Republican opposition.
Mitchell, Henry L. Letter Books. 1893-96. Florida State Library. Official gubernatorial correspondence of Mitchell. Copies of letters include party politics as
   well as governmental matters.
Munson, F. W. Diary. 1880s. In possession of Munson Family, Georgiana, Fla.
   Concerns the everyday existence of a Northern settler on Merritt Island in
   the Indian River country. Unlike most Northerners in Florida, Munson re-
   mained Republican in politics.
Perry, Edward A. Letter Books. 1885-88. Florida State Library. Official gubernatorial correspondence of Perry, mostly of routine nature.
St. Augustine, City of. Papers. St. Augustine Historical Society Library. Miscel-
   laneous files of the municipality of St. Augustine, mostly of routine nature.
Sanford, Henry S., to President Chester A. Arthur, 19 Nov., 1881. Florida Historical
   Society Library. A strong protest against the carpetbag leadership of Florida's
   Republican party. Sanford advocated that the Northern settler and the white
   disaffected Democrat replace the Negro in building for the future.
Sanford, Henry S. Papers. Box 136. 1872-89. Henry S. Sanford Memorial Library.
   Over 250 items, largely correspondence, relating to Florida politics and San-
   ford's efforts to reform the state's Republican party.
Savage and James, Plantiffs in Error v. the State of Florida, Defendant in Error.

Handwritten transcript in Florida Supreme Court Library. Letter from supreme court justice to defense attorney announcing retrial included in transcript.
Sherman, John. Papers. 1859-93. Manuscripts Division, Library of Congress. Included in this extensive collection are a number of letters from Florida Republican politicians who hoped to get on the Sherman presidential bandwagon in 1880.
Swann, Samuel A. Papers. 1853-1907. P. K. Yonge Library of Florida History, University of Florida. An extensive collection of letter books, business records, incoming correspondence of a large-scale real estate developer. Swann was also an associate of Yulee's in the building of the Florida Railroad.
Yulee, David L. Papers. 1840-98. P. K. Yonge Library of Florida History, University of Florida. An extensive collection consisting of personal, business, and political correspondence and records of a Democratic political leader and railroad builder who exerted a strong influence in Florida from the 1840s to the 1880s.

Official Records and Documents

Federal

Congressional Record. 44th through 52nd Congresses, 1875-93. Washington: Government Printing Office, 1877-97.
Department of Commerce, Bureau of the Census. *Negro Population 1790-1915.* Washington: Government Printing Office, 1918.
"Major General Meade's Report on the Ashburn Murder," published in the *Report of Major General Meade's Military Operation and Administration of Civil Affairs in the Third Military District and Dep't of the South.* Atlanta: Assistant Adjutant General's Office, 1868.
Rowell, Chester H. *A Historical and Legal Digest of All the Contested Election Cases in the House of Representatives of the United States from the First to the Fifty-Sixth Congress, 1789-1901.* H. Doc. 510, 56th Cong., 2d sess. Washington: Government Printing Office, 1901.
U.S. Congress. *Testimony Taken by the Joint Select Committee to Inquire into the Condition of Affairs in the Late Insurrectionary States, Miscellaneous and Florida.* Washington: Government Printing Office, 1872.
U.S. Congress, House. *Biographical Directory of the American Congress 1774-1927.* H. Doc. 783, 69th Cong., 2d sess. Washington: Government Printing Office, 1933.
———. *Bisbee v. Finley.* H. Misc. Doc. 11. 47th Cong., 1st sess. Washington: Government Printing Office, 1882.
———. *Bisbee v. Finley.* In *Digest of Election Cases,* H. Misc. Doc. 35, 47th Cong., 2d sess. Washington: Government Printing Office, 1883.
———. *Bisbee v. Hull.* H. Misc. Doc. 26, 46th Cong., 1st sess. Washington: Government Printing Office, 1879.
———. *Presidential Election Investigation, Testimony Taken by the Select Committee on Alleged Frauds in the Presidential Election of 1876.* Vol. 2, *Testimony Relating to Florida.* H. Misc. Doc. 31, Part 2, 45th Cong., 3d sess. Washington: Government Printing Office, 1879.
U.S. Congress, Senate. *Public Lands in Florida.* Sen. Report 2288, 50th Cong., 1st sess. Washington: Government Printing Office, 1888.
———. *Report of the Senate Committee on Privileges and Elections with the Testimony and Documentary Evidence on the Election in the State of Florida*

in 1876. Sen. Report 611, 44th Cong., 2d sess. Washington: Government Printing Office, 1877.

U.S. Electoral Commission. *Proceedings of the Electoral Commission and of the Two Houses of Congress in Joint Meeting Relative to the Count of Electoral Votes Cast December 6, 1876 for the Presidential Term Commencing March 4, 1877*. Washington: Government Printing Office, 1877.

Vose v. Reed, et. al. trustees (Woods 647). *Federal Cases Circuit and District Courts 1789-1880*. St. Paul: West Publishing Co., 1896. Book 28.

State

Brevard County. Deed Books A and F.

Bush, Allen H. *A Digest of the Statute Law of Florida*. Tallahassee: Charles H. Walton, State Printer, 1872.

Departmental Reports, 1872-94. Printed in appendices of Florida *Senate* and *Assembly Journals*, 1873-95. These include *Reports* of the Comptroller, State Treasurer, Secretary of the Board of Trustees of the Internal Improvement Fund, Treasurer of the Internal Improvement Fund, Superintendent of Public Instruction, Adjutant-General, Commissioner of Lands and Immigration, Surgeon of State Prison, Warden of State Prison, Attorney General, Secretary of State, Commissioner of Agriculture, and President of State Board of Health.

Drew v. State Canvassing Board, 16 Florida Reports 17.

Ex-parte Eagan, 18 Florida Reports 194.

Fleming, Francis P. *Message of Francis P. Fleming, Governor of Florida, to the Legislature, convened in Extra Session—February 5, 1889*. Tallahassee: N. M. Bowen, Printer, 1889.

Florida *Assembly Journal*, 1865, 1868, 1873-85. Tallahassee: State Printer. State Printers: 1865, Hart & Shober; 1868, Tallahassee *Sentinel*; 1873, S. B. McLin; 1874, Hamilton Jay; 1875, *Floridian*; 1877-79, C. E. Dyke, Sr.; 1881, Charles A. Finley; 1883-85, C. E. Dyke, Sr.

Florida Board of Commissioners of Public Institutions. *Minute Book*. 26 Oct., 1869 to 13 Feb., 1892. Florida State Library. Public institutions included the state prison, convict leasing, and the insane asylum.

Florida Board of Trustees Internal Improvement Fund. *Minutes of the Board of Trustees Internal Improvement Fund of the State of Florida*. Vol. 2. Tallahassee: J. B. Hilson, State Printer, 1904.

Florida Constitutional Convention. *Journal of Proceedings of the Convention of Florida, Begun and Held at the Capitol of the State at Tallahassee, Wednesday, October 25th, A.D. 1865*. Tallahassee: Dyke & Sparhawk, 1865.

———. *Journal of the Proceedings of the Constitutional Convention of the State of Florida, Begun and Held at the Capitol, at Tallahassee on Monday, January 20th, 1868*. Tallahassee: Edward M. Cheney, Printer, 1868.

———. *Journal of the Proceedings of the Constitutional Convention of the State of Florida which convened at the Capitol, at Tallahassee, Tuesday, June 9, 1885*. Tallahassee: N. M. Bowen, State Printer, 1885.

Florida, Department of Agriculture. *The Seventh Census of the State of Florida 1945*. Tallahassee: Commissioner of Agriculture [1945].

Florida *House Journal*, 1887-93, 1897: Tallahassee: State Printer. State Printers: 1887-89, N. M. Bowen; 1891, *Times-Union*; 1897, W. N. Shine.

Florida Laws, 1877-92.

Florida *Senate Journal*, 1865, 1868, 1873-93. Tallahassee: State Printer. See *Assembly* and *House Journal* entries for names of printers.

Florida State Government, 1885, An Official Directory, compiled by J. B. Whitfield. Tallahassee: Florida Steam Book and Job Office, 1885.

Hamilton County, Circuit Court Motion Docket, 1873-1905.

Holland v. Florida, 15 Florida Reports 455.

Mitchell, Henry L. *Message of Henry L. Mitchell, Governor of Florida, to the Legislature. Regular Session of 1893.* Tallahassee: Tallahasseean Book and Job Office, 1893.

Official Certificate of the Board of State Canvassers of the General Election held November 7th, A. D. 1882, published in the Tallahassee *Weekly Floridian,* 19 Dec., 1882.

Official Certificate of the Board of State Canvassers of the General Election Held on the Fourth Day of November, A.D. 1884, published in the Tallahassee *Weekly Floridian,* 9 Dec., 1884.

Official Certificate of the Board of State Canvassers of the General Election Held on the Fifth Day of May, A.D. 1885 for Delegates to the Constitutional Convention, published in the Tallahassee *Weekly Floridian,* 4 June, 1885.

Official Certificate of the Board of State Canvassers of the General Election Held on the 2nd Day of November A.D. 1886, published in the Tallahassee *Weekly Floridian,* 16 Dec., 1886.

Savage and James v. the State, 18 Florida Reports 909.

Newspapers

Daytona: *Halifax Journal,* 16 Oct., 1884.

DeLand: *Florida Agriculturist,* 1881, 1888-93. *Volusia County Record,* 5 Aug., ., 1891.

Fernandina: *Florida Mirror,* 1879-85.

Fort Myers Press, 1888.

Gainesville: *Weekly Bee,* 1883-84.

Green Cove Spring, 9 May, 1891.

Jacksonville: *Daily Florida Times,* 1882.

    Daily Florida Union, 1877, 1882.

    Evening Chronicle, 14 Nov., 1877.

    Evening Telegram, 1891.

    Florida Dispatch, 1890-93.

    Florida Journal, 1884.

    Florida Republican, 16 July, 1 Oct., 1892.

    Florida Sun, 16 Jan., 1877.

    Florida Times-Union, 1884-93.

    Florida Union, 1865, 1868.

    Florida Weekly Times, 31 Jan., 1884.

    News-Herald, 14 Apr., 1888.

    Southern Sun, 7 May, 1885.

Lake City Reporter, 7 Oct., 1887.

Madison: *New Era,* 7 Aug., 1884.

    Madison Recorder, 5 Nov., 1880, 4 Nov., 1882.

New York Times, 1877-91.

Ocala Banner, 1885-93.

Orange City: *Times,* 1889.

Palatka Daily News, 1884-86.

Pensacola: *Commercial,* 1882-87.

    Pensacola Daily News, 1889-93, 1896.

    Pensacolian, 1884.

Philadelphia Press, 1881.

    Public Ledger, 1 May, 1896.

    Philadelphia Sunday Times, 1876 [undated clipping]

Sanford Journal, 1884.

Starke: *Bradford County Telegraph*, 1890, 1892.
Tallahassee: *Daily Florida*, 1891.
    Florida Sentinel, 1868.
    Land of Flowers, 1884.
    Semi-Weekly Floridian, 1865–67.
    Tallahassee Sentinel, 1867.
    Tallahassean, 1885–86.
    Weekly Floridian, 1867–92.
Tampa Daily Tribune, 1892.
    Tampa Guardian, 1880.
    Sunland Tribune, 1880.
Titusville: *Florida Star*, 1881–93.

Travel Accounts, Reports, and Miscellaneous Writings

Barbour, George M. *Florida for Tourists, Invalids and Settlers*. New York: D. Appleton and Company, 1882.
Chamberlain, H. R. *The Farmers' Alliance, What It Aims to Accomplish*. New York: Minerva Publishing Co., 1891.
Davidson, James Wood. *The Florida of To-Day, A Guide for Tourists and Settlers*. New York: D. Appleton and Company, 1889.
Florida Annual, 1884. Edited by C. K. Monroe. New York: Vaux & Company, 1883.
Florida Industrial Record, Sept. 1901.
King, Edward. *The Southern States of North America: A Record of Journeys*. 4 vols. London: Blackie & Son, 1875.
Lanier, Sidney. *Florida: Its Scenery, Climate, and History*. Philadelphia: J. B. Lippincott & Co., 1876.
Poor, Henry V., comp. *Manual of the Railroads of the United States for 1882*. New York: H. V. and H. W. Poor, 1882.
Powell, J. C. *American Siberia*. Chicago: W. B. Conkey Co., 1891.
Report of the Jacksonville Auxiliary Sanitary Association of Jacksonville, Florida. Edited by Charles S. Adams. Jacksonville: Times-Union Print, 1889.
Stowe, Harriet Beecher. *Palmetto-Leaves*. Boston: J. R. Osgood and Company, 1873.
Wallace, John. *Carpetbag Rule in Florida*. Jacksonville: Da Costa Printing and Publishing House, 1888.
Webber, Carl. *The Eden of the South*. New York: Love & Alden, 1883.

Pamphlets

Annual: Farmers' Alliance Exposition at Ocala, Florida. Oakland: Appleyard, 1890.
Bailey, E. B. *Pasco Finale and Pasco's Pedigree*. Monticello: n.p., 1899
Bloxham, W. D. *The Disston Sale and the State Finances*. N.p., 1884.
Chipley, William D. *Review of Senator Call's Record*. N.p., 1890.
Descriptive List Catalogue of the Disston Lands in Florida. Philadelphia: Edward Stern & Co., 1885.
Fleming, Francis. *Did the Florida Legislature of 1891 Elect a Senator?*.Tallahassee: n.p., 1891.
Florida Atlantic and Gulf Ship-Canal Company Summary Report. New York: Evening Post Steam Presses, 1881.
Independent Platform and Record of the Candidates. N.p., 1884.
Rose, R. E. *The Swamp and Overflowed Lands of Florida*. Tallahassee: Appleyard, 1916.
Sanchez, E. C. F. *Opening Speech of the Hon. E. C. F. Sanchez, of Alachua*

County *in the Constitutional Convention, July 14, 1885.* Tallahassee: Tallahassean book and job print, 1885.

An *Address to the People of Florida Setting Forth the Objects and the Principles of the Republican Party.* Prepared by the Republican State Executive Committee of Florida. Tallahassee: Office of the Tallahassee *Sentinel,* 1875.

SECONDARY WORKS

Books

Brevard, Caroline Mays. *A History of Florida.* 2 vols. DeLand: Florida State Historical Society, 1925.

Browne, Jefferson B. *Key West, the Old and the New.* St. Augustine: Record Co., 1912.

Cash, W. T. *History of the Democratic Party in Florida.* Tallahassee: Democratic Historical Foundation, 1936.

_____. *The Story of Florida.* 4 vols. New York: American Historical Society, 1938.

Current, Richard N. *Three Carpetbag Governors.* Baton Rouge: Louisiana State University Press, 1967.

Davis, T. Frederick. *History of Jacksonville, Florida and Vicinity 1513 to 1924.* St. Augustine: Florida Historical Society, 1925.

Davis, William Watson. *The Civil War and Reconstruction in Florida.* Studies in History, Economics and Public Law, vol. 53. Edited by Faculty of Political Science of Columbia University. New York: Columbia University, 1913.

De Santis, Vincent P. *Republicans Face the Southern Question—The New Departure Years, 1877-1897.* Baltimore: Johns Hopkins Press, 1959.

Dickison, Mrs. Mary Elizabeth. *Dickison and His Men.* Louisville: Courier-Journal Job Printing Co., 1890.

Douglas, Marjory Stoneman. *The Everglades Rivers of Grass.* New York: Rinehart and Co., 1947.

Dovell, J. E. *Florida: Historic, Dramatic, Contemporary.* 4 vols. New York: Lewis Historical Publishing Co., 1952.

Eppes, Susan Bradford. *Through Some Eventful Years.* Macon: J. W. Burke Publishing Co., 1926.

Going, Allen Johnston. *Bourbon Democracy in Alabama 1874-1890.* Tuscaloosa: University of Alabama Press, 1951.

Grismer, Karl H. *Tampa: A History of the City of Tampa and the Tampa Bay Region of Florida.* St. Petersburg: St. Petersburg Printing Co., 1950.

Hanna, Alfred Jackson, and Hanna, Kathryn Abbey. *Florida's Golden Sands.* Indianapolis and New York: Bobbs-Merrill Co., 1950.

_____. *Lake Okeechobee: Wellspring of the Everglades.* Indianapolis and New York: Bobbs Merrill Co., 1948.

Hirshson, Stanley P. *Farewell to the Bloody Shirt: Northern Republicans & the Southern Negro, 1877-1893.* Bloomington: Indiana University Press, 1962.

Johnson, James Weldon. *Along This Way: The Autobiography of James Weldon Johnson.* New York: Viking Press, 1933.

Knauss, James Owen. *Territorial Florida Journalism,* DeLand: Florida State Historical Society, 1926.

Logan, Rayford W. *The Betrayal of the Negro: From Rutherford B. Hayes to Woodrow Wilson.* New York: Collier Books, 1965.

McKinnon, John L. *History of Walton County.* Atlanta: Byrd Printing Co., 1911.

Makers of America, Florida Edition. 4 vols. Atlanta: A. B. Caldwell, 1909.

Martin, Sidney Walter, *Florida's Flagler.* Athens: University of Georgia Press, 1949.

Mayer, George H. *The Republican Party 1854-1964*. New York: Oxford University Press, 1964.

Merritt, Webster. *A Century of Medicine in Jacksonville and Duval County*. Gainesville: University of Florida Press, 1949.

Morris, Allen, comp. *Florida Handbook, 1949-1950*. Tallahassee: Peninsula Publishing Co., 1949.

Overy, David H., Jr. *Wisconsin Carpetbaggers in Dixie*. Madison: State Historical Society of Wisxonsin, 1961.

Pettengill, George W., Jr. *The Story of the Florida Railroads*. Railway and Locomotive Historical Society Bulletin No. 86 (July 1952).

Proctor, Samuel. *Napoleon Bonaparte Broward, Florida's Fighting Democrat*. Gainesville: University of Florida Press, 1950.

Rerick, Roland H. *Memoirs of Florida*. 2 vols. Atlanta: Southern Historical Association, 1902.

Richardson, Leon B. *William E. Chandler: Republican*. New York: Dodd, Mead and Co., 1940.

Saloutos, Theodore. *Farmer Movements in the South 1865-1933*. Lincoln: University of Nebraska Press, 1960.

Skinner, Emory Fiske. *Reminiscences*. Chicago: Vestal Printing Co., 1908.

Soldiers of Florida in the Seminole Indian, Civil and Spanish-American Wars. Compiled by Fred L. Robertson. Live Oak: Democrat Book and Job Print, 1903.

Stanley, J. Randall, *History of Jackson County*. Marianna: Jackson County Historical Society, 1950.

Tebeau, Charlton W. *A. History of Florida*. Coral Gables: University of Miami Press, 1971.

Thrift, Charles Tinsley, Jr. *The Trail of the Florida Circuit Rider*. Lakeland: Florida Southern Press, 1944.

Woodward, C. Vann. *Origins of the New South, 1877-1913*. A History of the South, edited by Wendell H. Stephenson and E. Merton Coulter, vol. 9. Baton Rouge: Louisiana State University Press, 1951.

_____. *The Strange Career of Jim Crow*. 2d ed., rev. New York: Oxford University Press, 1966.

Articles

Abbey, Kathryn T. "Florida Versus the Principles of Populism 1896-1911." *Journal of Southern History* 4 (1938):462-75.

Bentley, George R., "The Political Activity of the Freedmen's Bureau in Florida." *Florida Historical Quarterly* 28 (1949-50):28-37.

Brown, C. K. "The Florida Investments of George W. Swepson." *North Carolina Historical Review* 5 (1928):275-88.

Bush, George Gary. "The Educational Outlook in Florida." *Education Magazine*, January 1889, pp. 312-23.

Cash, W. T. "The Lower East Coast, 1870-1890." *Tequesta: The Journal of the Historical Association of Southern Florida* 8 (1948):57-71.

Davis, T. Frederick. "The Disston Land Purchase." *Florida Historical Quarterly* 17 (1938-39):200-210.

"Dennis Eagan." *Florida Industrial Record*, September 1901, pp. 5-6.

De Santis, Vincent P. "President Arthur and the Independent Movements in the South in 1882." *Journal of Southern History* 19 (1953):346-63.

Fairlie, Margaret C. "The Yellow Fever Epidemic of 1888 in Jacksonville." *Florida Historical Quarterly* 19 (1940-41):95-108.

Interview with Henry B. Plant. *Success* [magazine], November 1898, pp. 5-6.

Knauss, James O. "The Farmers' Alliance in Florida." *South Atlantic Quarterly* 25 (1926):300-315.

Lewis, Elsie M. "The Political Mind of the Negro 1865-1900." *Journal of Southern History* 21 (1955):189-202.

Pasco, Samuel, Jr. "Samuel Pasco (1834-1917)." *Florida Historical Quarterly* 7 (1928-29):135-38.

Pennington, Edgar Legare. "The Episcopal Church in Florida, 1763-1892." *Historical Magazine of the Protestant Episcopal Church* 7 (1938):3-77.

Proctor, Samuel. "The National Farmers' Alliance Convention of 1890 and Its Ocala Demands." *Florida Historical Quarterly* 28 (1949-50):161-81.

Roberts, Albert H. "Wilkinson Call, Soldier and Senator." *Florida Historical Quarterly* 12 (1933-34):95-113, 179-97.

Sharp, Helen R. "Samuel A. Swann and the Development of Florida, 1855-1900." *Florida Historical Quarterly* 20 (1941-42):169-96.

Shofner, Jerrell H. "Florida in the Balance: The Electoral Count of 1876." *Florida Historical Quarterly* 47 (1968-69):122-50.

――――. "A Note on Governor George F. Drew." *Florida Historical Quarterly* 48 (1969-70):412-14.

Simkins, W. S. "Why the Ku Klux." *Alcade* 4 (June 1916):735-48.

Smith, J. D. "The Construction of the P & A." *The L & N Employees Magazine*, August 1926.

Webb, John N., and Fenlon, Paul E. "Florida's Early Industrial Development: 1850-1890. *Economic Leaflets* 11. No. 5 (April 1952).

Whitfield, J. B. "Notes on the Constitutional Conventions of Florida." *Tallahassee Historical Society Annual* 3 (1937):53-81.

Williamson, Edward C. "Black Belt Political Crisis: The Savage-James Lynching, 1882." *Florida Historical Quarterly* 45 (1966-67):402-9.

――――. "The Constitutional Convention of 1885." *Florida Historical Quarterly* 41 (1962-63):116-26.

――――. "George F. Drew, Florida's Redemption Governor." *Florida Historical Quarterly* 38 (1960-61):206-15.

――――. "Independentism: A Challenge to the Florida Democracy of 1884." *Florida Historical Quarterly* 27 (1948-49):131-56.

――――. "William D. Chipley, West Florida's Mr. Railroad." *Florida Historical Quarterly* 25 (1946-47):333-55.

Yulee, C. Wicliffe. "Senator Yulee." *Florida Historical Quarterly* 2 (July 1909):3-22.

Unpublished Material

Ackerman, Philip D. "Florida Reconstruction from Walker through Reed, 1865 to 1873." Master's thesis, University of Florida, 1948.

Carson, Ruby Leach. "William Dunnington Bloxham, Florida's Two-Term Governor." Master's thesis, University of Florida, 1945.

Collins, Eldridge R. "The Florida Constitution of 1885." Master's thesis, University of Florida, 1939.

Doherty, Herbert J., Jr. "The Florida Whigs." Master's thesis, University of Florida, 1949.

Dovell, J. E. "A History of the Everglades of Florida." Ph.D. diss., University of North Carolina, 1947.

Finley, J. J. Biographical File. 1812-94. Florida Historical Society Library. Consisting of typewritten extracts, based largely on the diary of an Indian fighter, congressman, judge, Confederate general, and candidate for U. S. Senate.

Gammon, William Lamar. "Governor John Milton of Florida Confederate States of America." Master's thesis, University of Florida, 1948.

Parker, Oswald L. "William N. Sheats, Florida Educator." Master's thesis, University of Florida, 1948.

Pratt, Kathleen Falconer, "The Development of the Florida Prison System." Master's thesis, Florida State University, 1949.

"Statement of swamp lands owned by the State of Florida, and what may accrue to the state and of the lands sold and granted to corporations up to January 1st, 1883," revised and corrected by Hugh A. Corley. Typewritten copy in the Florida Historical Society Library.

Statement of Thomas Moreno, 96-year-old Creole Negro, Federal Writer's Project, Pensacola, Fla., 1 June, 1937. Typewritten copy in the Florida Historical Society Library.

Stearns, Marcellus L. "Statement Concerning the 1876 State and National Election of the State of Florida." Unsigned and undated manuscript, Stearns's authorship certified by his nephew, Aretas E. Stearns. Typewritten copy in Florida Historical Society Library.

Interviews and Letters

Statement of Alston Cockrell, grandson of ex-Governor David S. Walker, personal interview, 29 Dec., 1945.

Statement of Jacob Disston, Jr., nephew of Hamilton Disston, personal interview, 26 Sept., 1947.

Statement of W. Lansing Gleason, grandson of ex-Lieutenant Governor William H. Gleason, personal interview, 16 Oct., 1952.

Statement of Mrs. William S. Jennings, daughter of "Farmer" Austin S. Mann, personal interview, 1 Apr., 1952.

Statement of Donald Brenham McKay, Tampa historian, personal interview, 20 May, 1949; letter from, 17 Nov., 1945.

Statement of Mrs. Frank W. Pope, Jr., personal interview, 16 Mar., 1952.

Statement of Elmer S. Roberts, personal interviews, 26 Sept., 2 Oct., 1947. As a youth Roberts was Hamilton Disston's office boy.

Statement of Carlton Smith, Madison, personal interview, 10 Mar., 1952.

Statement of Columbus Smith, brother-in-law of Frank W. Pope, personal interview, 16 Oct., 1948.

Statement of Benmont Tench, Gainesville, personal interview, 31 Oct., 1950.

Letter from J. B. Hill, president of the Louisville and Nashville Railroad Company, 19 Dec., 1945.

Index

227